NEW WAYS IN PSYCHOANALYSIS

NEW WAYS IN
PSYCHOANALYSIS

KAREN HORNEY, M.D.

W · W · NORTON & COMPANY · INC ·
PUBLISHERS · NEW YORK

W. W. Norton & Company, Inc. is also the publisher of the works of Erik H. Erikson, Otto Fenichel, Karen Horney, and the principal works of Sigmund Freud.

ISBN 0 393 00132 6 Paper Edition
ISBN 0 393 01015 5 Cloth Edition

PRINTED IN THE UNITED STATES OF AMERICA

8 9

CONTENTS

INTRODUCTION

MY desire to make a critical re-evaluation of psycho-analytical theories had its origin in a dissatisfaction with therapeutic results. I found that almost every patient offered problems for which our accepted psychoanalytical knowledge offered no means of solution, and which therefore remained unsolved.

As most analysts probably do, at first I attributed the resulting uncertainty to my own lack of experience, lack of understanding or blind spots. I remember pestering more experienced colleagues with questions such as what Freud or they understood by "ego," why sadistic impulses were interrelated with "anal libido," and why so many different trends were regarded as an expression of latent homosexuality—without, however, obtaining answers that seemed satisfactory.

I had my first active doubts as to the validity of psychoanalytical theories when I read Freud's concept of feminine psychology, doubts which were then strengthened by his postulate of the death instinct. But it was several years before I started to think through psychoanalytical theories in a critical way.

As will be seen throughout the book, the system of theories which Freud has gradually developed is so consistent that when one is once entrenched in them it is difficult to make observations unbiased by his way of thinking. It is only through recognizing the debatable premises on which this system is built that one acquires a clearer vision as to the sources of error contained in the individual theories. In all sincerity I may say that I regard myself qualified to make the criticisms contained in this book, because I consistently applied Freud's theories for a period of over fifteen years.

The resistance which many psychiatrists as well as laymen feel toward orthodox psychoanalysis is due not only to emotional sources, as is assumed, but also to the debatable character of many theories. The complete refutation of psychoanalysis which these critics often resort to is regrettable because it leads to discarding the valid with the dubitable and thereby prevents a recognition of what psychoanalysis essentially has to offer. I found that the more I took a critical stand toward a series of psychoanalytical theories, the more I realized the constructive value of Freud's fundamental findings and the more paths opened up for the understanding of psychological problems.

Thus the purpose of this book is not to show what is wrong with psychoanalysis, but, through eliminating the debatable elements, to enable psychoanalysis to develop to the height of its potentialities. As a result of both theoretical considerations and practical experience, I believe that the range of problems which can be understood is enlarged considerably if we cut loose from certain historically determined theoretical premises and discard the theories arising on that basis.

My conviction, expressed in a nutshell, is that psychoanalysis should outgrow the limitations set by its being an instinctivistic and a genetic psychology. As to the latter, Freud tends to regard later peculiarities as almost direct repetitions of infantile drives or reactions; hence he expects later disturbances to vanish if the underlying infantile experiences are elucidated. When we relinquish this one-sided emphasis on genesis, we recognize that the connection between later peculiarities and earlier experiences is more complicated than Freud assumes: there is no such thing as an isolated repetition of isolated experiences; but the entirety of infantile experiences combines to form a certain character structure, and it is this structure from which later difficulties emanate. Thus the analysis of the actual character structure moves into the foreground of attention.

As to the instinctivistic orientation of psychoanalysis: when character trends are no longer explained as the ultimate outcome of instinctual drives, modified only by the environment, the entire emphasis falls on the life conditions molding the character and we have to search anew for the environmental factors responsible for creating neurotic conflicts; thus disturbances in human relationships become the crucial factor in the genesis of neuroses. A prevailingly sociological orientation then takes the place of a prevailingly anatomical-physiological one. When the one-sided consideration of the pleasure principle, implicit in the libido theory, is relinquished the striving for safety assumes more weight and the role of anxiety in engendering strivings toward safety appears in a new light. The relevant factor in the genesis of neuroses is then neither the Oedipus complex nor any kind of infantile pleasure strivings but all those adverse influences which make a child feel helpless and defenseless and which make him conceive the world as potentially menacing. Because of his dread of potential dangers the child must develop certain "neurotic trends" permitting him to cope with the world with some measure of safety. Narcissistic, masochistic, perfectionistic trends seen in this light are not derivatives of instinctual forces, but represent primarily an individual's attempt to find paths through a wilderness full of unknown dangers. The manifest anxiety in neuroses is then not the expression of the "ego's" fear of being overwhelmed by the onslaught of instinctual drives or of being punished by a hypothetical "super-ego," but is the result of the specific safety devices' failure to operate.

The influence these basic changes in viewpoint have on individual psychoanalytical concepts will be discussed in successive chapters. It suffices here to point out a few general implications:

Sexual problems, although they may sometimes prevail in the symptomatic picture, are no longer considered to be in the dynamic center of neuroses. Sexual difficulties are the effect rather than the cause of the neurotic character structure.

Moral problems on the other hand gain in importance. To take at their face value those moral problems with which the patient is ostensibly struggling ("super-ego," neurotic guilt feelings) appears to lead to a blind alley. They are pseudo-moral problems and have to be uncovered as such. But it also becomes necessary to help the patient to face squarely the true moral problems involved in every neurosis and to take a stand toward them.

Finally, when the "ego" is no longer regarded as an

organ merely executing or checking instinctual drives, such human faculties as will power, judgment, decisions are reinstated in their dignity. The "ego" Freud describes then appears to be not a universal but a neurotic phenomenon. The warping of the spontaneous individual self must then be recognized as a paramount factor in the genesis and maintenance of neuroses.

Neuroses thus represent a peculiar kind of struggle for life under difficult conditions. Their very essence consists of disturbances in the relations to self and others, and conflicts arising on these grounds. The shift in emphasis as to the factors considered relevant in neuroses enlarges considerably the tasks of psychoanalytical therapy. The aim of therapy is then not to help the patient to gain mastery over his instincts but to lessen his anxiety to such an extent that he can dispense with his "neurotic trends." Beyond this aim there looms an entirely new therapeutic goal, which is to restore the individual to himself, to help him regain his spontaneity and find his center of gravity in himself.

It is said that the writer himself profits most through writing a book. I know that I have benefited through writing this one. The necessity to formulate thoughts has greatly helped me to clarify them. Whether others will profit, no one knows in advance. I suppose there are many analysts and psychiatrists who have experienced my uncertainties as to the validity of many theoretical contentions. I do not expect them to accept my formulations in their entirety, for these are neither complete nor final. Nor are they meant to be the beginning of a new psychoanalytical "school." I hope, however, that they are sufficiently clearly presented to permit others to test their validity for themselves. I also hope that those seriously interested in applying psychoanalysis to education, social work and anthropology will receive some help toward clarification of the problems with which they are confronted. Finally I hope that those laymen as well as psychiatrists who have tended to repudiate psychoanalysis as a construction of startling but unsubstantiated assumptions will gain from this discussion a perspective on psychoanalysis as a science of cause and effect and as a constructive tool of unique value for the understanding of ourselves and others.

During the time of my dimly perceived doubts as to the validity of psychoanalytical theories two colleagues encouraged and stimulated me, Harald Schultz-Hencke and Wilhelm Reich. Schultz-Hencke questioned the curative value of infantile memories and emphasized the necessity of analyzing primarily the actual conflict situation. Reich, though at that time engrossed in the contentions of the libido theory, pointed out the necessity of analyzing in the first instance the defensive character trends a neurotic has built up.

Other influences on the development of my critical attitude were more general. An elucidation of certain philosophical concepts brought home to me by Max Horkheimer helped me to recognize the mental premises of Freud's thinking. The greater freedom from dogmatic beliefs which I found in this country alleviated the obligation of taking psychoanalytical theories for granted, and gave me the courage to proceed along the lines which I considered right. Furthermore, acquaintance with a culture which in many ways is different from the European taught me to realize that many neurotic conflicts are ultimately determined by cultural conditions. In this respect my knowledge has been widened by acquaintance with the work of Erich Fromm, who in a series of papers and lectures has criticized the lack of cultural orientation in Freud's works. He also has given me a new perspective on many problems of individual psychology, such as the central significance which the loss of self entails for neuroses. I regret that at the time of writing this book his systematic presentation of the role of social factors in psychology has not yet been published, and that therefore I cannot quote him in many instances where I should have liked to do so.

I take this opportunity to express my thanks to Miss Elizabeth Todd, who has edited the book and has helped me greatly both by her constructive criticisms and by her suggestions as to a more lucid organization of the material. My thanks are due also to my secretary, Mrs. Marie Levy, whose untiring labors and fine understanding have been invaluable. Also I feel indebted to Miss Alice Schulz, who has given me a better understanding of the English language.

NEW WAYS IN PSYCHOANALYSIS

CHAPTER I

FUNDAMENTALS OF PSYCHOANALYSIS

OPINIONS are divided as to what constitutes the basic principles of Freud's psychology. Is it the attempt to make psychology a natural science, the attempt to ascribe our feelings and strivings ultimately to "instinctual" sources? Is it the extension of the concept of sexuality which has met with so much moral indignation? Is it the belief in the general importance of the Oedipus complex? Is it the assumption that the personality is divided into "id," "ego" and "super-ego"? Is it the concept of repetitional patterns in life which are formed in childhood, and the expectation of effecting a cure by reviving early experiences?

No doubt all these are important parts of Freud's psychology. But it depends on one's judgment of values whether one ascribes to them a central place in the whole system or regards them as more peripheral theoretical elaborations. As will be shown later on, all these theories are open to criticism and must be regarded rather as an historical burden which psychoanalysis carries than as its pivotal center.

What then are the constructive and—if I may venture to predict further development—the imperishable values Freud has given to psychology and psychiatry? To make a sweeping statement: nothing of importance in the field of psychology and psychotherapy has been done since Freud's fundamental findings without those findings being used as a directive for observation and thinking; when they have been discarded the value of new findings has been decreased.

One of the difficulties in presenting the basic concepts is that they are often entangled in doctrines which are debatable. In order to point out the essential content of these concepts it is necessary to divest them of certain theoretical implications. Hence what may look like a popular presentation is a purposeful attempt to elucidate the elementary principles.

I regard as the most fundamental and most significant of Freud's findings his doctrines that psychic processes are strictly determined, that actions and feelings may be determined by unconscious motivations and that the motivations driving us are emotional forces. As these doctrines are interrelated, one may start more or less arbitrarily with any one of them. Still, it seems to me that the doctrine of unconscious motivations, if taken seriously, deserves first place. It belongs among those concepts which are generally accepted but which, in their implications, are often not fully understood. Probably to anyone who has not had the experience of discovering within himself attitudes or goals whose power he was unaware of, this concept is difficult to grasp.

It is contended by critics of psychoanalysis that in reality we never uncover material which was entirely unconscious to the patient, that he has felt it to be existent, only he did not know how important it was in its effect upon his life. In order to clarify this issue let us recall what actually happens when a hitherto unconscious attitude is uncovered. To take a typical example: on the basis of observations made within the analytical situation, a patient is told that he seems to be compelled never to make any mistakes, that he must always be right and know everything better than anyone else, hiding all these strivings behind a screen of rational skepticism. When the patient realizes that this suggestion may perhaps be valid, he may recall that when reading mystery stories he is always thrilled by the infallibility of the master detective's observations and conclusions; that in high school he was very ambitious; that he is never good at discussions and is easily swayed by the opinions of others, but that he can ruminate for hours about the things he should have said; that once, having made a mistake in reading a time-table, he was seriously upset afterwards; that he is always inhibited in saying or writing anything that is not beyond doubt, and hence has not been as productive as he might have been; that he is sensitive to any form of criticism; that he has often doubted his own intelligence; that he would succumb to a deadly fatigue when he could not understand immediately the tricks he saw a magician perform.

What was the patient aware of and what was he unaware of? He was at times aware of the appeal that "to be right" had for him, but he was not in the least aware of the important effect this attitude had upon his life. He had regarded it as an insignificant peculiarity. He was also unaware that certain of his important reactions and inhibitions were in some way connected with it; nor, of course, did he know why he had to be always right. This means that the patient was not aware of all that was important on that score.

Objections to the concept of unconscious motivations are made from a much too formalistic standpoint. Awareness of an attitude comprises not only the knowledge of its existence but also the knowledge of its forcefulness and influence and the knowledge of its consequences and the functions which it serves. If this is missing it means that the attitude was unconscious, even though at times glimpses of knowledge may have reached awareness. The further objection that we never discover any truly unconscious trends is in numerous instances contradicted by fact. Consider, for instance, a patient whose conscious attitude to others is that of liking them indiscriminately. Our assertion that he does not like them but that he only feels obliged to do so may strike home at once; his feeling is that he was always dimly aware of this, but did not dare recognize it. Even our further suggestion that his prevailing feeling for others is contempt may not impress him as an entirely new revelation; he knew that occasionally he despised others, without realizing, however, the depth and extent of such feelings. But our added assertion that the contempt was the result of tendencies to disparage others may strike him as entirely alien.

The importance of Freud's concept of unconscious motivations lies not in the statement that unconscious processes exist, but in two particular aspects of it. The first is that to thrust strivings out of awareness, or not to admit them into awareness, does not prevent them from existing and from being effective. This means, for example, that we may be disgruntled or depressed without knowing why; that we may make our most important decisions without knowing the real motivations; that our interests, our convictions, our attachments may be determined by forces which we do not know. The other aspect, if divested of certain theoretical implications, is that unconscious motivations remain unconscious because we are interested in not becoming aware of them. Compressed into this general formula, the latter doctrine contains the key to both a practical and a theoretical understanding of psychic phenomena. It implies that if an attempt is made to unearth unconscious motivations we will have to put up a struggle because some interest of ours is at stake. This, in succinct terms, is the concept of "resistance" which is of paramount value for therapy. Differences in viewpoint as to the nature of those interests which bar drives from consciousness are of comparatively lesser importance.

It was only after Freud had recognized unconscious processes and their effects that he was able to arrive at another basic conviction which has since proved to be most constructive: the working hypothesis that psychic processes are as strictly determined as physical processes. It permitted the tackling of psychic manifestations which had hitherto been regarded as incidental, meaningless or mysterious, such as dreams, fantasies, errors of everyday life. It encouraged the venture into a psychological understanding of phenomena which hitherto had been ascribed to organic stimuli, for example, the

psychic foundation of anxiety dreams, the psychic consequences of masturbation, the psychic determination of
hysteria, the psychic determinants of functional diseases,
the psychic determinants of exhaustion through work.
It permitted a constructive approach to occurrences
which until then had been attributed to external factors
and hence had not even aroused psychological interest:
the psychic factors involved in incurring accidents, the
psychic dynamics of the reason for the formation and
retention of certain habits, the psychic understanding
of repetitive experiences formerly ascribed to fate.

The significance of Freud's thinking concerning this
range of problems is not in his solution of them—the
repetition compulsion, for example, is certainly far
from being a satisfactory solution—but in his having
made them accessible to understanding. As a matter of
fact, the doctrine that psychic processes are determined
is one of the premises without which we could not take
a single step in our daily analytical work. Without it
we could not hope to understand a single one of the
patient's reactions. Moreover, it makes it possible for
us to recognize the existence of gaps in our understanding of a patient's situation, and to raise questions
leading to a more complete grasp. We may find, for
example, that a patient who has exalted fantasies about
his own significance, and subsequent intense hostile reactions to the world around him because it does not
recognize his significance, develops feelings of unreality.
We find that the feelings of unreality develop during
such hostile reactions, and we may tentatively arrive at
an assumption that the feelings of unreality represent

an escape into fantasy and a thorough devaluation of an unbearable reality situation. When keeping in mind, however, the doctrine that psychic processes are determined, we are able to recognize that some specific factor or combination of factors must be lacking in our understanding, as we see other patients with a generally similar structure who do not develop feelings of unreality.

The same applies to the evaluation of quantitative factors. If, for example, an insignificant provocation, such as a slightly impatient tone in our voice, leads to a considerable increase in the patient's anxiety, then the disproportion between cause and effect will raise in the analyst's mind questions like these: if a slight and momentary impatience on our part can elicit such intense anxiety, then it may be that the patient feels basically uncertain about our attitude toward him; what accounts for this degree of uncertainty? Why is our attitude toward him of such paramount importance? Does he perhaps feel utterly dependent on us and if so, why? Is as great an uncertainty present in all his relationships or are there particular factors which have enhanced it in his relation to us? In short, the working hypothesis that psychic processes are strictly determined gives us a definite lead and encourages us to penetrate more deeply into psychological connections.

The third basic principle of psychoanalytical thinking, implied in part in the two already mentioned, has been called the dynamic concept of personality. More accurately, it is the general assumption that the motivations for our attitudes and behavior lie in emotional forces, and the specific assumption that in order to understand any personality structure we must recognize emotional drives of conflicting character.

As to the general assumption, it is scarcely necessary to point out its constructive value and its infinite superiority over psychologies dealing with rational motivations, conditioned reflexes and habit formations. According to Freud, these driving forces are instinctual in nature: sexual or destructive. If, however, we discard these theoretical aspects, and for "libido" substitute emotional drives, impulses, needs or passions, we see the essential kernel of the assumption and can appreciate its value in creating an understanding of personality.

The more specific assumption of the importance of inner conflicts has become the key to an understanding of neuroses. The debatable part of this finding concerns the nature of the conflicts involved. For Freud the conflicts are between the "instincts" and the "ego." He has entangled his theory of instincts with his concept of conflicts, and this combination has been subject to violent attacks. I too consider Freud's instinctivistic orientation as one of the greatest handicaps to psychoanalytical development. What has happened under the stress of these polemics, however, is that the emphasis has been shifted from the essential part of the concept— the central role of conflicts—to the debatable part, the theory of instincts. It is not expedient now to explain at length why I ascribe fundamental importance to this concept, but it will be elaborated throughout the book that even when dropping the whole theory of instincts the fact still remains that neuroses are essentially the result of conflicts. To have seen this in spite of the obstacle of theoretical assumptions is proof of Freud's vision.

Freud has not only revealed the importance of unconscious processes in the formation of character and neuroses, but he has taught us a great deal about the dynamics of these processes. The shutting out of awareness of an affect or impulse Freud has called repression. The process of repression can be compared to the ostrich policy: the repressed affect or impulse is as effective as it was before, but we "pretend" that it does not exist. The only difference between repression and pretense, in its usual meaning, is that in the former we are subjectively convinced that we do not have the impulse. Simply repressing a drive usually does not suffice, if it is of any consequence, to keep it in abeyance. For this purpose other defensive measures are necessary. Among these two groups may be roughly distinguished: those which effect a change in the drive itself, and those which do nothing but change its direction.

Strictly speaking, only the first group of defenses deserves fully to be called repression because it creates a positive lack of awareness of the existence of a certain affect or impulse. The two main kinds of defense in which this result is brought about are reaction-formations and projections. Reaction-formations may have a compensatory character. An existing cruelty may be compensated by presenting a façade of overkindliness. A tendency to exploit others, if repressed, may result in an attitude of being overmodest in one's demands or in a timidity with regard to asking for anything. An existing repressed antagonism may be covered up by dis-

interestedness; a repressed craving for affection, by an
"I don't care" attitude.

The same result is attained by projecting an affect
to others. The process of projection is not essentially
different from the tendency to assume naïvely that
others feel or react in the same manner as we ourselves
do. Sometimes a projection may be only that. If a patient, for example, despises himself for being entangled
in all sorts of conflicts, he cannot but assume that the
analyst despises him likewise. Thus far a projection is
in no way connected with unconscious processes. But a
belief that an impulse or feeling exists in another person
may be used in order to deny its existence in oneself.
Such a displacement has many advantages. If, for example, a husband's wishes for extramarital affairs are
projected to the wife, the husband not only has removed
his impulse from awareness, but as a result may also feel
superior to the wife and may feel justified in discharging on her in the form of suspicion and reproaches all
sorts of otherwise unwarranted hostile affects.

Because of all these advantages this defense is frequent. The only point that should be added is not a
criticism of the concept but a warning not to interpret
anything as a projection without having evidence for it,
and also to be meticulously careful in the search for the
factors which are projected. If, for example, a patient
firmly believes that the analyst does not like him, this
feeling may be a projection of the patient's dislike for
the analyst, but it may also be a projection of his own
dislike for himself. Finally, it may not be a projection
at all, but may serve essentially as the patient's justifica-
tion for not becoming emotionally involved with the

analyst, in the event that he considers this to imply the danger of dependency.

The other group of defenses leaves the impulse itself unaltered, but changes its direction. What is repressed in this group is not the affect itself, but its relation to a certain person or situation. The emotion is separated from that person or situation in any of several ways, of which the following are the most significant.

First, an affect related to a person may be displaced to another person. This is a most common occurrence in the case of anger, the reason usually being fear of the person concerned or dependency on the person toward whom the anger is actually felt; the reason may also lie in a dim awareness that anger toward the particular person is not warranted. Accordingly, anger may be displaced to persons of whom one is not afraid, such as children or maids, to persons on whom one is not dependent, such as in-laws or employees, or to persons concerning whom anger may be put on a justifiable basis, as in a displacement from the husband to a waiter who has cheated. Also, if an individual feels irritated at himself his irritation may appear against anyone in the environment.

Second, an affect concerning a person may be displaced to things, animals, activities, situations. A proverbial example is finding a cause for irritation in a fly on the wall. Anger may also be displaced from the person concerned to ideas or activities cherished by that person. Here too the principle that psychic processes are determined proves its usefulness, because the choice of the object to whom an affect is displaced is strictly determined. If, for example, a wife believes that she is entirely devoted to her husband but displaces to his occupation a factual resentment she feels toward him, it may be that her strivings to possess the husband entirely are the factor determining the displacement of resentment from the husband to his occupation.

Third, an affect related to another person may be turned toward the self. The outstanding example concerns reproaches of others which are turned into self-recriminations. The merit of this concept lies in Freud's having pointed out a problem which is crucial in many neuroses. The problem arises from the observation that there is a frequent connection between people's inability to express criticism, reproaches or resentment, and their inclination to find fault with themselves.

Fourth, an affect which is related to a definite person or situation can be made entirely vague and diffuse. A definite anger at the self or others may, for example, appear as a general diffuse state of irritation. An anxiety connected with a definite dilemma may appear as a vague anxiety without any content.

Another series of revealing information concerns the question as to how affects which are kept from awareness may be discharged. Freud saw four ways.

First, all the above defense measures, while they serve to keep from awareness the affect or its real meaning and direction, nevertheless permit it expression, though sometimes in a circuitous way. An overprotective mother, for instance, may through her very protectiveness discharge a good deal of hostility. If hostility is projected to someone else the individual's own hostility may still be discharged as a response to the alleged hostility of others. If an affect is merely displaced it can be discharged nevertheless, though in the wrong direction.

Second, repressed feelings or drives may be expressed if put on the basis of a rational formula, or more correctly, as Erich Fromm has put it, if they are made to appear in socially accepted forms.[1] A tendency to possess or to dominate may be expressed in terms of love; a personal ambition, in terms of devotion to a cause; a tendency to disparage, in terms of intelligent skepticism; a hostile aggression, in terms of an obligation to tell the truth. While in crude ways the process of rationalization has always been known, Freud has not only shown its extent and the subtlety with which it is used, but he has taught us to utilize it systematically for the purpose of uncovering unconscious drives in therapy.

In this latter respect it is important to know that rationalization is used also for the purpose of maintaining and justifying defensive positions. An incapacity to accuse someone or to defend one's own interests may appear in awareness as a kind consideration for the feelings of others, or as a capacity to understand people. An unwillingness to admit any unconscious forces within oneself may be rationalized as consideration for the sinfulness of not believing in free will. An incapacity to reach out for what one wants may appear as unselfishness; a hypochondriacal fear, as duty to take care of oneself.

The value of this concept is not diminished by the fact that in its practical application it is often misused. One cannot hold it against a good surgical knife that wrong operations may be performed with it. One should be aware, however, that to work with the concept of

[1] Erich Fromm's contribution in *Studien über Autorität und Familie,* edited by Max Horkheimer (1936).

rationalization is to work with a dangerous tool. It should not be assumed without evidence that an attitude or a conviction presented is a rationalization of something else. Rationalization is present if other motivations than those assumed in awareness are the real driving ones. If, for instance, someone does not accept a difficult but remunerative position because it would force him into compromises concerning his convictions, he may really feel his convictions so deeply that to defend them is more important to him than financial gain or prestige. The other possibility is that the primary motivation in his decision is not his convictions, though they exist, but is a fear that he will not be able to fill the position adequately, or that he will expose himself to criticism or attack. In the latter case he would have accepted the position in spite of necessary compromises, if it had not been for his fears. There are of course all sorts of variations possible as to the comparative weight of the two sorts of motivations. We can speak of a rationalization only if the fears are actually the more influential motivation. An indication that we might distrust a conscious motivation could be, for instance, our knowledge that at other times the person concerned did not hesitate to make compromises.

Third, a feeling or thought that is repressed may find expression in inadvertent behavior. Freud has pointed out such expressions in his findings concerning the psychology of wit and of the errors of everyday life; these findings, though disputable in many details, have become an important source of psychoanalytical information. Feelings and attitudes may also be expressed inadvertently in tone of voice and in gestures, in saying or doing something without realizing its meaning. Observations made accessible on this score form likewise a valuable part of psychoanalytical therapy.

Fourth, and finally, repressed wishes or fears may reappear in dreams and fantasies. A repressed impulse of revenge may be lived out in dreams; superiority over someone which one does not dare to establish in one's conscious thoughts may be realized in dreams. This con-cept will probably prove to be even more fruitful than it has been thus far, particularly if we enlarge it to make it comprise not only concrete dreams and fantasies but also unconscious illusions. From the point of view of therapy their recognition is important inasmuch as what is very often described as a patient's reluctance to get well is often his unwillingness to abandon his illusions.

As I shall not come back to Freud's theory of dreams, I shall take this opportunity to point out what I con-sider its paramount value. Leaving aside many detailed peculiarities of dreams which Freud has taught us to understand, I regard as his most important contribution on this score his working hypothesis that dreams are the expression of wish-fulfilling tendencies. A dream often gives the clue to the existing dynamics if, after its latent content is understood, one considers what tendency the dream expresses and what underlying need made it necessary to express that particular tendency.

Suppose, as a simplified example, that the essence of a patient's dream is a representation of the analyst as ignorant, presumptuous and ugly. The assumption that tendencies are expressed in dreams shows us, first, that this dream contains a disparaging tendency versus, for example, an opinion, and second, that we must seek for the actual need that drives the patient to disparage the analyst. This question in turn may lead to a recognition that the patient has felt humiliated by something the analyst has said, or that he has felt his supremacy endangered and by disparaging the analyst he was able to reassert it. Recognizing such a sequence of reactions may lead to the further question as to whether this is the patient's typical way of reacting. In neuroses the most important function of dreams is the attempt to find either reassurance for an anxiety or compromise solutions for conflicts insoluble in real life. If such an attempt fails, an anxiety dream may ensue.

Freud's theory of dreams has frequently been disputed. It seems to me, however, that two aspects of such polemics have often been confused: the principle according to which interpretations should be made; and the factual interpretations arrived at. Freud has given us methodological points of view which are necessarily of a formal nature. The factual results arrived at on the basis of these principles will depend entirely on what drives, reactions, conflicts one holds to be essential in an individual. Hence the same principle may be the basis of different interpretations without the principle being invalidated by these differences.

Another basic contribution of Freud's lies in his having opened a path for the understanding of the nature of neurotic anxiety and of the role it plays in neuroses. As this point will be discussed later in detail, it is sufficient merely to mention it here.

For the same reason I can be brief about Freud's findings concerning the influence of childhood experiences. The disputable aspects of these findings concern mainly three assumptions: that an inherited set of reactions is more important than the influence of the environment; that the influential experiences are sexual in nature; that later experiences to a large extent represent a repetition of those had in childhood. Even if these debatable issues are discarded the essence of Freud's findings still remains: that character and neuroses are molded by early experiences to an extent hitherto unthought of. It is needless to point out the revolutionary influence which this discovery has had, not only on psychiatry but also on education and ethnology.

The reason for enumerating among the debatable issues Freud's emphasis on sexual experiences will be elaborated later. In spite of all objections to Freud's evaluation of sexuality, however, it should not be forgotten that Freud did clear the way for the consideration of sexual problems in a matter of fact fashion and for the understanding of their meaning and significance.

Not least in importance, Freud has given us basic methodological tools for therapy. The main concepts which have contributed to psychoanalytical therapy are those relating to transference, to resistance and to the method of free association.

The concept of transference—divested of the theoretical controversies as to whether transference is essentially a repetition of infantile attitudes—contends that observation, understanding and discussion of the patient's emotional reactions to the psychoanalytical situation constitute the most direct ways of reaching an understanding of his character structure, and consequently of his difficulties. It has become the most powerful, and indeed the indispensable, tool of analytical therapy. I believe that quite apart from its value to therapy, much of the future of psychoanalysis depends on a more accurate and a deeper observation and understanding of the patient's reactions. This conviction is based on the assumption that the essence of all human psychology resides in understanding the processes operating in human relationships. The psychoanalytical relationship, which is one form of human relations, provides us with unheard-of possibilities in understanding these processes. Hence a more accurate and profound understanding of this one relationship will constitute the greatest contribution to psychology which psychoanalysis will eventually have to offer.

By resistance is meant the energy with which an individual protects repressed feelings or thoughts against their integration into conscious awareness. This concept, as mentioned before, is based on our knowledge that the patient has good reasons not to become aware of certain drives. That there are debatable questions, and in my opinion wrong conceptions, as to the nature of these interests does not detract from the basic importance of recognizing their existence. Much work has been done in studying the ways in which the patient defends his positions, how he struggles, retreats, evades the issue; and the more we are able to recognize the numerous individual forms of such struggles, the more rapid and the more effective psychoanalytical therapy will become.

The specific factor in psychoanalysis which renders an accurate observation possible is the obligation for the patient to express everything he thinks or feels, regardless of any intellectual or emotional objections. The working principle used in this fundamental rule of psychoanalytical therapy is that a continuity of thoughts and feelings exists even if it is not apparent. It forces the analyst to be keenly attentive to the sequence in which thoughts and feelings arise, and it enables him gradually to make tentative conclusions as to the tendencies or reactions which are motivating the patient's manifest expressions. The idea of free associations, as it is used in therapy, belongs among those analytical concepts whose potential value is far from exhausted. My experience is that the more we progress in our knowledge of possible psychic reactions and connections and of possible forms of expression, the more valuable this concept proves to be.

Observation of the content and sequence of the patient's expressions, together with general observations of his behavior—gestures, tone of voice and the like—allows inferences as to the underlying processes. If these inferences, in the form of more or less tentative interpretations, are communicated to the patient, they in turn set new associations going, proving or disproving the analyst's assumptions, widening them by showing new aspects or narrowing them down to more specific conditions, and in general revealing emotional reactions to these interpretations.

This method has been attacked with the argument that interpretations are arbitrary, that associations following an interpretation are provoked and influenced by them, and that hence the whole procedure is extremely subjective in character. If such objections have any meaning, apart from a cry for a kind of objectivity which in the psychological field is impossible to attain, it can concern only the following possibility: a wrong interpretation, made in an authoritative way to a suggestible patient, may mislead the patient in much the same manner as a suggestible student is misled when he believes he sees something through the microscope if the teacher has told him what to look for. That, of course, is possible. The danger of misleading interpretations cannot be excluded. It can only be diminished. This danger will be the slighter the more psychological knowledge and understanding the analyst has, the less he looks for confirmation of established theories, the less authoritative his interpretation is and the less his own problems interfere with his observations. The danger will be further diminished if the patient's possible compliance is constantly taken into account and is eventually analyzed.

This preliminary discussion does not mean to present exhaustively the productive findings of Freud. It concerns only those fundamentals of psychological approach which in my experience have proved to be most constructive. It was possible to make their presentation comparatively brief, since they are the tools with which I am working and since in each succeeding chapter their validity and use will be unfolded. They are, so to speak, the mental background of the whole book. Many other pioneering observations of Freud's will be pointed out later on.

CHAPTER II

SOME GENERAL PREMISES
OF FREUD'S THINKING

IT is one of the characteristics of a genius to have the power of vision and the courage to recognize current prejudices as such. In this sense as in others Freud certainly deserves to be called a genius. It is almost incredible how often he freed himself from venerable ways of thinking and looked upon psychic connections in a new light.

It sounds like a banality to add that on the other hand no one, not even a genius, can entirely step out of his time, that despite his keenness of vision his thinking is in many ways bound to be influenced by the mentality of his time. To recognize this influence on Freud's work is not only interesting from an historical viewpoint but it is also important for those who strive to understand more fully the intricate and seemingly abstruse structure of psychoanalytical theories.

My historical interest as well as my knowledge of the history of psychoanalysis and philosophy is much too limited to allow a complete understanding of how Freud's thinking was determined by philosophical ideologies prevailing in the nineteenth century, or by the psychological schools of that time. My intention is merely to concentrate on certain premises of Freud's thinking for the sake of understanding better his peculiar way of tackling and solving psychological problems. As those psychoanalytical theories which were molded largely by implicit philosophical premises will be discussed later on, the purpose of this chapter is not to follow up in detail the influence of these premises but rather to survey them in brief.

One is Freud's biological orientation. Freud has always prided himself on being a scientist and has emphasized that psychoanalysis is a science. Hartmann, who has given an excellent presentation of the theoretical bases of psychoanalysis,[1] has declared, "That psychoanalysis is based on biology is its most significant methodological advantage." When evaluating Adler's theories, for example, Hartmann expresses the opinion that it would have been of enormous gain had Adler succeeded in finding an organic basis for the striving for power, which he assumed to be the all-important factor in neuroses.

The influence of Freud's biological orientation is threefold: it is apparent in his tendency to regard psychic manifestations as the result of chemical-physiological forces; in his tendency to regard psychic experiences and the sequence of their occurrence as determined primarily by constitutional or hereditary factors; finally, in his tendency to explain psychic differences between the two sexes as the result of anatomical differences.

The first tendency is the determining factor in

[1] Heinz Hartmann, *Die Grundlagen der Psychoanalyse* (1927).

Freud's theory of instincts: the libido theory and the theory of the death instinct. In so far as Freud is con-vinced that psychic life is determined by emotional drives and in so far as he assumes these to have a physiological basis, he belongs among the instinct theo-rists.[2] Freud conceives instincts as inner somatic stimuli which are continually operating and which tend toward a release of tension. He has repeatedly pointed out that this interpretation puts the instincts on the borderline between organic and psychic processes.

The second tendency—his emphasis on constitutional or hereditary factors—has greatly contributed to the doctrine that the libido develops in certain stages pre-scribed by heredity: the oral, anal, phallic and genital stages. It also is greatly responsible for the assumption that the Oedipus complex is a regular occurrence.

The third tendency is one of the decisive factors in Freud's views on feminine psychology. It is most pointedly expressed in the phrase "anatomy is destiny," [3] which appears also in Freud's concept of bisexuality, and it is apparent, for instance, in the doctrine that a woman's wish to be a man is essentially a wish to possess a penis, and that man's protest against exhibiting cer-tain "feminine" attitudes is ultimately his dread of castration.

A second historical influence is a negative one. It is

[2] This fact has been emphasized by Erich Fromm in an unpublished manuscript. The term instinct theorist is used here in its obsolete sense. In its modern meaning the term instinct is used to denote "in-herited modes of reaction to bodily need or external stimulus" (W. Trotter, *Instincts of the Herd in Peace and War*, 1915).

[3] Sigmund Freud, "Some Psychological Consequences of the Anatomi-cal Distinction Between the Sexes," in *International Journal of Psycho-analysis* (1927).

only recently that, as a result of the research work of sociologists and anthropologists, we have lost our naïveté in the matter of cultural questions. In the nineteenth century there was little knowledge regarding cultural differences, and the prevailing trend was to ascribe peculiarities of one's own culture to human nature in general. In accordance with these views Freud believes that the human being he sees, the picture which he observes and tries to interpret, has a general validity the world over. His insufficient cultural orientation is closely intertwined with his biological premises. Concerning the influence of the environment—the family in special, the culture in general—he is interested mostly in the ways in which it molds what he regards as instinctual drives. On the other hand, he is inclined to regard cultural phenomena as the result of essentially biological instinctual structures.

A third characteristic of Freud's approach to psychological problems is his explicitly refraining from any value judgment, his abstaining from moral evaluation. This attitude is consistent with his claim to being a natural scientist and as such justified only in recording and interpreting observations. In part, as Erich Fromm has pointed out,[4] it is influenced by the doctrine of tolerance prevailing in the economic, political and philosophical thinking of the liberal era. We shall see later how decisively this attitude influenced certain theoretical concepts, such as that of the "super-ego," as well as psychoanalytical therapy.

A fourth basis of Freud's thinking is his tendency to

[4] Erich Fromm, "Die gesellschaftliche Bedingtheit der psychoanalytischen Therapie" in *Zeitschrift für Sozialforschung* (1935).

view psychic factors as pairs of opposites. This dualistic thinking, likewise deeply ingrained in the philosophical mentality of the nineteenth century, shows throughout Freud's theoretical formulations. Each instinct theory he propounds tends to make the totality of psychic manifestations comprehensible under two rigidly contrasting groups of trends. The most significant expression of this mental premise is in the dualism he finds between instincts and the "ego," a dualism which Freud regards as the basis of neurotic conflicts and neurotic anxiety. His dualistic thinking appears also in his conception of "femininity" and "masculinity" as opposite poles. The rigidity involved in this type of thinking lends it a certain mechanistic quality, in contrast to dialectic thinking. On this basis we can understand Freud's assumption that elements contained in one group are alien to the opposite group, for instance, that the "id" contains all emotional strivings for satisfaction, while the "ego" has but a censoring and checking function. In reality—granting the classification—the "ego" as well as the "id" not only may but regularly does contain energetic strivings toward certain goals. The habit of mechanistic thinking explains also the idea that energies spent in one system automatically impoverish the opposite system, as for instance the idea that giving love to others engenders an impairment in one's self-love. Finally, this type of thinking is apparent in the belief that certain contradictory trends once established remain as they are, as opposed to a realization that there may be constant interaction between them, for instance in the form of "vicious circles."

A final important characteristic, closely akin to the

one just mentioned, is Freud's mechanistic-evolutionistic thinking. Because its implications are not generally known, and because of its special importance for an understanding of central psychoanalytical theories, I shall present it a little more circumstantially than the other premises.

By evolutionistic thinking I mean the presupposition that things which exist today have not existed in the same form from the very beginning, but have developed out of previous stages. These preceding stages may have little resemblance to the present forms, but the present forms would be unthinkable without the preceding ones. This evolutionism dominated scientific thinking through the eighteenth and nineteenth centuries, and it was greatly in contrast to the theological thinking of that time. It was applied primarily to inanimate matters of the physical universe, but also to biological and organic phenomena. Darwin was its most outstanding representative in the biological field. It exercised a strong influence also on psychological thought.

Mechanistic-evolutionistic thinking is a special form of evolutionistic thinking. It implies that present manifestations not only are conditioned by the past, but contain nothing except the past; nothing really new is created in the process of development; what we see today is only the old in a changed form. The following passage from William James is illustrative of mechanistic thinking: "The point which as evolutionists we are bound to hold fast to is that all the new forms that make their appearance are really nothing more than the results of the redistribution of the original and unchanged materials." [5] Speaking of the development of consciousness James declares: "In this story no new natures, no factors not present at the beginning are introduced at any later stage." Consciousness, he holds, could not have appeared as a new quality during the development of animals, and hence this quality must be ascribed to the monocellular beings. This example is indicative also of the focus of attention in mechanistic thinking. The focus is genetic, implying questions as to when and in what forms a thing has previously appeared, and in what forms it reappears or repeats itself.

The difference in emphasis between mechanistic and non-mechanistic thinking may be illustrated by many familiar examples. In the conversion of water into steam the mechanistic presupposition would emphasize the fact that steam is merely water appearing in another form. Non-mechanistic thinking, on the other hand, would emphasize that though steam has developed out of water, in doing so it has assumed an entirely new quality, regulated by different laws and having different effects. In considering the development of the machine from the eighteenth to the twentieth century, mechanistic thinking would point out mainly the various types of machines and factories which had already been in existence in the early eighteenth century, and would look at this development solely as one of quantity. Non-mechanistic thinking would emphasize that the increase in quantity brought with it a change in quality; that the quantitative development brought with it entirely new problems, such as a new scale of production, the rise of an entirely new group of employees, new types of labor

[5] William James, *Principles of Psychology* (1891).

problems and so on; that change is not simply a question of growth but brings with it entirely new factors. In other words, stress would be laid on the point that quantity is converted into quality. The non-mechanistic viewpoint would be that in organic development there can never be a simple repetition or regression to former stages.

In psychology the simplest example demonstrating these differences in viewpoint is the question of age. The mechanistic presupposition would consider the ambition of a man of forty as a repetition of the same ambition existing at the age of ten. Non-mechanistic thinking would hold that though elements of the infantile ambition are most certainly contained in the adult ambition, the implications in the latter are entirely different from those in the ambition of the boy, precisely because of the factor of age. The boy, having grandiose ideas about his future, has the hope of some day realizing such fantasies. A man of forty may either have a vague realization or may be well aware of the impossibility of ever fulfilling these ambitions. He will be aware of lost opportunities, of limitations within himself or of external difficulties. If he persists nevertheless in his ambitious fantasies, they will necessarily carry with them a connotation of hopelessness and despair.

Freud is evolutionistic in his thinking, but in a mechanistic way. In a schematized form, his assumption is that nothing much new happens in our development after the age of five, and that later reactions or experiences are to be considered as a repetition of past ones. This premise appears in many ways in psychoanalytic literature. Perceiving the problem of anxiety, for instance, Freud inquired as to where we may be able to find former manifestations of it; following this trend of thought he arrived at the conclusion that birth is a first manifestation of anxiety, and that later forms of anxiety are to be viewed as a repetition of the original anxiety of birth. This way of thinking accounts also for Freud's great interest in speculating about stages of development as repetitions of phylogenetic happenings—as for instance, considering the "latency" period as a residue of the ice period. It accounts in part too for his interest in anthropology. In *Totem and Taboo* he declares that the psychic life of primitives is of special interest because it represents well-preserved pre-stages of our own development. Theoretical attempts to explain that sensations in the vagina are transferred from sensations in the mouth or in the anus, though not important, may be mentioned as a further illustration of this kind of thinking.

The most general expression of Freud's mechanistic-evolutionistic thinking is in his theory of repetition compulsion. In more detail its influence can be seen in his theory of fixation, implying the doctrine of the timelessness of the unconscious, in his theory of regression, in his concept of transference. Generally speaking it accounts for the extent to which trends are designated as infantile and for the tendency to explain the present by the past.

I have presented these basic premises of Freud's thinking without critical comment. Nor shall I try to discuss their validity later on, because it is beyond the competence and also beyond the interest of a psychiatrist to do so. For the psychiatrist interest in these philosophical premises lies in investigating whether or not they lead to constructive and useful concepts. If I may anticipate the discussion of these concepts and their results, my judgment is that psychoanalysis has to rid itself of the heritage of the past if its great potentialities are to develop.

CHAPTER III

THE LIBIDO THEORY

THE doctrine that psychic forces are chemical-physio-logical in origin appears in Freud's instinct theories. Freud has successively propounded three dualistic instinct theories. In this dualism he has consistently believed one of the instincts to be the sexual one, but concerning the other he has changed his viewpoint. Among the instinct theories that of the libido takes a special place because it is a theory of sexuality, of the development of sexuality and of its influence on the personality.

It was on the basis of clinical observations that Freud's attention became focused on the significance of sexuality in creating mental disturbances. Hypnotic therapy, which he applied to hysterical patients, showed that forgotten sexual occurrences were often at the root of the trouble. Later observations seemed to confirm the first ones, inasmuch as the majority of neurotic persons factually have sexual difficulties of some sort. In some neuroses sexual problems are in the foreground of the picture, as for example in impotence or in perversions.

Freud's first instinct theory was that our lives are determined mainly by the conflict between the sexual

instinct and the "ego drives." By the latter he meant
the sum total of drives pertaining to self-preservation
and self-assertion, and it was his contention that every
drive or attitude which does not pertain to the sheer
necessities of existence is sexual in origin.

But even when this much influence on psychic life
was attributed to sexuality it was impossible to interpret
on a sexual basis the manifold strivings and attitudes
which apparently have nothing to do with sexuality—
for instance, attitudes of greediness, stinginess, defiance or other character peculiarities, artistic strivings,
irrational hostilities, anxieties. The sexual instinct as
we are accustomed to regard it could not possibly cover
this enormous field. If Freud desired to explain all these
psychic phenomena on a sexual basis he was forced to
enlarge the concept of sexuality. This was at any rate
the theoretical necessity for such an enlargement. Freud
himself has always declared that it was on the basis of
his empirical findings that he had to enlarge the concept of sexuality. It is true that he had gathered a great
number of clinical observations before he began to pro-
pound his libido theory.

The libido theory contains two basic doctrines which
may be designated briefly as an enlargement of the concept of sexuality and the concept of the transformation
of instincts.

The data according to which Freud felt entitled to
enlarge the concept of sexuality were, briefly, the following. Sexual strivings are not exclusively directed
toward heterosexual objects; they may be directed toward persons of the same sex, toward the self or toward
animals. Also, the sexual aim is not always toward the

union of the genitals, but other organs, particularly the mouth and the anus, may replace the genitals. And sexual excitement is promoted not only by a partner with whom intercourse is wanted, but also by sadistic, masochistic, voyeuristic, exhibitionistic practices, to mention the most important ones. Such practices are not restricted to sexual perverts but signs of them are found in otherwise healthy persons. Under the stress of long frustration normal persons may, for instance, turn to the same sex; immature persons may be seduced to any perversion; traces of such practices may occur in the normal sexual foreplay, as in kissing or aggressive actions; they occur also in dreams and fantasies and often seem to be an essential element in neurotic symptoms. Finally, infantile pleasure strivings have a certain resemblance to strivings occurring in perversions, such as thumb-sucking, intense pleasurable attention to the processes of defecation or urination, sadistic fantasies and activities, sexual curiosity, the pleasure of showing oneself naked or of observing others naked.

Freud concluded that since sexual drives can be easily attached to various objects, and since sexual excitement and satisfaction can be found in various ways, the sexual instinct itself is not a unit but a composite. Sexuality is not an instinctual drive directed toward the opposite sex, aiming at genital satisfaction; the heterosexual genital drive is only one manifestation of a non-specific sexual energy, the libido. The libido may be concentrated at the genitals, but it may be localized with equal intensity at the mouth or the anus or at other "erogenic" zones, lending these zones the value of genitals.

Besides the oral and anal drives Freud stipulated other component drives of sexuality—sadism and masochism, exhibitionism and voyeurism—which despite many endeavors could not be satisfactorily located in any bodily zone. Since the extra-genital expressions of libido prevail in early childhood, they are called "pre-genital" drives. Around the age of five, in a normal development, they are subordinated to the genital drives, thus forming the unit which is usually called sexuality.

Disturbances in the libido development may occur in two principal ways: either by fixation—some of the component drives may resist integration into "adult" sexuality because they are too strong constitutionally; [1] or by regression—under the stress of frustration a composite sexuality already achieved may split into its constituent drives. In both cases the genital sexuality is disturbed. The individual then pursues sexual satisfaction along the paths prescribed by the pre-genital drives.

The basic contention implicit in the libido theory—though not explicitly stated—is that all bodily sensations of a pleasurable nature, or strivings for them, are sexual in nature. These strivings comprise mere organ pleasure, such as pleasure in sucking, in defecating, in digestion, in muscular movements, in skin sensations, and also pleasure experienced in connection with others, such as in being beaten, in exposing oneself to others, in observing others or their physical functions, in inflicting injury on others. Freud recognized that this con-

[1] By "constitutional" Freud means both inherited and acquired through early experiences. This at any rate is the definition he gives in his paper "Analysis Terminable and Interminable," *International Journal of Psychoanalysis* (1937).

tention could not be proved on the grounds of childhood observation. What then is his evidence?

Freud points out that a baby's expression of satisfaction after being nursed is similar to that of a person
after intercourse. Certainly he did not mean to present
this analogy as conclusive evidence. But one cannot help
wondering why it is presented at all, because no one
has ever doubted that pleasure can be derived from
sucking, eating, walking and the like; the analogy,
therefore, omits the dubitable point as to whether the
baby's pleasure is sexual. According to Freud, although
the sexual nature of pleasurable sensations in the body
or of strivings for them cannot be ascertained from
childhood, it is suggested by the fact that such sensations may be intimately connected with definite adult
sexual activities as they occur in perversions, in sexual
foreplay or in masturbation fantasies. This is true; but
one has to consider that in perversions as well as in
sexual foreplay the ultimate satisfaction rests with the
genitals. According to Freud's assumption the excitement of the mouth in *fellatio* should be similar in quality and intensity to that of the vagina. In reality, in
fellatio as in kissing, the excitement of the mucous
membrane of the mouth is of minor importance. Oral
activity is merely a condition for genital satisfaction,
just as there may be a condition for genital excitement
in beating or being beaten, in exhibiting oneself or seeing the naked body or parts of it, or seeing others in
certain postures. Freud recognized this objection but
did not consider it as evidence against his theory.

In short, Freud has greatly contributed to our knowledge concerning the variety of factors which may stimu-

late sexual excitement or may become the condition for satisfaction. But he has not proved that these factors themselves are sexual. Furthermore, inadvertent generalizations are involved in his reasoning. From the fact that certain types derive sexual satisfaction from witnessing acts of cruelty it does not follow that cruelty is an integral part of the sexual drive in general.

As further evidence for the sexual nature of physical pleasure strivings, Freud points out that sometimes nonsexual bodily cravings may alternate with sexual hunger. Neurotics may have periods of compulsory eating alternating with periods of sexual activities; persons preoccupied with food and digestion often have but a scant interest in sexual intercourse. I shall return later to these observations and to the conclusions drawn from them. Only this much here: Freud has neglected as a possible explanation the fact that a substitution of one pleasure striving for another does not prove that the second is in any way akin to the first. If a person wants to go to the movies but cannot do so and instead listens to the radio, it does not follow that the pleasure in seeing the movies and the pleasure of listening to the radio are similar in nature. If a monkey cannot obtain a banana and finds a substitute pleasure in swinging, this is not conclusive evidence that the swinging is a component drive of eating, or of the pleasure found in eating.

In view of all the above considerations it is to be concluded that the libido concept is unproved. What is offered as evidence consists of unwarranted analogies and generalizations, and the validity of the data concerning the erogenic zones is highly dubitable.

If the libido concept led only to a peculiar interpretation of sexual deviations or of infantile pleasure strivings the question of its validity would not be so important. But its real significance lies in its doctrine of the transformation of instincts, which makes it possible to attribute to a libidinous source the majority of character traits, strivings and attitudes toward the self and others, in so far as they do not pertain to a mere struggle for existence. The tendency implied in this doctrine appears still more conspicuously in Freud's second instinct theory, which concerns the dualism between narcissism and object libido, and remains conspicuous in his third, his theory of the dualism between the libido and a destructive instinct. As both these theories shall be taken up later on I shall neglect, in the following discussion of the forms of libido expression, the fact that some of the attitudes mentioned as libidinous in origin—such as sadism and masochism—were subsequently regarded by Freud as admixtures of libidinal and destructive drives.

Freud suggests several ways in which the libido molds character and directs attitudes and strivings. Some attitudes are considered to be aim-inhibited libidinous drives. Thus not only the striving for power, but every kind of self-assertion is interpreted as an aim-inhibited expression of sadism. Any kind of affection becomes an aim-inhibited expression of libidinal desires. Any kind of submissive attitude toward others becomes suspect of being the expression of a latent passive homosexuality.

Closely akin to the concept of aim-inhibited strivings is that of the sublimation of libidinal drives. According to this concept a libidinous excitement and satisfaction, originally localized in some "pre-genital" drive, may be carried over to non-sexual strivings of a similar character, thus transforming the original libidinal energy into a nondescript form of energy. As a matter of fact, there is no sharp distinction between sublimation and aim-inhibition; the common denominator of both concepts is the dogmatic assertion that various traits, though not libidinal themselves, are to be regarded as an expression of desexualized libido. One reason why the distinction is not sharp is that the term sublimation originally contained the notion of transforming an instinctual drive into something socially valuable. It would be difficult to say, however, whether such a transformation as the use of narcissistic self-love for the formation of ego-ideals is a sublimation or an aim-inhibited form of self-love.

The term sublimation is reserved mostly for the transformation of "pre-genital" drives into non-sexual attitudes. In the view of this theory character traits, such as stinginess, are a sublimated anal-erotic pleasure, consisting of holding on to faeces; pleasure in painting is a desexualized pleasure in playing with faeces; sadistic strivings may reappear in a predilection for surgery or for executive jobs, and they may also show in general non-sexual tendencies to subdue, to hurt, to abuse; sexual masochistic drives may be transformed into such character traits as a propensity to feel unfairly treated or to feel insulted or humiliated; oral libidinal cravings may be converted into a general attitude of receptivity, acquisitiveness or greediness; urethral eroticism may be transformed into ambition. Also, competitiveness is regarded as the desexualized continuation of a sexual rivalry with parents or siblings; the wish to create something is explained partly as a desexualized wish for a child from one's father, partly as an expression of narcissism; sexual curiosity may be sublimated into a propensity for doing scientific research, or may be the reason for inhibitions on that score.

Certain attitudes are regarded not as a direct or modified outcome of libidinal drives, but as patterned after a similar attitude in sexual life. Freud speaks of the *Vorbildlichkeit* of sexual drives for life in general. The practical consequence of this concept is the expectation that difficulties in the non-sexual sphere will be solved if difficulties in the sexual sphere are removed, an expectation which frequently fails to be realized. Schematically, the interpretation required by this concept is that the reason for a compulsion to restrain feelings, for example, lies in an inability to abandon oneself sexually. The original frigidity would also be attributed to sexual factors, such as the aftermath of early sexual traumata or of incestuous fixations, homosexual trends, sadistic or masochistic elements, the latter being regarded as essentially sexual phenomena.

Again a difficulty arises as to classification: is a certain type of behavior masochistic because it follows automatically the sexual pattern? [2] Or are the non-sexual masochistic tendencies a desexualized aim-inhibited expression of the sexual ones? But actually these differences do not matter, as all the groups concerned are but various expressions of the same basic conviction: man

[2] *Cf.* Sandor Rado, "Fear of Castration in Women" in *Psychoanalytic Quarterly* (1933).

is primarily and peremptorily driven to fulfill certain elemental instincts; they are so powerful that they force him, not only directly but in the most devious ways, toward the goals they prescribe. Even when man believes himself to have the most sublime feelings, such as religious ones, or to pursue the most noble activities, as art or science, he still serves inadvertently his masters, the instincts.

The same dogmatic conviction underlies the tendency to regard certain character traits as a residue of past libidinal relationships or as an expression of actual latent libidinal attitudes toward others. The two main problems on this score concern attempts to explain attitudes as the result of a previous identification with someone or as the expression of latent homosexuality.

Other character traits are regarded as reaction-formations against libidinal strivings. Reaction-formations are supposed to take their energy from the libido itself: thus cleanliness or orderliness represents a reaction-formation against anal-erotic impulses; kindliness, a reaction-formation against sadism; modesty, a reaction-formation against exhibitionism or greediness.

A further group of feelings or character traits are considered to be the unavoidable consequence of instinctual desires. Thus an attitude of dependence on others is regarded as a direct result of oral-erotic cravings; inferiority feelings appear as a result of impoverishment of the "narcissistic" libido, for instance, as a consequence of not receiving "love" in return for having bestowed libido on others. Stubbornness is related to the anal-erotic sphere and is regarded as a result of a clash with the environment on that basis.

Finally, important feelings such as fear and hostility are understood to be reactions to a frustration of libidinal drives. When the main positive drives are conceived as libidinal in origin, it follows that it is the frustration of libidinal wishes of any kind which is the danger to be feared. Hence the fear of loss of love, for example, which to Freud is equal to the fear of losing a libidinal gratification expected from certain persons, is regarded as one of the basic fears. And hostility, when not interpreted as an expression of sexual jealousy, is one-sidedly related to frustration. Neurotic anxiety is regarded as ultimately resulting from frustration, inasmuch as frustration of instinctual drives, whether imposed by external circumstances or by internal factors such as fear and inhibition, is supposed to create instinctual pent-up tension. In his first concept of anxiety Freud believed that anxiety could be aroused if libido were prevented from discharge, by either inner or outer reasons, a concept which he later changed into a more psychological one. But anxiety remained an expression of pent-up libido, though it was defined as the individual's feelings of fear and helplessness toward such a pent-up libido tension.

To sum up, according to Freud a character trait, an attitude or a striving may be a direct, an aim-inhibited or a sublimated expression of libidinal drives. It may be modeled on sexual peculiarities; it may represent a reaction-formation to libidinal impulses or to their frustration; it may be the internal residue of libidinal attachments. In view of this attempt to ascribe to the libido such overwhelming influence in psychic life, the accusation of pan-sexuality has often been raised against psychoanalysis.[3] This has been refuted with the argument that libido is different from what is usually understood by sexuality, and that furthermore psychoanalysis also considers forces within the personality which prohibit sexual drives. It seems to me that such arguments are rather futile. What matters is the question whether sexuality actually has as much influence on character as Freud assumes. In order to answer this question we must critically discuss each of the ways in which Freud believes that attitudes are generated or motivated by the instinctual drives.

The assumption that certain feelings or drives are aim-inhibited expressions of sexuality contains some valuable clinical findings. Affection and tenderness may be aim-inhibited sexuality; they may be the forerunner of sexual desires; and a sexual relationship may pass into a merely affectionate one. The desire to control others and to run their lives may be a mitigated and, as it were, a rationalized form of sadistic trends, though the sexual origin and nature of the latter are dubitable. But there is no evidence for the generalization that therefore all trends toward affection or power are aim-inhibited instinctual drives. It is not proved that affection may not grow out of various non-libidinal sources, that it may not be, for example, an expression of maternal care and protection. What is neglected entirely is that a need for affection can be a means of reassurance against anxiety, in which case it is an entirely different phenomenon, essentially having nothing to do with sex-

[3] Cf., for instance, J. Jastrow, The House That Freud Built (1932).

uality—even though it may take on a sexual coloring.[4] Similarly, the desire to control, while it may be an aim-inhibited expression of sadistic impulses, nevertheless may be entirely different from sadism. A sadistic striving for power is born of weakness, anxiety and revenge impulses, while a non-sadistic striving for power is born of a feeling of strength, a capacity for leadership or devotion to a cause.

The dogmatic conviction that sexual elements determine strivings and attitudes appears perhaps still more blatantly in the doctrine of sublimation. The data for this assumption are scant and inconclusive. Observation shows that a child may ask for everything under the sun when his sexual curiosity is awakened, and that his general curiosity may subside when his sexual curiosity is satisfied. But to conclude that therefore every thirst for knowledge is a "desexualized" form of sexual curiosity is an unwarranted generalization. A particular interest in any kind of research may have many roots. Some of these will often date back to specific experiences in childhood, but even so, they are not necessarily or prevailingly sexual in nature. When against such criticism the objection is raised that psychoanalysis has never overlooked "overdetermining" factors, the issue is only befogged. It is a safe assumption that every psychic phenomenon is determined in multiple ways. Arguments like these do not touch the debatable contention, which is that the libidinal root is the essential one.

It is pointed out, again on the basis of good evidence,

[4] *Cf.* Karen Horney, *The Neurotic Personality of Our Time* (1937), chs. 6-9.

that drives or habits in the non-sexual sphere often co-exist with similar peculiarities in the libidinal sphere. A person who "devours" books and is greedy in money matters may be similarly greedy in eating or drinking, may have disturbances in appetite or functional stomach troubles. A miserly person may sometimes suffer from constipation. A person inclined to masturbation may have the same compulsory need to play solitaire, the same feeling of shame about it, the same repetitive determination to stop it.

It is, of course, tempting to an instinct theorist, when finding that organic manifestations such as those mentioned are often combined with similar psychic attitudes, to regard the former as the instinctual basis and the latter as emanating from it in one way or another. As a matter of fact, it is more than tempting; on the basis of the theoretical premises of an instinct theory not much more evidence than the combined occurrences of the two series of factors is required to prove a causal connection. If one does not share these premises, however, the frequent coincidence of these traits is no proof at all. It is as little proof as the frequent coincidence of tears and grief is proof that grief is an emotional result of tears, as was assumed by former instinct theorists.[5] Today we would assume that tears are a physical expression of grief, and not that grief is an emotional result of tears.

In other words, should not the greediness shown in eating or drinking be one of many expressions of a general greediness, rather than its cause? Should not a

[5] William James, *Principles of Psychology* (1891).

functional constipation [6] be one of many expressions of a general trend toward possessiveness, control? The same anxiety which may compel a person to masturbate may compel him to play solitaire. It is not at all self-evident that the shame in playing solitaire results from the fact that in the last analysis he is pursuing a forbidden sexual pleasure. If he is, for instance, a type for whom the appearance of perfection is more important than anything else,[7] the implication of self-indulgence and lack of self-control may be sufficient to determine his self-condemnation.

According to this viewpoint, there is no causal connection to be deduced from a similarity between nonsexual drives or habits and libidinal manifestations. The greediness, the possessiveness, the compulsory playing of solitaire have to be accounted for otherwise. It would lead us too far astray to go into detail. Roughly, in the compulsory playing of solitaire, for example, other factors have to be considered, similar to those that may be involved in gambling: a person's resistance against having to make efforts of his own because of an inner insistence to be carried on someone's shoulders, together with a feeling that he is a helpless prey of chance and must therefore attempt to put his energy into forcing chance on his side, to outwit the odds.

In the case of greediness or possessiveness, one would think of those character structures which in the psychoanalytical literature are described as "oral" or "anal"; but instead of relating these traits to the "oral" or

---

[6] *Cf.* C. P. Oberndorf, "The Psychogenic Factors in Asthma" in *New York State Journal of Medicine* (1935).

[7] *Cf.* Chapter XIII, The Concept of the "Super-Ego."

"anal" sphere, one would understand them as a response to the sum total of experiences in the early environment. As a result of these experiences the individual acquires, in both cases, a deep feeling of helplessness toward a world conceived as potentially hostile, a lack of spontaneous self-assertion and a disbelief in his own capacity to create or master something of his own accord. Then one would have to understand why one individual develops tendencies to hang on to others and to try to get out of them what he can—and also the means by which he makes others willing to let themselves be exploited, whether by a captivating smile, by intimidation or by promises made explicitly or implicitly—and why another person finds safety and satisfaction in withdrawing from others and in shutting himself off from the world by a wall of pride and defiance. In the latter type there will often be other physical expressions of tightness; it may show, for instance, in tight lips as well as in constipation.

Thus the difference in point of view may be expressed in this way: a person does not have tight lips because of the tenseness of his sphincter, but both are tight because his character trends tend toward one goal—to hold on to what he has and never give away anything, be it money, love or any kind of spontaneous feeling. When in dreams an individual of this type symbolizes persons through faeces, the libido-theory explanation would be that he despises people because they represent faeces to him, while I should say that representing people in symbols of faeces is an expression of an existing contempt for people. I should seek the reasons for this contempt in his general attitude to others and to himself: such as, for instance, self-contempt because of neurotic weaknesses, the fear of being despised by others as well, and the resulting attempts to establish, by despising others, an equilibrium favorable to the self-esteem. Furthermore, on a deeper layer there are often sadistic impulses to triumph over others by degrading them. Similarly, if a man looks upon sexual intercourse as upon a form of bowel evacuation, one may in a merely descriptive way speak of an "anal" concept of intercourse, but an interpretation in terms of the dynamics of the situation would consider the entirety of emotional disturbances in his relation to women and probably to men as well. The "anal concept of intercourse" is then seen as an expression of sadistic impulses to defile women.

The thinness of the data for the doctrine of sublimation is evident also in the fact that frequently the assumed physical basis for sublimation exists only in theory. Just as grief may be experienced without the shedding of tears, possessiveness may exist without any peculiarities in bowel movements or other physical functions, a thirst for knowledge without any peculiarities in eating or drinking, a deep interest in research without sexual curiosity having ever been a problem.

The doctrine that emotional life is patterned after sexual life has served the important function of revealing similarities between a person's general attitude and his sex life or sexual functions. No one has ever thought before that an incapacity to slide down hill on skis or a disparaging attitude toward men had anything in common with frigidity, or that feeling abused sexually had any connection with a propensity to feel cheated and humiliated by an employer. There is indeed a great deal of evidence that sexual disturbances and similar difficulties appear in general character traits. When a person generally tends to keep apart emotionally from others he will prefer sexual relations in which he can maintain his detachment. A disgruntled person who tends to begrudge others the pleasure they derive from something may also begrudge the satisfaction he gives to a sexual partner. A sadistic person who generally tends to arouse expectations in others, and then disappoints them, may also tend to deprive a sexual partner of the expected satisfaction—a tendency which may be one element constituting *ejaculatio praecox*. A woman with a general tendency to play the role of martyr may visualize the sexual act too as a form of cruelty and humiliation, and may react to such imaginings with a protest sufficient to prevent any satisfaction.

Freud's contention, however, goes beyond the statement that sexual and non-sexual difficulties are coincidental. He maintains that the sexual peculiarities are the cause and other peculiarities the result. This theory has led to the wrong belief that an individual is all right if only his sexual functions are satisfactory. Actually sex functions may be, but need not be, disturbed in neuroses. There are quite a number of severe neurotics whose conflicts may incapacitate them for productive work, who are haunted by anxieties, who have typical obsessive or schizoid trends, but notwithstanding all that receive the most complete satisfaction from sexual intercourse. I do not infer this fact from superficial assertions made by patients, but from the fact that these patients are able to distinguish clearly between having and not having a full orgasm.

Analysts adhering to the libido theory have disputed this fact. The wish to dispute it is understandable because it is a pivotal point. What hinges on it is not only the special contention of the *Vorbildlichkeit* of sexuality for other attitudes, but the basic contention of the libido theory: the power of sexuality to determine character. The theory of regression also hinges on it. Neuroses, according to Freud, are mainly the result of a regression from the "genital" level to "pre-genital" levels. Hence good sexual functioning cannot concur with neurotic disturbances. In order to reconcile this fact with the libido theory it is contended that although the sexual functions of some neurotics may be satisfactory it is in a merely physiological way, and the individuals are always disturbed "psychosexually," that is, there are always disturbances in the psychic relations with the sexual partner.

This argument is fallacious. Of course in every neurosis there are disturbances in the psychic relations with the sexual partner. But these allow a different interpretation. To those who, as I do, regard neuroses as the ultimate outcome of disturbances in human relationships, these disturbances must of necessity appear in every relationship, sexual or non-sexual. Furthermore, the contention of the libido theory is that even physiologically a good sexual functioning is possible only after "pre-genital" drives have been sufficiently overcome. Therefore the fact that a person can function well sexu-

ally and yet have neurotic disturbances shows the fundamental error of the libido theory, which is, to repeat,
to regard the personality as largely dependent on the
nature of the individual's sexuality.

The discovery that attitudes may be a reaction-
formation against existing opposite drives would be
most constructive if it were not stiffened into a generalization. That overkindliness may be a reaction-
formation against sadistic trends does not preclude the
possibility of a genuine kindliness which arises out of
basically good relations to others. That generosity may
be a reaction-formation against greediness does not dis-
prove the existence of genuine generosity.[8]

As to Freud's tendency to put frustration into the
center of discussion, this is misleading in many ways.
The fact that a neurotic person feels frustrated all the
time is caused by special conditions and does not allow
a generalization as to the significance of frustration.
The reasons why the neurotic feels frustrated so easily,
and why he reacts disproportionately to this feeling, lie
mainly in three factors: many of his expectations and
demands are prompted by anxiety, whereby they become imperative and thus make frustration a threat to
his security; furthermore, his expectations are often not
only excessive but also contradictory and hence render
their fulfillment in reality impossible; finally, his wishes
are often prompted by unconscious impulses to triumph
maliciously over others by imposing his will upon them,
so that if frustration is felt as a humiliating defeat, the
ensuing hostile reactions are a response not to the frus-

[8] *Cf.* Chapter XI. The "Ego" and the "Id."

tration of wishes but to the humiliation which the person subjectively experiences.

In Freud's theory frustration as such is supposed to arouse hostility. Actually, however, healthy persons— children as well as adults—are well able to endure a considerable amount of frustration without any reaction of hostility. This overemphasis on frustration has one practical implication in education: it is likely to divert attention from those factors in the parents' attitudes which are relevant in engendering hostility— briefly, the parents' own deficiencies [9]—and hence induce educators and anthropologists as well to put emphasis on unessential factors, such as weaning, education in cleanliness, birth of siblings. The emphasis should be not on the "what" but on the "how."

Moreover, frustration, as the source of instinctual tension, is believed to be the ultimate cause of neurotic anxiety.[10] This interpretation has done much to befog the understanding of neurotic anxiety, inasmuch as it prevents one from seeing that neurotic anxiety is not the "ego's" response to an increased instinctual tension but is the result of conflicting trends within the personality.

Also, the doctrine of frustration has done much to impair the potentialities of psychoanalytical therapy. The role ascribed to frustration has led to the advice that a technique of frustration should be used in analysis in order to bring to the foreground the patient's reaction to it. The implications of this procedure will

9 *Cf.* Chapter IV, The Oedipus Complex.
10 *Cf.* Chapter XII, Anxiety.

be discussed in connection with other problems of therapy.[11]

To come finally to Freud's use of latent homosexuality as an explanatory principle for such traits as submissiveness and parasitic propensities, or reactions against them, such an interpretation is in my opinion due to a failure to understand the basic masochistic character structure,[12] and this failure is in turn due largely to the conception of masochism as an ultimately sexual phenomenon.

In short, then, the libido theory in all its contentions is unsubstantiated. This is the more remarkable since it is one of the cornerstones on which psychoanalytical thinking and therapy rest. The assumption that every striving for pleasure is at bottom a striving for libidinal satisfaction is arbitrary. What is offered as evidence are unwarranted and often gross generalizations of certain good observations. Similarities existing between physiological functions and mental behavior or mental strivings are used to demonstrate that the former determine the latter. Peculiarities in the sexual sphere are off-hand assumed to engender similar coexisting peculiarities in character traits.

Its lack of substantial evidence is not, however, the severest criticism against the libido theory. A theory may be unsubstantiated but may still be a useful tool to widen and deepen the scope of our understanding. In other words, it may still be a good working hypothesis. As a matter of fact, Freud himself realizes that the

[11] *Cf.* Chapter IX, The Concept of Transference.
[12] *Cf.* Chapter XV, Masochistic Phenomena.

theory does not stand on too firm ground when he calls it "our mythology," [13] but still he does not feel that such an admission deters him from using it as an explanatory principle. To some extent the libido theory has been a constructive lead in making certain observations. It has helped us to regard sexual difficulties in an unprejudiced way and to recognize their importance; it has helped us to recognize similarities between character traits and sexual peculiarities and to see the frequent coincidence of certain trends (oral and anal character). It has been instrumental in shedding light on certain functional disturbances coexisting with these trends.

Nor does its basic weakness lie in the contention of a sexual origin for many attitudes and drives. As a matter of fact, one can drop not only the physiological origin of the "pre-genital" drives [14] but even the doctrine that these are sexual in nature without relinquishing the essence of the whole theory. Alexander, though not explicitly stating it, has practically abandoned the theory of pre-genital sexuality and has propounded instead a doctrine of three elementary tendencies which he designates as: to receive or take, to retain, and to give or eliminate.[15]

But whether we speak of sexual drives or, with

13 Sigmund Freud, *New Introductory Lectures on Psychoanalysis* (1933).

14 Lately Freud himself has been more reserved as to the specific somatic source of oral and anal drives: "Whether the relation to a somatic source gives the instinct any specific character and if so which is not at all clear" (*New Introductory Lectures on Psychoanalysis,* chapter on "Anxiety and Instinctual Life").

15 Franz Alexander, "The Influence of Psychologic Factors upon Gastro-Intestinal Disturbances" in *Psychoanalytic Quarterly* (1934).

Alexander, of elementary tendencies, whether we call them oral-libidinal or elementary tendencies to receive or take, does not essentially alter the basic mode of thinking. Though Alexander's attempt constitutes a definite progress, the essential assumption remains that man is driven to fulfill certain primary, biologically given needs, and that these are powerful enough to exert a decisive influence on his personality and thus on his life as a whole.

This assumption is what constitutes the real danger of the libido theory. Its main characteristic and its main deficiency lie in the fact that it is an instinct theory. Although it enables us to see the manifold ways in which a single trend manifests itself in a personality, it engenders the illusion that the libidinal manifestations are the ultimate source of all trends. This illusion is fostered by the notion that only such interpretations are "deep" which show presumably biological roots for a trend. The claim of psychoanalysis that it is a depth psychology is warranted by its dealing with unconscious motivations: an interpretation is deep when it reaches down to repressed strivings, feelings, fears. But to regard only those interpretations as deep which establish a connection with infantile drives is an illusion born of theoretical preconceptions. It is a harmful illusion too, for three main reasons.

First, it contributes toward a distorted perspective on human relationships, on the "ego," on the nature of neurotic conflicts, neurotic anxieties, on the role of cultural factors. These implications will be discussed in later chapters.

Second, it constitutes a temptation to understand a

whole machine out of one wheel, instead of trying to understand how the interrelation of all parts brings about certain effects, and in the process to understand also why one wheel is located where it is and why it has to function as it does. Instead of seeing sexual masochistic trends, for example, as one expression of a whole character structure, the latter and its complexity are explained as the result of the individual having been sexually excited in painful experiences, such as being beaten. Or instead of understanding a woman's wish to be a man—if there is any—from her entire personality, and understanding the latter from the totality of her life circumstances, particularly in childhood, the opposite way is followed: the entire structure is seen as a result of penis-envy. Such intricate features as destructive ambitions, feelings of inadequacy, hostility toward men, self-sufficiency, general discontentment, difficulties in menstruation or in pregnancy, masochistic trends, are regarded as the ultimate outcome of one allegedly biological source: penis-envy.

Third, it leads to seeing final limitations in therapy where they do not exist. By regarding biological factors as the *ultima causa movens,* one is bound to come to rock bottom in therapy because, as Freud points out, one cannot change what is determined by biology.[16]

What to put in its place has been indicated in discussing the individual contentions of the libido theory, and will be further suggested throughout the book. In principle there are two answers to the question: a more

16 *Cf.* Sigmund Freud, "Analysis Terminable and Interminable," *op. cit.*

specific one, concerning the power of the drives which Freud regards as instinctual; and a more comprehensive one, concerning the nature of the drives themselves.

The observation underlying the conviction that certain drives are instinctual or elemental is their seemingly irresistible strength, their enforcing themselves on the individual and driving him willy-nilly toward certain goals. The instinctual drives seek satisfaction even though in order to obtain it they may go against the interests of the individual as a whole. The theoretical basis for this part of the libido theory is that man is ruled by the pleasure principle.

But it is neurotic patients who exhibit this seemingly unreasonable and blind urge of certain drives. Freud realizes that there is a difference in this regard between the neurotic and the non-neurotic person. The healthy individual can postpone satisfaction if it is not available at the time being, and he can make sustained and purposeful efforts to obtain it at some future time. For the neurotic all these drives may be imperative and not postponable. To account for this difference Freud introduces two subsidiary hypotheses. One is that the neurotic is more stringently ruled by the pleasure principle and is bound to obtain immediate satisfaction at any price because he is infantile. The other is that the libido in neurotics has a queer kind of adhesiveness. I shall have opportunity later on to discuss the all too generous use of infantilism as an explanatory principle. The hypothesis of the tenacity of the neurotic libido is merely speculative and should be resorted to only if there are no psychological explanations for the phe-nomenon.

As far as neurotic persons are concerned, Freud's observations as to the irresistibility of certain drives are not only valid but may rightly be numbered among his constructive findings. In neuroses such drives as those toward self-inflation and toward having a parasitic existence can be stronger than the sexual instinct proper and can largely determine a person's life. The question, however, is how to account for such strength. As pointed out, Freud ascribes it to the instinctual search for satisfaction.

Actually, however, what lends all the drives their peculiar strength is the fact that they serve both satisfaction and safety. Man is ruled not by the pleasure principle alone but by two guiding principles: safety and satisfaction.[17] Since the neurotic has more anxiety than the mentally healthy individual he has to put an infinitely greater amount of energy into maintaining his security, and it is the necessity for obtaining reassurance against a lurking anxiety which lends his strivings their strength and tenacity.[18] People can renounce food, money, attention, affection so long as they are only renouncing satisfaction, but they cannot renounce these things if without them they would be or feel in danger of destitution or starvation or of being helplessly exposed to hostility, in other words, if they would lose their feeling of safety.

That the driving force is not only satisfaction but anxiety can be shown with an accuracy approximating

[17] The importance of these two principles has been emphasized by Alfred Adler and H. S. Sullivan, among others, but neither of them sufficiently recognizes the role of anxiety, which accounts for the stringency of the striving for safety.

[18] *Cf.* Karen Horney, *op. cit.,* ch. 5.

that of an experiment. Types with prevailingly receptive, grabbing or parasitic trends, for instance, react
with anxiety—more or less admixed with rage—when
the afflux of money, help or affection is stopped. The
prospect of standing on their own is frightening. Accordingly anxiety is allayed when they obtain what they
want. It can be allayed by eating, by buying something,
by receiving any sign of attention or care. Types with
a predominant striving to assume control over others,
and to be always right, not only enjoy righteousness
and power but become positively frightened when they
have made an error in judgment or when they are part
of a crowd (fear in subways). Retentive types not only
treasure money, collections, knowledge, but become
frightened in any situation implying the intrusion of
others into their privacy or their opening up to others;
they may develop anxiety at sexual intercourse; they
may feel love as a danger; they may anxiously ruminate
after having told others even insignificant data concerning their own life, particularly their own feelings. Similar data will be presented later on concerning narcissistic and masochistic attitudes. They show uniformly
that all these strivings, while they yield overt or concealed satisfaction, yet derive their character of "have
to," of insistence that it should be so and not otherwise,
from being a defensive strategy aiming at allaying
anxiety.

The anxiety against which these defenses are built
up is what I have described in a previous publication [19]
as basic anxiety, defined as a feeling of helplessness

[19] Karen Horney, op. cit., chs. 3-5.

toward a potentially hostile world. This concept is alien
to psychoanalytical thinking in so far as the latter is
oriented on the libido theory. The psychoanalytical
concept which is nearest to it is what Freud calls "real"
anxiety. This too is a fear of the environment but it is
related entirely to the individual's instinctual drives.
Its main implication is that the child is afraid the environment will punish him with castration or loss of
love for any pursuit of forbidden instinctual drives.

The concept of basic anxiety is more comprehensive
than Freud's "real" anxiety. It contends that the environment is dreaded as a whole because it is felt to
be unreliable, mendacious, unappreciative, unfair, un-
just, begrudging and merciless. According to this concept the child not only fears punishment or desertion
because of forbidden drives, but he feels the environment as a menace to his entire development and to his
most legitimate wishes and strivings. He feels in danger
of his individuality being obliterated, his freedom taken
away, his happiness prevented. In contrast to the fear
of castration this fear is not fantasy,[20] but is well
founded on reality. In an environment in which the
basic anxiety develops, the child's free use of energies
is thwarted, his self-esteem and self-reliance are undermined, fear is instilled by intimidation and isolation,
his expansiveness is warped through brutality, standards
or overprotective "love."

The other essential element in the basic anxiety is
that a child is rendered helpless to defend himself adequately against infringements. Not only is he biologi-

20 Cf. Anna Freud, *Das Ich und die Abwehrmechanismen* (1936).

cally helpless [21] and dependent on the family, but every kind of self-assertion is discouraged. He is usually too intimidated to express his resentment or his accusations, and when he does express them he is made to feel guilty. The hostility which has to be repressed precipitates anxiety, because hostility is a danger when directed against someone on whom one feels dependent.

In the face of these circumstances the child resorts to building up certain defensive attitudes—one might say strategies—which enable him to cope with the world and at the same time allow him certain possibilities of gratification. What attitudes he develops depend entirely on the combination of factors present in the whole situation: whether his prevailing striving will be for assuming control, for being submissive, for being unobtrusive, or for walling himself in and drawing a magic circle around himself, preventing intrusion into his privacy, depends on which ways are in reality closed to him and which are accessible.

In spite of Freud's recognition of anxiety as "the central problem of neuroses," he has nevertheless not seen the all-pervasive role of anxiety as a dynamic factor driving toward certain goals. With recognition of this role of anxiety the role of frustration appears in another light. It becomes clear not only that we can accept frustration of pleasure much more easily than Freud assumes, but that we may even greatly prefer it, provided it guarantees safety.

In this case the need to facilitate understanding prevails over my reluctance to introduce new terms. I sug-

[21] A helplessness which in psychoanalytical literature is one-sidedly emphasized.

gest that those strivings whose power is determined mainly by a search for safety be designated as "neurotic trends." In many ways the neurotic trends coincide with what Freud considers instinctual drives and "super-ego." Freud regards the "super-ego" as a composite of various instinctual drives, while I regard it primarily as a safety-device, that is, as a neurotic trend toward perfectionism; Freud holds narcissistic or masochistic drives to be instinctual in nature, while in my judgment they are neurotic trends toward self-inflation and self-disparagement.

The advantage of equating Freud's "instinctual drives" to my "neurotic trends" is that it becomes then less difficult to compare his viewpoints with the ones I suggest. But we have to consider that this equivalence is inaccurate in two respects. According to Freud, all kinds of hostile aggression are instinctual in nature. As I see it, aggressiveness is a neurotic trend only if a neurotic's feeling of safety rests on being aggressive. Otherwise I would regard hostility in neuroses not as a neurotic trend but as a reaction to such trends. The hostility of a narcissistic person, for example, is his reaction to the fact that others do not accept his inflated notions about himself. The hostility of the masochistic person is his reaction to his feeling of being abused or to his wish for a vindictive triumph for being abused.

The other inaccuracy is rather self-evident. Needless to say, sexuality in the usual sense is not a neurotic trend but is an instinct. But sexual drives, too, can take the coloring of a neurotic trend inasmuch as many neurotics need sexual satisfaction (masturbation or intercourse) in order to allay anxiety.

A more comprehensive interpretation of the nature of the drives regarded as instinctual has been formulated by Erich Fromm,[22] on the assumption that particular needs which are relevant to understanding the personality and its difficulties are not instinctual in character but are created by the entirety of conditions under which we live. Freud does not neglect environmental influences but considers them only as a factor molding instinctual drives. The formulation I have sketched above puts the environment and its perplexities into the center. Among the environmental factors, however, that which is most relevant to character formation is the kind of human relationships in which a child grows up. In regard to neuroses this means that the conflicting trends constituting them are determined ultimately by disturbances in human relationships.

To formulate the difference in viewpoint with the utmost condensation: Freud regards the neurotic's irresistible needs as instincts or their derivatives; he believes that the influence of the environment is restricted to giving the instinctual drives their special form and strength. The concept I have outlined holds that these needs are not instinctual but grow from the child's need to cope with a difficult environment. Their power, which Freud ascribes to elemental instinctual forces, is due to the fact that they are the only means for the individual to have some feeling of safety.

[22] He has elaborated it in lectures, particularly in reference to sociological problems, and in a manuscript not yet published.

CHAPTER IV

THE OEDIPUS COMPLEX

BY Oedipus complex Freud means sexual attraction to one of the parents with a concomitant jealousy toward the other parent. Freud regards this experience as biologically determined, though in the individual it is engendered by the parents' care of the physical needs of the child. Its numerous variations depend on the individual constellation actually existing in the particular family. Libidinal desires directed toward the parents vary in nature according to the stages of libido development. They culminate in genital desires toward the parents.

The assumption that such a constellation is biologically conditioned, and hence ubiquitous, has made two further assumptions necessary for its support. Finding no traces of the Oedipus complex in the majority of healthy adults, Freud assumed that in these persons the complex had been successfully repressed, a conclusion which, as McDougall has already pointed out,[1] is not convincing to those who do not share Freud's belief in the biological nature of the complex. Furthermore, find-

[1] William McDougall, *Psychoanalysis and Social Psychology* (1936).

ing many instances in which the major tie occurred between mother and daughter, or father and son, Freud
propounded an enlargement of the concept according to
which the homosexual—inverted—Oedipus complex is
equal in importance to the heterosexual—normal—one;
thus, for example, the homosexual tie, in the case of a
girl, is a normal precursor of a later attachment to the
father.

Freud's conviction of the ubiquitous occurrence of
the Oedipus complex rests on the presuppositions given
by the libido theory, so much so that anyone accepting
the libido theory must accept also the doctrine of the
universality of the Oedipus complex. As indicated before, according to the libido theory every human relationship is based ultimately on instinctual drives.

When this theory is applied to the child-parent relationship it suggests several conclusions: the wish to be
like a parent may be a derivate of wishes toward oral
incorporation; a dependent clinging to a parent may
be the expression of an intensified oral organization; [2]

[2] To quote Otto Fenichel: "A young girl had suffered as an infant
from a gastric affection, on account of which she had been put on a
starvation diet. This engendered in her peculiarly strong oral cravings.
In the period immediately following this illness, she had contracted the
habit of throwing her bottle, when she had finished the milk in it, on
the floor and breaking it, a gesture which I construe as an expression
of some such thought as this: What good is an empty bottle to me? I
want a full one! As a little child she was very greedy. *The oral fixation
manifested itself in an intense dread of a loss of love and a passionate
clinging to her mother* [italics mine]. It was therefore a great disappointment to her, at the age of three, when her mother became preg-
nant" (Otto Fenichel, "The Scopophilic Instinct and Identification" in
International Journal of Psychoanalysis, 1937).

The implicit assumption in the report can only be that the passionate clinging to the mother, the fear of losing her love, the outbreaks

any kind of submissive devotion to a parent of the same sex is probably the expression of passive homosexuality or of sexual masochistic trends, while a rebellious rejection of a parent of the same sex is probably an inner fight against existing homosexual desires; more generally, any kind of affection or tenderness toward a parent is by definition aim-inhibited sexuality; fears concern mainly punishment for forbidden instinctual desires (incestuous desires, masturbation, jealousy), and the anticipated danger is the prohibition of physical satisfaction (fear of castration, fear of loss of love); finally, hostility toward a parent, if not related to the frustration of instinctual drives, may be understood as the ultimate expression of sexual rivalry.

As some of these feelings or attitudes are present in every child-parent relationship—as they are in every human relationship—the evidence for an omnipresent Oedipus complex is overwhelming indeed to anyone accepting the theoretical premise. There is no doubt that persons who later develop a neurosis or a psychosis may be closely tied to the parents, whether the nature

of temper and the hatred of the mother are the results of a reinforced oral libido. All factors which in my estimation are relevant to the picture are omitted. While it is possible that the starvation diet was important, in so far as it focused the child's attention on food, I should like to hear in the first place about the manner in which the mother treated the child. By analogy I should assume that here was a child in whom, because of the treatment accorded it, intense anxiety and hostility were engendered, resulting in an enhanced need for affection and thus in claims for unconditional love, enhanced jealousy and a great fear of rejection and desertion. Furthermore, I should assume that the hostility appearing in temper tantrums and in destructive fantasies was partly an expression of the hostility provoked by the mother and partly an expression of rage because possessive love claims were not fulfilled.

of this tie be sexual or not. It is Freud's merit to have seen this in spite of existing social tabus and to have recognized its implications. The question remains, however, as to whether fixations on the parents arise in a child for biological reasons or whether they are the product of describable conditions. I firmly believe that the latter is true. There are in the main two series of conditions provoking a stronger attachment to one of the parents. They may or may not be allied, but both are created by the parents.

One of them is, briefly, sexual stimulation by the parents. This may consist in a gross sexual approach to the child; it may arise from sexually-tinged caresses, or from an emotional hothouse atmosphere surrounding all members of the family or including some members and excluding others who are regarded with animosity. Such a parental attitude is not only the result of the parents' emotional or sexual dissatisfaction, but according to my experience it has also other more complicated causes, which I do not wish to elaborate here as it would lead us too far astray.

The other series of conditions is entirely different in nature. While in the above group there is a genuinely sexual response to stimulation, the second group is connected in no way with either spontaneous or stimulated sexual desires of the child, but with its anxiety. Anxiety, as we shall see later, is an outcome of conflicting tendencies or needs. The typical conflict leading to anxiety in a child is that between dependency on the parents—enhanced by the child's feeling of being isolated and intimidated—and hostile impulses against the parents. Hostility may be aroused in a child in many ways: by the parents' lack of respect for him; by unreasonable demands and prohibitions; by injustice; by unreliability; by suppression of criticism; by the parents dominating him and ascribing these tendencies to love; by misusing children for the sake of prestige or ambitious goals. If a child, in addition to being dependent on his parents, is grossly or subtly intimidated by them and hence feels that any expression of hostile impulses against them endangers his security, then the existence of such hostile impulses is bound to create anxiety.[3]

One way to allay this anxiety is to cling to one of the parents, and a child will do so if there is any chance of thus receiving reassuring affection. Such a hanging-on to a person out of sheer anxiety is easily confounded with love, and in the child's own mind seems like love. It does not necessarily take on a sexual coloring, but it may easily do so. It certainly assumes all the characteristics of a neurotic need for affection, that is, a need for affection conditioned by anxiety, as we see it in adult neurotics: dependency, insatiability, possessiveness, jealousy toward anyone who does or might interfere.

The resulting picture may look exactly like what Freud describes as the Oedipus complex: passionate clinging to one parent and jealousy toward the other or toward anyone interfering with the claim of exclusive possession. In my experience the vast majority of infantile attachments to parents, as they are retrospectively revealed in the analysis of adult neurotics, belongs to this group. But the dynamic structure of these at-

[3] *Cf.* Lawrence F. Woolley, "The Effect of Erratic Discipline in Childhood on Emotional Tensions" in *Psychiatric Quarterly* (1937).

tachments is entirely different from what Freud conceives as the Oedipus complex. They are an early
manifestation of neurotic conflicts rather than a primarily sexual phenomenon.

A comparison between this situation and one primarily determined by a stimulated sexual attachment
to the parent shows several significant differences. In
the attachment created mainly by anxiety the sexual
element is not essential; it may be present, but it may
be entirely missing. In the incestuous attachment the
goal is love, but in the attachment conditioned by
anxiety the main goal is security. Hence, in the first
kind, attachment goes to the parent who elicits love or
sexual desires; in the second group it usually goes to the
parent who is the more powerful or the more awe-
inspiring, for the winning of his affection promises the
greatest chance of protection. If in the latter case the
same clinging attitude a girl had toward a domineering
mother reappears in her relation to her husband, this
means not that to the girl the husband represents the
mother but that for reasons which have to be analyzed
the girl is still full of anxiety and tries to allay it in the
same way she did in childhood, clinging now to the
husband instead of to the mother.

In both groups the attachment to the parents is not a
biologically given phenomenon but a response to provocations from the outside. This contention that the
Oedipus complex is not of a biological nature seems to
be confirmed by anthropological observations, the results of which indicate that the generation of such a
complex depends on the whole set of factors operating
in family life, such as the role of authority of the par-

ents, seclusion of the family, size of the family, sexual prohibitions and the like.

There still remains the question whether spontaneous sexual feelings for the parents arise at all under "normal" conditions, that is, when there is no special provocation by either stimulation or anxiety. Our knowledge is restricted to neurotic children and adults. But I should be inclined to think that there is no good reason why a child born with its sexual instincts should not have sexual inclinations toward the parents or siblings. It is questionable, however, whether without other factors these spontaneous sexual attractions ever reach an intensity sufficient to meet Freud's description of an Oedipus complex—which is the presence of sexual desire strong enough to arouse so much jealousy and fear that they can be dissolved only by repression.

The theory of the Oedipus complex has greatly influenced present-day education. On the positive side, it has helped to make parents conscious of the lasting harm inflicted on children by exciting them sexually and also by being overindulgent, overprotective and too prohibitive in sexual matters. On the negative side, it has fostered the illusion that it is enough to enlighten children sexually and to refrain from forbidding masturbation, from whipping them, from letting them witness parental intercourse and from attaching them too strongly to parents. The danger lies in the one-sidedness of such suggestions. Even if they are all religiously adhered to, the germs for later neuroses may be laid. Why? The answer is in principle the same as the answer to the charge that psychoanalytical therapy is insuffi-

ciently successful: too many factors extremely relevant
to a child's growth are regarded as comparatively superficial, and hence are not given the weight they deserve.
I am thinking of such parental attitudes as having real
interest in a child, real respect for it, giving it real
warmth, and of such qualities as reliability and sincerity.

It may be, however, that the actual damage done by a
one-sided sexual orientation is less harmful than would
appear at first thought. At least the psychoanalytical
suggestions to the educator are reasonable and can be
followed easily, as they consist mainly in avoiding certain concrete errors. But suggestions concerning more
important factors, such as those I have mentioned—factors which create an atmosphere favorable to growth—
are infinitely more difficult to follow as they entail
changes in character.

The theory of the Oedipus complex is significant
mainly because of the bearing the complex is assumed
to have on later relationships. Freud believes that later
attitudes to people are largely a repetition of the oedipal
one. Thus, for example, a man's defiant attitude toward
other men would suggest that he is warding off homosexual tendencies which he had toward his father or
brother; a woman's incapacity to love her children spontaneously would be interpreted as an identification with
her own mother.

The debatable points in this kind of thinking will be
discussed in connection with the theory of repetition
compulsion. Only this much here: if it is an unwarranted belief that incestuous attachment to parents is a
normal incident of childhood, then the validity of interpretations relating later peculiarities to infantile inces-

tuous wishes, and reactions to them, is likewise dubitable. Interpretations of this kind serve mainly to strengthen the interpreter's conviction as to the regular occurrence of the Oedipus complex and its powerful after-effects. But the evidence thus found results from a process of circular reasoning.

If we discard the theoretical implications of the theory, what remains is not the Oedipus complex but the highly constructive finding that early relationships *in their totality* mold the character to an extent which can scarcely be overestimated. Later attitudes to others, then, are not repetitions of infantile ones but emanate from the character structure, the basis of which is laid in childhood.

CHAPTER V

THE CONCEPT OF NARCISSISM

THE phenomena which in psychoanalytical literature are called narcissistic are most divergent in character. They include vanity, conceit, craving for prestige and admiration, a desire to be loved in connection with an incapacity to love others, withdrawal from others, normal self-esteem, ideals, creative desires, anxious concern about health, appearance, intellectual faculties. Thus a clinical definition of narcissism would be an embarrassing task. All that the above phenomena have in common is concern about the self, or perhaps merely attitudes pertaining to the self. The reason for this bewildering picture is that the term is used in a purely genetic sense to signify that the origin of these manifestations is assumed to be the narcissistic libido.

In contrast to the vagueness of the clinical definition, the genetic one is precise: a person is narcissistic who at bottom is in love with himself. In the words of Gregory Zilboorg: "The term 'narcissism' does not mean mere selfishness, or egocentricity, as is assumed; it denotes specifically that state of mind, that spontaneous attitude of man, in which the individual himself happens to choose only himself instead of others as the object to love. Not that he does not love, or that he hates, others and wants everything for him; but he is inwardly in love with himself and seeks everywhere for a mirror in which to admire and woo his own image." [1]

The core of the concept is the postulate that concern with one's self or overvaluation of one's self is an expression of infatuation with the self. Are we not just as blind, Freud argues, toward shortcomings in another person, and just as inclined to overrate his good qualities, when we are infatuated with him? Therefore persons tending toward self-concern or self-overvaluation must undoubtedly at bottom be in love with themselves. This postulate is in accordance with the libido theory. On this basis it is conclusive indeed to regard egocentricity as an expression of self-love and also to regard normal self-esteem and ideals as its desexualized derivatives. But if we do not accept the libido theory the postulate appears to be a merely dogmatic contention.[2] Clinical evidence, with few exceptions, is not in its favor.

If narcissism is considered not genetically but with reference to its actual meaning it should, in my judgment, be described as essentially self-inflation. Psychic inflation, like economic inflation, means presenting greater values than really exist. It means that the person loves and admires himself for values for which

1 Gregory Zilboorg, "Loneliness" in *Atlantic Monthly* (January 1938).
2 *Cf.* Michael Balint, "Frühe Entwicklungsstadien des Ichs" in *Imago* (1937).

there is no adequate foundation.[3] Similarly, it means that he expects love and admiration from others for qualities that he does not possess, or does not possess to as large an extent as he supposes. According to my definition, it is not narcissistic for a person to value a quality in himself which he actually possesses, or to like it to be valued by others. These two tendencies—appearing unduly significant to oneself and craving undue admiration from others—cannot be separated. Both are always present, though in different types one or the other may prevail.

Why must people aggrandize themselves? If we are not content with a speculative biological answer—which means relating the tendency to an instinctual source—we must find some other answer. As in all neurotic phenomena we find at the basis disturbances in the relationships to others, disturbances acquired in childhood through the environmental influences mentioned in previous chapters.[4] The factor which contributes most fundamentally to the development of narcissistic trends appears to be the child's alienation from others, provoked by grievances and fears. His positive emotional ties with others become thin; he loses the capacity to love.

The same unfavorable environment produces disturbances in his feeling for self. In more severe cases these

[3] The emphasis rests on the fact that the foundation is not adequate. The illusory picture a person presents to himself and to others is not altogether fantastic, but may be an exaggerated picture of the potentialities he actually has.

[4] Cf. Chapter III, The Libido Theory, and Chapter IV, The Oedipus Complex.

mean more than a mere impairment of self-esteem; they bring about a complete suppression of the spontaneous individual self.[5] Various influences operate to this effect: the unquestioned authority of righteous parents, creating a situation in which the child feels compelled to adopt their standards for the sake of peace; the attitudes of self-sacrificing parents who elicit the feeling from the child that he has no rights of his own and should live only for the parents' sake; parents who transfer their own ambitions to the child and regard the boy as an embryonic genius or the girl as a princess, thereby developing in the child the feeling that he is loved for imaginary qualities rather than for his true self. All these influences, varied as they are, make the child feel that in order to be liked or accepted he must be as others expect him to be. The parents have so thoroughly superimposed themselves on the mind of the child that he complies through fear, thus gradually losing what James calls the "real me." His own will, his own wishes, his own feelings, his own likes and dislikes, his own grievances, become paralyzed.[6] Therefore he gradually loses the capacity to measure his own val-

[5] Erich Fromm in his lectures on authority was the first to point out the significance which this loss of self has for neuroses. Also it seems that Otto Rank, in his concept of will and creativeness, has similar factors in mind; cf. Otto Rank, *Will Therapy* (1936).

[6] Strindberg describes this process in one of his fairy tales, "Jubal ohne Ich" (in *Märchen und Fabeln*, 1920). A boy was naturally possessed of a strong will; at an earlier age than other boys he spoke of himself in the first person. But his parents told him that he had no self. When he grew a little older he said: I will. But his parents told him that he had no will. Having a strong will he was amazed at this verdict but he accepted it. When he grew up his father asked him what he wanted to be, but he did not know because he had ceased to will as it had been forbidden.

ues. He becomes dependent on the opinion of others. He is bad or stupid when others think he is bad or stupid, intelligent when others order him to be intelligent, a genius when others consider him one. While in all of us self-esteem is to some extent dependent upon the estimate of others, in this case nothing but the estimate of others counts.[7]

Such a development is fostered also by other influences, such as direct blows to the self-esteem, derogatory attitudes of parents who miss no opportunity to make a child feel that he is no good, the parents' preference for other siblings, which undermines his security and makes him concentrate on outshining them. There are also all those factors which directly impair a child's self-sufficiency, self-reliance and initiative.

There are several ways in which a child tries to cope with life under such distressing conditions: by defiantly conforming with the standards ("super-ego"); by making himself unobtrusive and dependent on others (masochistic trends); by self-inflation (narcissistic trends). Which way is chosen, or prevailingly chosen, depends on the peculiar combination of circumstances.

What does an individual gain by self-aggrandizement?

He escapes the painful feeling of nothingness by molding himself in fancy into something outstanding. This is achieved whether he indulges in an active conscious play of fantasy—thinking of himself as a prince, a genius, a president, a general, an explorer—or is aware only of an inarticulate feeling of his own significance. The more he is alienated, not only from others but also

[7] In William James' term, what remains is the "social self": "A man's social self is the recognition which he gets from his mates."

from himself, the more easily such notions acquire a psychic reality. Not that he discards reality because of them—as the psychotic does—but reality takes on a provisional character, as life does for a Christian who expects his real life to begin in heaven. His notions of himself become a substitute for his undermined self-esteem; they become his "real me."

By creating a fantasy world of his own in which he is the hero he also consoles himself for not being loved and appreciated. He may feel that though others reject him, look down on him, do not love him for what he really is, it is because he is too far above their understanding. My personal impression is that the illusions do far more than give secret substitute satisfactions. I often wonder whether they do not save the individual from being crushed entirely and thus whether they are not literally life-saving.

Finally, self-inflation represents an attempt to put relationships to others on a positive basis. If others do not love and respect the individual for what he is they should at least pay attention to him and admire him. The obtainment of admiration is substituted for love— a consequential step. From then on he feels unwanted if he is not admired. He loses any understanding of the fact that friendliness and love can include an objective or even a critical attitude. What falls short of blind adoration is to him no longer love; he will even suspect it of being hostility. He will judge others according to the admiration or flattery he receives from them. People who admire him are good and superior, people who do not are not worth bothering with. Thus his main gratification lies in being admired. but also his security rests on it, because it gives him the illusion that he is strong and that the world around is friendly. It is a security on a rickety basis, however. Any failure may bring to the surface all the underlying insecurity. In fact, not even a failure is needed to elicit this effect; admiration paid to someone else may be sufficient to bring it about.

Thus there develops a certain combination of character trends which for the sake of facilitating understanding one might call the basic narcissistic trends. Their further development depends on the extent of alienation from self and others, and on the degree of anxiety produced. If the early experiences were not too decisive, and if later conditions are favorable, these basic trends may be outgrown. If not, they tend to be reinforced in time through three main factors.

One of them is an increasing unproductivity. A striving for admiration may be a powerful motor toward achievement, or toward developing qualities which are socially desirable or which make a person lovable, but it involves the danger that everything will be done with both eyes on the effect it has on others. An individual of this type chooses a woman not for her own sake but because her conquest would flatter him or add to his prestige. A piece of work is done not for its own sake but for the impression it might make. Brilliancy becomes more important than substance. Hence the danger that superficiality, showmanship, opportunism will choke productivity. Even if the individual succeeds in winning prestige this way, he rightly feels that it cannot last, though he is not aware of the reasons for his uneasiness about it. The only available means for silencing his uneasiness is to reinforce the narcissistic trends: to chase for more success and to build up more inflated notions about himself. Sometimes a baffling capacity is developed to transform shortcomings and failures into something glorious. If his writings are not recognized sufficiently it is because he is far ahead of his time; if he cannot get along with his family or friends it is because of their shortcomings.

Another factor increasing the individual's basic narcissistic trends is the development of excessive expectations as to what the world owes him. He feels he should be recognized as a genius without having to give evidence of it by actual work. Women should single him out without his actively doing anything about it. Deep down he may feel, for example, that it is inconceivable that any woman knowing him could fall in love with another man. The characteristic feature of these attitudes is the expectation that devotion or glory can be obtained without effort and initiative of his own. This peculiar type of expectation is strictly determined. It is necessary because of the damage that has been done to the individual's spontaneity, originality and initiative, and because of his fear of people. The factors which originally pushed him toward self-inflation also paralyze his inner activity. Hence the inner insistence that fulfillment of his wishes should come from others.[8]

8 H. Schultz-Hencke in *Schicksal und Neurose* (1931) points out the significance of this process for neuroses. He claims that a sequence which can be briefly characterized as fears, inertia, excessive demands, is the essential process in every neurosis. Also N. L. Blitzsten in "Amphithymia" (*Archives of Neurology and Psychiatry*, 1936) stresses the significance of unreasonable demands on others, and of the wish for accomplishment without having to make any efforts.

This process, which is unconscious in its implications, leads in two ways to a reinforcement of narcissistic trends: the claims made on others must be justified by emphasis on his own alleged values; and this emphasis must be renewed in order to cover up the disappointments which inevitably ensue from his exaggerated expectations.

A last source feeding the basic narcissistic trends is the increasing impairment of human relationships. The individual's illusions about himself, and his peculiar kind of expectations of others, are bound to make him vulnerable. Since the world does not recognize his secret claims he often feels hurt and develops greater hostility toward others, becomes more isolated and as a result is driven again and again to take refuge in his illusions. Grievances toward others also may grow because he holds them responsible for his failures to realize his illusions. As a consequence he develops traits which we regard as morally objectionable, such as pronounced egoism, vindictiveness, distrust, disregard for others if they do not serve his own glory. These traits, however, are incompatible with his notion that he is a wonderful being, far above the average of human frailties. Therefore they must be covered up. They are either repressed, in which case they appear only in disguise, or they are simply denied.[9] Self-inflation thus acquires the function of concealing the existing disparity, in line with the maxim: it is out of the question that I, this superior

[9] Repressions resulting from self-inflation seem to be less radical than those resulting from perfectionistic strivings (cf. Chapter XIII, The Concept of the "Super-Ego"); frequently trends not fitting into the individual's inflated picture of himself are merely denied or embellished.

being, have such shortcomings, and therefore they are nonexistent.

In order to understand the differences that are found in types with pronounced narcissistic trends we have to consider two main factors. One of them is how far the phantom of admiration is pursued in reality or only in the realm of fantasy; this difference ultimately boils down to quantitative factors in genesis, briefly, to the extent to which the individual's spirit has been broken. The other factor is the way in which narcissistic trends are combined with other character trends; they may be entangled, for example, with perfectionistic, masochistic [10] and sadistic trends. The frequency of these combinations is accounted for by the fact that all of them emanate from a similar source, that they represent different solutions for similar calamities. The bewildering number of contradictory qualities attributed to narcissism in psychoanalytical literature results in part from a failure to recognize that narcissism is but one specific trend within a personality structure. It is the combination of trends which gives a personality a certain coloring.

Narcissistic trends may be combined also with a tendency to withdraw from people, a tendency that is found in the schizoid personality. In psychoanalytical literature withdrawal from others is regarded as inherently a narcissistic trend; but while alienation from others is inherent in narcissistic trends withdrawal is not. On the contrary, a person with pronounced narcissistic trends,

[10] *Cf.* Fritz Wittels, "The Mystery of Masochism" in the *Psychoanalytic Review* (1937).

though incapable of love, nevertheless needs people as a source of admiration and support. Thus it would be more accurate in these cases to speak of a combination of narcissistic trends with a tendency to withdraw from others.

Narcissistic trends are frequent in our culture. More often than not people are incapable of true friendship and love; they are egocentric, that is, concerned with their security, health, recognition; they feel insecure and tend to overrate their personal significance; they lack judgment of their own value because they have relegated it to others. These typical narcissistic features are by no means restricted to persons who are incapacitated by neuroses.

Freud accounts for the frequency of these trends by his assumption of their biological origin. This assumption is evidence again of Freud's faith in the concept of instincts, but it also reveals his habitual failure to take cultural factors into consideration. Actually the two sets of factors engendering narcissistic trends in neuroses are generally operative in our culture. There are many cultural factors creating fears and hostile tensions among people and thereby alienating them from one another. There are also many general influences tending to curtail individual spontaneity, such as the standardization of feelings, thoughts and behavior, and the fact that people are valued rather for what they appear to be than for what they are. Furthermore, the striving for prestige as a means of overcoming fears and inner emptiness is certainly culturally prescribed.

Summing up, the observations which Freud has taught us to make [11] concerning self-aggrandizement and egocentricity permit a different interpretation from that suggested by him. I believe that—here as in other psychological problems—the postulate that an instinct is the generating cause prevents a perception of the meaning and significance which particular trends have for a personality. According to my view, narcissistic trends are not the derivative of an instinct but represent a neurotic trend, in this case an attempt to cope with the self and others by way of self-inflation.

Freud assumes that both normal self-esteem and self-aggrandizement are narcissistic phenomena, the difference being merely one of quantity. In my opinion this failure to distinguish clearly between the two attitudes toward the self befogs the issue. The difference between self-esteem and self-inflation is not quantitative but qualitative. True self-esteem rests on qualities which a person actually possesses, while self-inflation implies presenting to the self and to others qualities or achievements for which there is no adequate foundation. If the other conditions are present narcissistic trends may arise if self-esteem and other qualities pertaining to the individual's spontaneous self are smothered. Hence self-esteem and self-inflation are mutually exclusive.

Finally, narcissism is an expression not of self-love

[11] Sigmund Freud, "Narcissism: An Introduction" in *Collected Papers,* Vol. IV (1914). *Cf.* also the excellent observations reported by Ernest Jones, "Der Gottmensch-Komplex" in *Internationale Zeitschrift für ärztliche Psychoanalyse* (1913), and Karl Abraham, "Über eine besondere Form des neurotischen Widerstandes gegen die psychoanalytische Methodik" in *ibid.* (1919).

but of alienation from the self. In rather simplified terms, a person clings to illusions about himself because, and as far as, he has lost himself. As a consequence the correlation between love for self and love for others is not valid in the sense that Freud intends it. Nevertheless, the dualism which Freud assumes in his second theory of instincts—the dualism between narcissism and love—if divested of theoretical implications contains an old and significant truth. This is, briefly, that any kind of egocentricity detracts from a real interest in others, that it impairs the capacity to love others. Freud, however, means something different by his theoretical contention. He interprets the tendency toward self-inflation as originating in self-love, and he believes that the reason why the narcissistic person does not love others is that he loves himself too much. Freud thinks of narcissism as a reservoir which is depleted to the extent that the individual loves (that is, gives libido to) others. According to my view, a person with narcissistic trends is alienated from self as well as from others, and hence to the extent that he is narcissistic he is incapable of loving either himself or anyone else.

CHAPTER VI

FEMININE PSYCHOLOGY

FREUD believes that psychic peculiarities and difficulties in the two sexes are engendered by bisexual trends in both of them. His contention is, briefly, that many psychic difficulties in man are due to his rejection of "feminine" trends in himself, and that many peculiarities in woman are due to her essential wish to be a man. Freud has elaborated this thought in more detail for the psychology of woman than for that of man, and therefore I shall discuss only his views of feminine psychology.

According to Freud the most upsetting occurrence in the development of the little girl is the discovery that other human beings have a penis, while she has none. "The discovery of her castration is the turning point in the life of the girl." [1] She reacts to this discovery with a definite wish to have a penis too, with the hope that it will still grow, and with an envy of those more fortunate beings who possess one. In the normal development penis-envy does not continue as such; after recog-

[1] Sigmund Freud, *New Introductory Lectures on Psychoanalysis* (1933), chapter on "The Psychology of Women." The following interpretation of Freud's point of view is based primarily on this source.

nizing her "deficiency" as an unalterable fact, the girl transfers the wish for a penis to a wish for a child. "The hoped-for possession of a child is meant as a compensation for her bodily defect." [2]

Penis-envy is originally a merely narcissistic phenomenon, the girl feeling offended because her body is less completely equipped than the boy's. But it has also a root in object relations. According to Freud the mother is the first sexual object for the girl as well as for the boy. The girl wishes to have a penis not only for the sake of narcissistic pride, but also because of her libidinal desires for the mother, which, in so far as they are genital in nature, have a masculine character. Not recognizing the elemental power of heterosexual attraction, Freud raises the question as to why the girl has any need at all to change her attachment to the father. He gives two reasons for this change in affection: hostility toward the mother, who is held responsible for the lack of a penis, and a wish to obtain this desired organ from the father. "The wish with which girls turn to their father is, no doubt, ultimately the wish for the penis." Thus originally both boys and girls know only one sex: the masculine.

Penis-envy is assumed to leave ineradicable traces in woman's development; even in the most normal development it is overcome only by a great expenditure of energy. Woman's most significant attitudes or wishes derive their energy from her wish for a penis. Some of Freud's principal contentions intended to illustrate this may be briefly enumerated.

[2] Karl Abraham, "Ausserungsformen des weiblichen Kastrationskom-plexes" in *Internationale Zeitschrift für Psychoanalyse* (1921).

Freud considers the wish for a male child to be woman's strongest wish, because the wish for a child is heir to the wish for a penis. The son represents a sort of wish-fulfillment in the sense of penis possession. "The only thing that brings a mother undiluted satisfaction is her relation to a son: the mother can transfer to her son all the ambition which she has had to suppress in herself and she can hope to get from him the satisfaction of all that has remained to her of her masculinity complex."

Happiness during pregnancy, particularly when neurotic disturbances that are otherwise present subside during this time, is referred to as symbolic gratification in the possession of a penis (the penis being the child). When the delivery is delayed for functional reasons, it is suspected that the woman does not want to separate herself from the penis-child. On the other hand, motherhood may be rejected because it is a reminder of femininity. Similarly, depressions and irritations occurring during menstruation are regarded as the result of menstruation being a reminder of femininity. Cramps in menstruation are often interpreted as the result of fantasies in which the father's penis has been swallowed.

Disturbances in the relationship to men are regarded as ultimate results of penis-envy. As women turn to men mainly in the expectation of receiving a gift (penis-child), or in the expectation of having all their ambitions fulfilled, they easily turn against men if they fail to live up to such expectations. Envy of men may show itself also in the tendency to surpass them or in any kind of disparaging or in a striving for independence in so far as it implies disregarding man's help. In the sexual sphere the refutation of the feminine role may appear openly after defloration; the latter may arouse animosity to the partner because it is experienced as a castration.

In fact, there is scarcely any character trait in woman which is not assumed to have an essential root in penis-envy. Feminine inferiority feelings are regarded as an expression of contempt for the woman's own sex because of the lack of a penis. Freud believes that woman is more vain than man and attributes this to her necessity for compensation for the lack of a penis. Woman's physical modesty is born ultimately of a wish to hide the "deficiency" of her genitals. The greater role of envy and jealousy in woman's character is a direct out-come of penis-envy. Her tendency toward envy accounts for woman having "too little sense of justice," as well as for her "preference for mental and occupational in-terests belonging to the sphere of men." [3] Practically all of woman's ambitious strivings suggest to Freud her wish for a penis as the ultimate driving force. Also ambitions which are usually regarded as specifically feminine, such as the wish to be the most beautiful woman or the wish to marry the most prominent man, are, according to Abraham, expressions of penis-envy.

Although the concept of penis-envy is related to ana-tomical differences it is nevertheless contradictory to biological thinking. It would require tremendous evi-dence to make it plausible that woman, physically built for specifically female functions, should be psychically determined by a wish for attributes of the other sex.

[3] Karl Abraham, *op. cit.*

But actually the data presented for this contention are scant, consisting of three main observations.

First, it is pointed out that little girls often express the wish to have a penis or the hope that it will still grow. There is no reason, however, to think that this wish is any more significant than their equally frequent wish to have a breast; moreover the wish for a penis may be accompanied by a kind of behavior which in our culture is regarded as feminine.

It is also pointed out that some girls before puberty not only may wish to be a boy, but through their tomboyish behavior may indicate that they really mean it. Again, however, the question is whether we are justified in taking these tendencies at their face value; when they are analyzed we may find good reasons for the apparently masculine wishes: opposition, despair at not being attractive as a girl, and the like. As a matter of fact, since girls have been brought up with greater freedom this kind of behavior has become rare.

Finally, it is pointed out that adult women may express a wish to be a man, sometimes explicitly, sometimes by presenting themselves in dreams with a penis or penis symbol; they may express contempt for women and attribute existing inferiority feelings to being a woman; castrative tendencies may be manifest or may be expressed in dreams, in disguised or undisguised form. These latter data, however, though their occurrence is beyond doubt, are not as frequent as is suggested in some analytical writings. Also they are true only of neurotic women. Finally, they permit of a different interpretation and hence are far from proving the contention beyond dispute. Before discussing them critically let us first try to understand how it is that Freud and many other analysts see such overwhelming evidence for the decisive influence of penis-envy on woman's character.

In my estimation two main factors account for this conviction. On the basis of theoretical biases—which coincide to some extent with existing cultural prejudices —the analyst regards the following trends in women patients as off-hand suggestive of underlying penis-envy: tendencies to boss man, to berate him, to envy his success, to be ambitious themselves, to be self-sufficient, to dislike accepting help. I suspect that these trends are sometimes imputed to underlying penis-envy without further evidence. Further evidence may easily be found, however, in simultaneous complaints about feminine functions (such as menstruation) or frigidity, or in complaints about a brother having been preferred, or in a tendency to point out certain advantages of man's social position, or in dream symbols (a woman carrying a stick, slicing a sausage).

In reviewing these trends, it is obvious that they are characteristic of neurotic men as well as of neurotic women. Tendencies toward dictatorial power, toward egocentric ambition, toward envying and berating others are never-failing elements in present-day neuroses though the role they assume in a neurotic structure varies.

Furthermore, observation of neurotic women shows that all the trends in question appear toward other women or toward children as well as toward men. It appears dogmatic to assume that their expression in relation to others is merely a radiation from their relation to men.

Finally, as to dream symbols, any expression of wishes for masculinity is taken at its face value instead of being regarded skeptically for a possible deeper meaning. This procedure is contrary to the customary analytical attitude and can be ascribed only to the determining power of theoretical preconceptions.

Another source feeding the analyst's conviction of the significance of penis-envy lies not in himself but in his women patients. While some women patients are not impressed by interpretations which point to penis-envy as the origin of their troubles, others take them up readily and quickly learn to talk about their difficulties in terms of femininity and masculinity, or even to dream in symbols fitting this kind of thinking. These are not necessarily patients who are particularly gullible. Every experienced analyst will notice whether a patient is docile and suggestible and by analyzing these trends will diminish errors springing from that source. And some patients view their problems in terms of masculinity and femininity without any suggestion from the analyst, for naturally one cannot exclude the influence of literature. But there is a deeper reason why many patients gladly seize upon explanations offered in terms of penis-envy: these explanations present comparatively harmless and simple solutions. It is so much easier for a woman to think that she is nasty to her husband because, unfortunately, she was born without a penis and envies him for having one than to think, for instance, that she has developed an attitude of righteousness and infallibility which makes it impossible to tolerate any questioning or disagreement. It is so much easier for a patient to think that nature has given her an unfair deal than to realize that she actually makes excessive demands on the environment and is furious whenever they are not complied with. It seems thus that the theoretical bias of the analyst may coincide with the patient's tendency to leave her real problems untouched.

If wishes for masculinity may screen repressed drives, what then renders them fit to serve in this way?

Here we come to see cultural factors. The wish to be a man, as Alfred Adler has pointed out, may be the expression of a wish for all those qualities or privileges which in our culture are regarded as masculine, such as strength, courage, independence, success, sexual freedom, right to choose a partner. To avoid misunderstanding let me state explicitly that I do not mean to say that penis-envy is nothing but a symbolic expression of the wish to have the qualities regarded as masculine in our culture. This would not be plausible, because wishes to have these qualities need not be repressed and hence do not require a symbolic expression. A symbolic expression is necessary only for tendencies or feelings shoved out of awareness.

What then are the repressed strivings which are covered up by the wish for masculinity? The answer is not an all-embracing formula but must be discovered from an analysis of each patient and each situation. In order to discover the repressed strivings it is necessary not to take at face value a woman's tendency in one way or another to base her inferiority feelings on the fact that she is a woman; rather it must be pointed out to her that every person belonging to a minority group or to a less privileged group tends to use that status as a cover for inferiority feelings of various sources, and that the important thing is to try to find out these sources. According to my experience, one of the most frequent and effective sources is a failure to live up to certain inflated notions about the self, notions which in turn are necessary because various unrecognized pretenses have to be covered up.

Furthermore, it is necessary to bear in mind the possibility that the wish to be a man may be a screen for repressed ambition. In neurotic persons ambition may be so destructive that it becomes loaded with anxiety and hence has to be repressed. This is true of men as well as of women but as a result of the cultural situation a repressed destructive ambition in a woman may express itself in the comparatively harmless symbol of a wish to be a man. What is required of psychoanalysis is to uncover the egocentric and destructive elements in the ambition and to analyze not only what led up to this kind of ambition but also what consequences it has for the personality in the way of inhibitions to love, inhibitions to work, envy of competitors, self-belittling tendencies, fear of failure and of success.[4] The wish to be a man drops out of the patient's associations as soon as we tackle the underlying problems of her ambition and exalted opinion about what she is or should be. It is then no longer possible for her to hide behind the symbolic screen of masculinity wishes.

In short, interpretations in terms of penis-envy bar

[4] *Cf.* Karen Horney, *The Neurotic Personality of Our Time* (1937) chs. 10-12.

the way to an understanding of fundamental difficulties, such as ambition, and of the whole personality structure linked up with them. That such interpretations befog the real issue is my most stringent objection to them, particularly from the therapeutic angle. And I have the same objection to the assumed importance of bisexuality in man's psychology. Freud believes that in man's psychology what corresponds to penis-envy is his "struggle against the passive or feminine attitude toward other men." [5] He calls this fear the "repudiation of femininity" and makes it responsible for various difficulties which in my estimation belong to the structure of types who need to appear perfect and superior.

Freud has made two other suggestions, closely interrelated, concerning inherent feminine characteristics. One is that femininity has "some secret relationship with masochism." [6] The other is that the basic fear in woman is that of losing love, and that this fear corresponds to the fear of castration in man.

Helene Deutsch has elaborated Freud's assumption and generalized it in calling masochism the elemental power in feminine mental life. She contends that what woman ultimately wants in intercourse is to be raped and violated; what she wants in mental life is to be humiliated; menstruation is significant to the woman because it feeds masochistic fantasies; childbirth represents the climax of masochistic satisfaction. The pleasures of motherhood, inasmuch as they include certain sacrifices and a concern for the children, constitute a

[5] Sigmund Freud, "Analysis Terminable and Interminable," op. cit.
[6] Sigmund Freud. New Introductory Lectures.

long drawn out masochistic gratification. Because of these masochistic strivings women, according to Deutsch, are more or less doomed to be frigid unless in intercourse they are or feel raped, injured or humiliated.[7] Rado holds that woman's preference for masculinity is a defense against feminine masochistic strivings.[8]

Since according to psychoanalytic theory psychic attitudes are molded after sexual attitudes, the contentions concerning a specifically feminine basis of masochism have far-reaching implications. They entail the postulate that women in general, or at least the majority of them, essentially desire to be submissive and dependent. In support of these views is the impression that in our culture masochistic trends are more frequent in women than in men. But it must be remembered that the available data concern only neurotic women.

Many neurotic women have masochistic notions about intercourse, such as that women are prey to man's animal desires, that they have to sacrifice themselves and are debased by the sacrifice. There may be fantasies about being physically injured by intercourse. A few neurotic women have fantasies of masochistic satisfaction in childbirth. The great number of mothers who play the role of martyr and continually emphasize how much they are sacrificing themselves for the children may certainly be proof that motherhood can offer a masochistic satisfaction to neurotic women. There are

[7] Helene Deutsch, "The Significance of Masochism in the Mental Life of Women" (Part I, "Feminine Masochism in Its Relation to Frigidity") in *International Journal of Psychoanalysis* (1930).

[8] Sandor Rado, "Fear of Castration in Women" in *Psychoanalytic Quarterly* (1933).

also neurotic girls who shrink from marriage because they visualize themselves as enslaved and abused by the potential husband. Finally, masochistic fantasies about the sexual role of woman may contribute to a rejection of the female role and a preference for the masculine one.

Assuming that there is indeed a greater frequency of masochistic trends in neurotic women than in neurotic men, how may it be accounted for? Rado and Deutsch try to show that specific factors in feminine development are responsible. I refrain from discussing these attempts because both authors introduce as the basic factor the lack of a penis, or the girl's reactions to the discovery of this fact, and I believe this to be a wrong presupposition. In fact, I do not believe it is possible at all to find specific factors in feminine development which lead to masochism, for all such attempts rest on the premise that masochism is essentially a sexual phenomenon. It is true that the sexual aspect of masochism, as it appears in masochistic fantasies and perversions, is its most conspicuous part and was the first to attract the attention of psychiatrists. I hold, however—and this contention will be elaborated later on—that masochism is not a primarily sexual phenomenon, but is rather the result of certain conflicts in interpersonal relations. When masochistic tendencies are once established they may prevail also in the sexual sphere and here may become the condition for satisfaction. From this point of view masochism cannot be a specifically feminine phenomenon, and the analytical writers who have tried to find specific factors in feminine development accounting for masochistic attitudes in women are not to be blamed for the failure to find them.

In my opinion, one has to look not for biological reasons but for cultural ones. The question then is whether there are cultural factors which are instrumental in developing masochistic trends in women. The answer to this question depends on what one holds to be essential in the dynamics of masochism. My concept, briefly, is that masochistic phenomena represent the attempt to gain safety and satisfaction in life through inconspicuousness and dependency. As will be discussed later on, this fundamental attitude toward life determines the way in which individual problems are dealt with; it leads, for instance, to gaining control over others through weakness and suffering, to expressing hostility through suffering, to seeking in illness an alibi for failure.

If these presuppositions are valid there are indeed cultural factors fostering masochistic attitudes in women. They were more relevant for the past generation than for the present one, but they still throw their shadow today. They are, briefly, the greater dependency of woman; the emphasis on woman's weakness and frailty; the ideology that it is in woman's nature to lean on someone and that her life is given content and meaning only through others: family, husband, children. These factors do not in themselves bring about masochistic attitudes. History has shown that women can be happy, contented and efficient under these conditions. But factors like these, in my judgment, are responsible for the prevalence of masochistic trends in feminine neuroses when neuroses do develop.

Freud's contention that woman's basic fear is that of losing love is in part not separate from, for it is implicitly contained in, the postulate that there are specific factors in feminine development leading to masochism. Inasmuch as masochistic trends, among other characteristics, signify an emotional dependence on others, and inasmuch as one of the predominant masochistic means of reassurance against anxiety is to obtain affection, a fear of losing love is a specific masochistic feature.

It seems to me, however, that in contrast to Freud's other two contentions concerning feminine nature—that of penis-envy and that of a specifically feminine basis for masochism—this last one has some validity also for the healthy woman in our culture. There are no biological reasons but there are significant cultural factors which lead women to overvaluate love and thus to dread losing it.

Woman lived for centuries under conditions in which she was kept away from great economic and political responsibilities and restricted to a private emotional sphere of life. This does not mean that she did not carry responsibility and did not have to work. But her work was done within the confines of the family circle and therefore was based only on emotionalism, in contradistinction to more impersonal, matter of fact relations. Another aspect of the same situation is that love and devotion came to be regarded as specifically feminine ideals and virtues. Still another aspect is that to woman—since her relations to men and children were her only gateway to happiness, security and prestige—love represented a realistic value, which in man's sphere can be compared with his activities relating to earning capacities. Thus not only were pursuits outside the emotional sphere factually discouraged, but in woman's own mind they assumed only secondary importance.

Hence there were, and to some extent still are, realistic reasons in our culture why woman is bound to overrate love and to expect more from it than it can possibly give, and why she is more afraid of losing love than man is.

The cultural situation which has led woman to regard love as the only value that counts in life has implications which may throw light on certain characteristics of modern woman. One of them is the attitude toward aging: woman's age phobia and its implications. Since for such a long time woman's only attainable fulfillments—whether they involved love, sex, home or children—were obtained through men, it necessarily became of paramount importance to please men. The cult of beauty and charm resulting from this necessity might be registered, at least in some respects, as a good effect. But such a concentration on the importance of erotic attractiveness implies an anxiety for the time when it might eventually diminish in value. We should consider it neurotic if men became frightened or depressed when they approached the fifth decade. In a woman this is regarded as natural, and in a way it is natural so long as attractiveness represents a unique value. While age is a problem to everyone it becomes a desperate one if youthfulness is the center of attention.

This fear is not limited to the age which is regarded as ending woman's attractiveness, but throws its shadow over her entire life and is bound to create a great feeling of insecurity toward life. It accounts for the jealousy often existing between mothers and adolescent daughters, and not only helps to spoil their personal relationships but may leave a remnant of hostility toward all women. It prevents woman from evaluating qualities which are outside the erotic sphere, qualities best characterized by the terms maturity, poise, independence, autonomy in judgment, wisdom. Woman can scarcely take the task of the development of her personality as seriously as she does her love life if she constantly entertains a devaluating attitude toward her mature years, and considers them as her declining years.

The all-embracing expectations that are joined to love account to some extent for that discontentment with the female role which Freud ascribes to penis-envy. From this point of view the discontentment has two main reasons. One is that in a culture in which human relationships are so generally disturbed it is difficult to attain happiness in love life (by that I do *not* mean sexual relations). The other is that this situation is likely to create inferiority feelings. Sometimes the question is raised whether in our culture men or women suffer more from inferiority feelings. It is difficult to measure psychic quantities, but there is this difference: as a rule man's feeling of inferiority does not arise from the fact that he is a man; but woman often feels inferior merely because she is a woman. As mentioned before, I believe that feelings of inadequacy have nothing to do with femininity but use cultural implications of femininity as a disguise for other sources of inferiority feelings which, in essence, are identical in men and women. There remain, however, certain cultural reasons why woman's self-confidence is easily disturbed.

A sound and secure self-confidence draws upon a broad basis of human qualities, such as initiative, courage, independence, talents, erotic values, capacity to master situations. As long as homemaking was a really big task involving many responsibilities, and as long as the number of children was not restricted, woman had the feeling of being a constructive factor in the economic process; thus she was provided with a sound basis for self-esteem. This basis, however, has gradually vanished, and in its departure woman has lost one foundation for feeling herself valuable.

As far as the sexual basis of self-confidence is concerned, certainly the puritanical influences, however one may evaluate them, have contributed toward the debasement of women by giving sexuality the connotation of something sinful and low. In a patriarchal society this attitude was bound to make woman into the symbol of sin; many such allusions may be found in early Christian literature. This is one of the great cultural reasons why woman, even today, considers herself debased and soiled by sexuality and thus lowered in her own self-esteem.

There remains, finally, the emotional basis of self-confidence. If, however, one's self-confidence is dependent on giving or receiving love, then one builds on a foundation which is too small and too shaky—too small because it leaves out too many personality values, and too shaky because it is dependent on too many external factors, such as finding adequate partners. Besides, it very easily leads to an emotional dependence on other people's affection and appreciation, and results in a feeling of unworthiness if one is not loved or appreciated.

As far as the alleged given inferiority of woman is concerned, Freud has, to be sure, made a remark which it is quite a relief to hear from him: "You must not forget, however, that we have only described women in so far as their natures are determined by their sexual function. The influence of this factor is, of course, very far-reaching, but we must remember that *an individual woman may be a human being apart from this*" (italics mine). I am convinced that he really means it, but one would like to have this opinion of his assume a broader place in his theoretical system. Certain sentences in Freud's latest paper on feminine psychology indicate that in comparison with his earlier studies he is giving additional consideration to the influence of cultural factors on women's psychology: "But we must take care not to underestimate the influence of social conventions, which also force women into passive situations. The whole thing is still very obscure. We must not overlook one particularly constant relation between femininity and instinctual life. The repression of their aggressiveness, which is imposed upon women by their constitutions and by society, favors the development of strong masochistic impulses, which have the effect of binding erotically the destructive tendencies which have been turned inwards."

But since he has a primarily biological orientation Freud does not, and on the basis of his premises cannot, see the whole significance of these factors. He cannot see to what extent they mold wishes and attitudes, nor can he evaluate the complexity of interrelations between cultural conditions and feminine psychology.

I suppose everyone agrees with Freud that differences in sexual constitution and functions influence mental life. But it seems unconstructive to speculate on the exact nature of this influence. The American woman is different from the German woman; both are different from certain Pueblo Indian women. The New York society woman is different from the farmer's wife in Idaho. The way specific cultural conditions engender specific qualities and faculties, in women as in men— this is what we may hope to understand.

CHAPTER VII

THE DEATH INSTINCT

IN his third and final theory of instincts Freud abandons the dualism between "ego-libido" and "object-libido" and instead takes up again his former contrast between libidinal and non-libidinal drives, but with one significant difference. Formerly Freud had assumed that drives toward self-preservation—"ego" drives—were the counterpart of sexual drives. Now this role of counterpart is ascribed to exactly the opposite kind of instincts, that is, to instincts of self-destruction. In its main clinical implication the dualism is now between the sexual instincts, comprising narcissism as well as object-love, and a destruction instinct.

What suggested the concept of a destruction instinct is the frequency of cruelty in the history of mankind: in wars, revolutions, religious persecutions, in any kind of authoritative relationship, in crime. These facts convey the impression that people have to have some outlet for hostility and cruelty and that they seize upon the slightest opportunity to discharge it. Furthermore, a great deal of subtle and gross cruelty goes on daily in our culture: exploiting, cheating, disparaging, suppression of the defenseless, of children and of the poor.

Even in those relationships in which love or friendship should prevail, undercurrents of hostility are often the determining factors. Freud believes only one human relationship to be free from hostile admixtures: that of the mother to the son. The making of even that exception looks like wishful thinking. And as much cruelty and plain destructiveness appear in fantasies as appear in actuality. After a seemingly slight offense we may have dreams in which the offender is torn to pieces or is exposed to a deadly humiliation.

Finally, not only is there much destructiveness against others, but often much cruelty seems to be discharged against the self. We may kill ourselves; psychotics may inflict severe injuries on themselves; the average neurotic seems to have a tendency to torment, to belittle, to jeer at himself, to deprive himself of pleasure, to demand the impossible of himself and to condemn himself with inexorable severity if such impossible demands are not fulfilled.

Formerly Freud interpreted impulses and manifestations of hostility as related to sexuality. He believed that they were partly the expression of sadism, that is, of a component drive of sexuality, and partly reactions to frustrations or expressions of sexual jealousy. Later he recognized that these explanations did not suffice. There was much more destructiveness than could be accounted for by relating it to sexual instincts.

"I know that we have always had before our eyes manifestations of the destruction instinct fused with eroticism, directed outwards and inwards in sadism and masochism; but I can no longer understand how we could have overlooked the universality of non-erotic aggression and destruction, and could have omitted to give it its due significance in our interpretation of life." [1]

The assumption of a destruction instinct independent of sex did not necessitate any fundamental changes in the libido theory. The only theoretical change involved was that sadism and masochism were now regarded as fusions or admixtures of libidinal and destructive drives, instead of as wholly libidinal drives.

If the destructive drives are instinctual in nature, what is their organic basis? To answer this question Freud resorted to certain biological considerations which he himself calls speculations. These originated with his concept concerning the nature of instincts and his theory of repetition compulsion. An instinct, according to Freud, is caused by organic stimuli; its aim is to extinguish the disturbing stimulation and re-establish the equilibrium as it was before the stimulation interfered. By repetition compulsion, which Freud believes to represent a basic principle of instinctual life, he understands the compulsion to repeat former experiences or former stages of development, regardless of whether these were pleasurable or painful. This principle, Freud argues, seems to be the expression of a tendency, inherent in organic life, to restore an earlier form of existence and to return to it.

From these considerations Freud jumps to a daring conclusion: since there is an instinctual tendency to regress, to re-establish former stages, and since the inorganic existed prior to the organic, prior to the development of life, there must be an innate tendency to

[1] Sigmund Freud, *Civilization and Its Discontents* (1929).

ward re-establishing the inorganic state; since the condition of non-living existed earlier than the condition of living, there must be an instinctual drive toward death. "The goal of life is death." This is the theoretical way in which Freud comes to assume a death instinct; he believes that the fact that living organisms die from internal causes can be used to substantiate the assumption of an instinct driving toward self-destruction. The physiological basis of the instinct he sees in the catabolic processes in metabolism.

If there were nothing to counteract this instinct, the fact that we guard ourselves against dangers would be unintelligible. The intelligible thing to do would be to die. Perhaps what appears as a drive toward self-preservation would then be nothing but the will of the organism to die in its own way. But there is something to counteract the death instinct: the life instinct, which Freud thinks is represented by the sexual drives. Thus the basic dualism, according to this theory, is that between the life instinct and the death instinct. Their organic representation is in the germ-plasm and in the soma. There are no clinical observations to prove the existence of a death instinct because "it works silently within the organism toward its disintegration." What we are able to observe are fusions, an alliance of the death instinct with the sexual instinct. It is this alliance which prevents the death instinct from destroying us, or at least postpones this destruction. At the outset the death instinct becomes alloyed with the narcissistic libido, and these together form what Freud calls primary masochism.

The alliance with the sexual instincts, however, is not

in itself sufficient to prevent self-destruction. If that is to be prevented a considerable part of the self-destructive tendencies has to be turned toward the outside world. *We have to destroy others in order not to destroy ourselves.* By this deduction the destruction instinct becomes a derivate of the death instinct. The destructive drives can be turned inward again and appear in drives to harm oneself: these are clinical manifestations of masochism.[2] If the flow outward is inhibited, self-destruction is intensified. The evidence for this latter assumption Freud sees in the fact that neurotic persons torment themselves if their piled-up resentment cannot be discharged outward.

Though Freud himself recognizes that the theory of the death instinct rests on mere speculation, and though there is no evidence to support it, Freud feels nevertheless that the theory is far more fruitful than previous assumptions. Moreover, it meets all his requirements of an instinct theory: it is dualistic; both sides can be put on an organic basis; the two instincts and their derivates seem to embrace all psychic manifestations.

More particularly, the assumption of a death instinct and its derivate, a destruction instinct, seems to Freud to explain the amount of hostile aggression in neuroses, which could not be accounted for by his previous point of view; the amount of suspicion, fear of hostility from others, accusation, scornful rejection of all efforts, remained a puzzle when tackled only with the tools of the libido theory. And the early appearance of destruction fantasies, as observed by Melanie Klein and other

[2] Sigmund Freud, "The Economic Problem in Masochism" in *Collected Papers*, Vol. II (1924).

English analysts, seemed now with this theory to find a satisfactory foundation. Also the phenomenon of masochism, which had remained a puzzle so long as it was understood as a turned-in sadism, seemed to be better explained now; the alliance of sexual drives with self-destructive drives suggests that masochism has a function or, as Freud puts it, that it has an economic value, that of preventing self-destruction.[3]

Finally, the new theory allows a theoretical foundation for the concept of the "super-ego" and of the need for punishment. By "super-ego" Freud understands an autonomous agency within the personality, the main function of which is to prohibit the pursuit of instinctual drives. It is assumed to be a carrier of hostile aggression against the self, to impose frustrations, to begrudge pleasure, to make inexorable demands on the self and to punish their non-fulfillment with relentless severity. In brief, it owes its energy to the aggressions which are not discharged outward.[4]

In the following I shall restrict the discussion to the derivate of the death instinct: the destruction instinct. Freud has left no doubt about its meaning: man has an innate drive toward evil, aggressiveness, destructiveness, cruelty. "The bit of truth behind all this—one so eagerly denied—is that men are not gentle, friendly creatures wishing for love, who simply defend themselves if they are attacked, but that a powerful measure of desire for aggression has to be reckoned as part of their instinctual endowment. The result is that their

---

[3] *Cf.* Sigmund Freud, "The Economic Problem in Masochism," *op. cit.*
[4] *Cf.* Chapter XIII, The Concept of the "Super-Ego."

neighbor is to them not only a possible helper or sexual object, but also a temptation to them to gratify their aggressiveness on him, to exploit his capacity for work without recompense, to use him sexually without his consent, to seize his possessions, to humiliate him, to cause him pain, to torture and to kill him. Homo homini lupus; who has the courage to dispute it in the face of all the evidence in his own life and in history?" [5] "Hatred is at the bottom of all the relations of affection and love between human beings." "Hatred in relation to objects is older than love." [6] In the earliest stage of development, the "oral" stage, it appears in the tendency to incorporate the object, that is, to annihilate its existence. In the "anal" stage the relation to the object is determined by tendencies to get hold of it or to overpower it, an attitude which can scarcely be distinguished from hatred. It is only on the "genital" level that love and hatred appear as a pair of opposites.

Freud has anticipated emotional objections to such an assumption by declaring that we prefer to believe man good by nature. In arguing this way, however, he fails to see that disputing the contention that man is destructive by nature does not mean asserting the contrary, that he is good by nature. Freud also fails to see that the assumption of a destruction instinct may appeal to people emotionally because it can relieve them of feelings of responsibility and guilt, and because it can free them from the necessity of facing the real reasons for their destructive impulses. The important ques-

[5] Sigmund Freud, *Civilization and Its Discontents*.

[6] Sigmund Freud, "Triebe und Triebschicksale" in *Internationale Zeitschrift für Psychoanalyse* (1915).

tion is not so much whether or not we like the assumption, but whether it is in accord with our psychological knowledge.

The disputable point in Freud's assumption is not the declaration that man can be hostile, destructive and cruel, nor the extent and frequency of these reactions, but is the declaration that the destructiveness manifesting itself in actions and fantasies is instinctual in nature. The extent and frequency of destructiveness are *not* proof that it is instinctual.

The assumption implies that hostility will appear under any conditions, that it "lies in wait for some provocation," that "we feel ill at ease if we are deprived of that satisfaction," that is, the satisfaction of discharging hostility. Therefore, the question which must be discussed is whether we are ever hostile or destructive without adequate reasons for being so. If adequate reasons exist for being hostile, if hostility is an adequate reaction to the situation, the assumption of a destruction instinct loses even the scant evidence it has for its support.

On the surface there is much to be said in favor of Freud's belief that there is more hostility or cruelty than is warranted by the provocation. A child may be treated cruelly without its having given any provocation; a colleague may disparage one's character or achievements without one's ever having crossed his path; a patient may be hostile even though he has been helped considerably; the mob may be fascinated by acts of cruelty without the victims having ever harmed the individuals rejoicing in their sufferings.

But while there is often a disproportion between external provocation and the hostility displayed, the question remains whether there are not always adequate reasons for hostility. The best material for answering this question is provided by psychoanalytical therapy.

No doubt a patient may disparage the analyst in the most vicious fashion in spite of intellectually realizing that he has been helped. He may wish to ruin the analyst's reputation or may even attempt to do so. He may respond to the analyst's efforts with a rigid suspicion that the analyst is going to mislead him, harm him, exploit him. The analyst feels he has done nothing to warrant such hostility. Of course he may have been lacking in tact or patience; he may have given interpretations which were not to the point. But even if no mistakes are made—a fact established by retrospective common agreement—all this hostility may continue to be thrust at the analyst. This then would be a good example of hostility not provoked from the outside.

But is this really so? Because of the unique advantage of the psychoanalytical situation—the fact that it allows one to recognize pretty accurately what is going on in the partner—we can give an unequivocally negative answer. The gist of the situation is that the patient's hostility is defensive and that its extent is absolutely in proportion to the degree in which he feels hurt and endangered. The patient may, for instance, on the basis of a vulnerable pride, feel the whole process of analysis as a constant humiliation. Or he may have such high expectations as to what psychoanalysis should give him that comparatively he feels cheated and foiled. Or he may need an excessive amount of affection because of his anxiety, and feel that the analyst is constantly rejecting him or is even repelled by him. Or he may project to the analyst his own relentless demands for perfection and for unlimited achievements, and feel that the analyst is expecting the impossible of him or is accusing him unfairly. His hostility is then the logical and adequate reaction to the analyst's behavior not as it actually is but as the patient feels it to be.

It appears reasonably safe to assume that the process is similar in many other situations in which hostility or cruelty seems to be unprovoked. But what about situations in which cruelty is exerted toward a victim quite unrelated to the aggressor? Let us consider, for example, the child who tortures an animal. The question here is how much impotent rage and hatred which could not possibly be evinced toward stronger ones has been previously stimulated in such a child by the environment? The same question has to be answered concerning the sadistic fantasies of small children: it has to be proved that such hostility is not a reaction to the provoking influence of the environment, or, to put it positively, it has to be shown whether sadistic behavior and fantasies in small children ever appear in children who feel happy and safe because they are treated with warmth and respect.

There is another experience in analytical practice which seems to contradict the assumption of a destruction instinct. The more anxiety is released by psychoanalysis, the more the patient becomes capable of affection and genuine tolerance for himself and others. He is no longer destructive. But if the destructiveness were instinctual, how could it vanish? After all, we cannot perform miracles. According to Freud's theory, we should expect that when a patient after he has been analyzed grants himself more gratifications in life, the turned-in aggression concentrated heretofore in the "super-ego" should now be turned toward the outside world. While he is rendered less masochistic, he has become more destructive toward others. But what actually happens after a successful analysis is that he becomes less destructive. Here the analyst believing in the death instinct would object that although the patient indeed becomes less destructive toward others in his behavior and fantasies, nevertheless it is clear that in comparison with his state before the analysis he can assert himself better, will stand up for his rights, reach out for the things he wants to have, make reasonable demands, is better able to master a situation; all this is often described as becoming more "aggressive," and this "aggression" is regarded as an aim-inhibited expression of the destruction instinct.

Let us examine this objection and the postulate it is based on. It seems to me that this postulate contains the same fallacy as that of affection as an aim-inhibited expression of sexual drives. To a neurotic person, with his pent-up repressed hostility, any kind of self-assertion, such as expressing a wish for matches with his cigarettes, may represent an aggressive act indeed, and he may therefore be incapable of asking for matches. But does this allow the conclusion that all "aggression," or as I should rather say, all self-assertion, is an aim-inhibited destructiveness? It seems to me that any kind of self-assertion is the expression of a positive, expansive, constructive attitude toward life and toward the self.

Finally, Freud's assumption implies that the ultimate

motivation for hostility or destructiveness lies in the impulse to destroy. Thus he turns into its opposite our belief that we destroy in order to live: we live in order to destroy. We should not shrink from recognizing error even in an age-old conviction if new insight teaches us to see it differently, but this is not the case here. If we want to injure or to kill, we do so because we are or feel endangered, humiliated, abused; because we are or feel rejected and treated unjustly; because we are or feel interfered with in wishes which are of vital importance to us. That is, if we wish to destroy, it is in order to defend our safety or our happiness or what appears to us as such. Generally speaking, it is for the sake of life and not for the sake of destruction.

The theory of a destruction instinct is not only unsubstantiated, not only contradictory to facts, but is positively harmful in its implications. In regard to psychoanalytical therapy it implies that making a patient free to express his hostility is an aim in itself, because, in Freud's contention, a person does not feel at ease if the destruction instinct is not satisfied. It is true that to the patient who has repressed his accusations, his egocentric demands, his impulses of revenge, it is a relief if he can express these impulses. But if analysts took Freud's theory seriously, a wrong emphasis would have to ensue. The main task is not to free these impulses for expression but to understand their reasons and, by removing the underlying anxiety, remove the necessity of having them. Furthermore, the theory helps to maintain the confusion that exists between what is essentially destructive and what essentially pertains to something constructive, that is, self-assertion. For example, a patient's critical attitude toward a person or cause may be primarily an expression of hostility arising from unconscious emotional sources; if, however, every critical attitude suggests to the analyst a subversive hostility, interpretations expressing such possibilities may discourage the patient from developing his faculties for critical valuations. The analyst should try instead to distinguish between hostile motivations and attempts toward self-assertion.

Equally harmful are the cultural implications of the theory. It must lead anthropologists to assume that whenever in a culture they find people friendly and peaceful, hostile reactions have been repressed. Such an assumption paralyzes any effort to search in the specific cultural conditions for reasons which make for destructiveness. It must also paralyze efforts to change anything in these conditions. If man is inherently destructive and consequently unhappy, why strive for a better future?

CHAPTER VIII

THE EMPHASIS ON CHILDHOOD

ONE of the most far-reaching premises of Freud's doctrines is what I have described as his evolutionistic-mechanistic thinking. To repeat briefly, this kind of thinking implies that present manifestations are not only conditioned by the past, but contain nothing except the past—that they are, in other words, a repetition of the past. The theoretical formulation of this premise is in Freud's concept of the timelessness of the unconscious and in his hypothesis of the repetition compulsion.

The concept of the timelessness of the unconscious means that fears and desires or entire experiences which are repressed in childhood are, because of the repression, dissociated from the continuity of the present day, that they do not participate in the development of the individual and remain uninfluenced by further experiences or growth. They retain unaltered their intensity and their specific quality. The doctrine may be compared with myths dealing with persons who are transplanted into some mountain cave, where they remain unchanged for hundreds of years while life around them continues its course.

This theory is the basis for the clinical concept of fixation. If a person in the early environment gains paramount emotional importance for a child, and essential parts of the feelings directed toward this person have been repressed, then the child may remain tied to him. When, for instance, a little boy has repressed his desires for his mother, as well as the accompanying jealousy and fear of the father, these desires in unchanged intensity may still be effective in his adulthood. They may account for the fact that he keeps away from women altogether, that he marries an older woman, that he wants to have relations only with married women, or that he develops what Freud calls the split in male love life. By the latter Freud understands a man's incapacity to desire sexually a woman whom he admires and his being sexually attracted to women whom he despises, as for instance prostitutes. Freud explains this phenomenon as a direct outcome of a fixation on the mother, the two types of women representing different images of the mother, one to be desired sexually, the other to be only revered.

A fixation not only may pertain to a certain person of the early environment, but also may concern a whole stage of libido development. While a person develops in other respects, his "sexual" wishes remain concentrated on some pre-genital strivings. Such a fixation may, for instance, concern the oral libido, either because of constitutional factors or because of incidental experiences such as difficulties in weaning or early gastro-intestinal disturbances. A child in that case may refuse to eat if a younger sibling is born; it may at a later period develop greediness in eating; it may cling to the mother's apron strings; in adolescence it may, if a girl, show a greater interest in candies than in boys; it may later on develop neurotic symptoms, such as vomiting or drinking; there may be inordinate emphasis on questions of diet; there may be dreams of swallowing others; there may be an insatiable need for affection, but a frigidity in sexual life.

The clinical observations underlying the concept of fixation are of a pioneering character, a fact which is often insufficiently appreciated by critics of psychoanalysis. The debatable points concern questions of interpretation. They will be discussed later on in connection with the concepts of repetition compulsion and of transference.

The idea of the timelessness of the unconscious not only led to the concept of fixation, but also is contained in the hypothesis of repetition compulsion. It represents, as it were, the implicit precondition for the latter. If Freud had believed that a special attachment to the mother, for instance, were an integral factor in the whole development, it would have been meaningless for him to assume that any particular manifestation was merely a repetition of that particular complex. Only by assuming that this complex remains isolated and unaltered could he regard later attachments of a similar kind as repetitions of this first one.

Briefly, the concept of repetition compulsion means that psychic life is regulated not only by the pleasure principle but by a more elemental principle: the tendency of instincts to repeat experiences or reactions already established. Freud finds evidence for this tendency in the following data.

First, children show a marked tendency to repeat previous experiences, even though these were unpleasant ones, such as a medical examination or an operation. They also insist on stories being retold in exactly the same fashion in which they were originally related.

Second, in traumatic neuroses dreams frequently appear in which the traumatic incident is re-experienced in detail. These dreams seem to contradict the wishful thinking which otherwise operates in fantasy life, for the traumatic incidents were painful ones.

Third, in the analytical situation, according to Freud, the patient repeats former experiences, even though these were painful. Freud argues that it would be quite understandable on the basis of the pleasure principle if the patient in the analytical situation tried to reach out for goals which he had wished for as a child. Patients seem to be under the compulsion, however, to repeat also painful experiences. A patient may, for instance, insist upon feeling rejected by the analyst, and in this way repeat the painful experience of having been rejected by a parent. A more complicated example is provided by a patient who in her childhood did not receive the help she might reasonably have expected when she felt miserable. For instance, when she had tonsilitis accompanied by high fever, her mother who slept in the same room refused to give her a compress she asked for. In the analytical situation this patient neither recognizes nor accepts the help offered her, and acts as if the same childhood situation still prevails, as if she is still miserable and no one helps her.

Fourth, many persons have distinctly repetitive experiences in the course of their lives. A woman in three marriages may marry an impotent man each time. A person may have several times the identical experience of making sacrifices for others and receiving ingratitude in return; he may repeatedly worship some idol and be disappointed each time.

Let us regard the validity of these data. The repetitive games of children Freud himself does not regard as convincing evidence, since he admits the possibility that by repeating painful experiences in games children might wish to master the unpleasant situation which in reality they had to bear passively. With regard to repetitive traumatic incidents in dreams, Freud himself considers another explanation: the operation of masochistic drives. This possibility, however, does not hold for him such importance as altogether to invalidate the assumption of a repetition compulsion, which in my opinion it does.

Concerning repetitive painful experiences in a person's life, we understand them easily, without having to assume a mysterious repetition compulsion, if we consider that certain drives and reactions in a person are bound to bring with them repetitive experiences.[1] For instance, a propensity for hero-worship may be determined by such conflicting drives as an exorbitant ambition so destructive in character as to render the individual afraid to pursue it, or a tendency to adore successful persons, to love them and to participate in their success without the individual having to accomplish anything himself, and at the same time an excessively destructive and hidden envy toward them. It is

[1] McDougall has already advanced this argument in *Psychoanalysis and Social Psychology* (1936).

not necessary to have recourse to any hypothetical repetition compulsion in order to understand that such a person will easily have repetitive experiences in which either he finds idols and is disappointed in them, or he deliberately makes idols of people in order to crush them afterward.

His most convincing evidence Freud derives from the assumption that patients in the analytical situation compulsorily repeat childhood experiences. According to him, the patient repeats with "fatiguing regularity" experiences of his childhood. This argument too is debatable, as we shall see later when discussing the concept of transference.

Freud formulated his hypothesis of repetition compulsion later than his theories of fixation, regression and transference, which belong to the same category. To him it must have appeared like a theoretical formulation derived from clinical experience. Actually, however, the experience itself, or rather his interpretations of his observations, were already determined by the same philosophical premise which is expressed in the concept of repetition compulsion.

It is therefore not so important to see whether or not Freud has succeeded in substantiating the theory of repetition compulsion. What is important is to understand how psychoanalytical thinking, the formation of theories, and therapy are influenced by this type of approach.

In the first place, the kind of thinking represented by the theory of repetition compulsion accounts for the degree of emphasis put on the importance of childhood factors. If later experiences are a repetition of past ones, a minute knowledge of the past must be of paramount importance for understanding the present. It is appropriate then to regard infantile memories of any kind as the most valuable material offered in the patient's associations. It is logical to discuss and rediscuss the question of how far back memories can be recovered. It is most important to reconstruct some early constellation out of present manifestations.

We can understand too why all trends not fitting the rational picture of what the average adult is supposed to feel, to think or do are designated as infantile. If it were not for the assumption of repetition compulsion it would be difficult to realize why a destructive ambition, for instance, or miserliness or inordinate demands made upon the environment should be considered infantile trends. They are alien to a healthy child and are found only in children who are already neurotic. But if trends like the first two are regarded as derivatives of the anal-sadistic stage, and trends like the last are regarded as a derivative of infantile helplessness or of the narcissistic stage, it is understandable why they should be called infantile.

Finally, we can understand one of the foremost therapeutic expectations, the expectation mentioned before that the patient will understand his present difficulties when he recognizes their connection with infantile experiences, that his awareness of the infantile trends involved will enable him to reject them as something that is antiquated and hence out of gear with his adult views and strivings. Also we see that it is consistent not to consider a patient cured so long as some infantile period is not elucidated.[2]

In brief, we can understand now why psychoanalysis is a genetic psychology, and must necessarily be, as long as it follows the type of thinking represented by the theory of repetition compulsion. But such thinking, even assuming there are indeed distinct similarities between present attitudes and past ones, is open to several serious criticisms.[3]

Let us take as an example a woman patient who easily felt unfairly treated, felt pushed aside, cheated, taken advantage of, treated with ingratitude or with disrespect, though a careful analysis of the situation showed that either she reacted in an exaggerated way to comparatively slight provocations, or that her feeling of being unfairly treated resulted from her making an unwarranted interpretation of the situation. As a child she was indeed unfairly treated. She grew up in the shadow of a beautiful, egocentric mother and a greatly preferred sister. She could not give vent to any resentment directly, because the mother was self-righteous and could not stand anything but blind adoration. Moreover, she was ridiculed for resenting any unfair treatment, was teased as playing the martyr role.

[2] I may tell a little story which, though a caricature, illustrates this type of thinking. An American girl who had been analyzed abroad came to see me with a wish to continue her analysis. I asked her why she wanted it, expecting to hear what difficulties there were in her actual life and what symptoms were still left. The reason she gave, however, was that there was still an amnesia for the first five years of her life. Frequently it is thus assumed that recovering infantile memories is an aim in itself, while actually it is a means to an end, that is, to an understanding of the present.

[3] *Cf.* criticisms made on this score by Otto Rank, David Levy, Frederick Allen, F. B. Karpf, A. Adler, A. C. Jung and others.

There was thus a clear similarity between her past attitudes and her present ones. Similarities of this kind can be observed frequently, and we owe it to Freud that we have learned to observe them. Pampered as a child—excessive demands on others as an adult; experiencing as a child that things can be obtained only by compliance—as an adult an attitude of compliance and an expectation of being taken care of in return. But why do the childhood attitudes sometimes persist into adulthood? After all, most persons grow out of them. If they are not outgrown, we must look for the reasons. Thus we are led to the question of what factors in the present character structure demand the persistence— even though it may be in a different form—of attitudes developed in the past. This question is of paramount importance, not only from the point of view of understanding, but particularly from that of therapy, because any therapeutic change hinges on knowing and getting hold of these factors. The answer Freud gives is the hypothesis of repetition compulsion. Let us examine now, on the basis of the example mentioned above, whether the later experiences are essentially repetitions of the old ones.

We shall assume that we do not know much about the patient's childhood situation. Her information about it is that she had a happy childhood and an adorable mother. Freud would suggest that even with scant knowledge of the infantile situation we can reconstruct it from the present set of reactions. Let us assume that by following that suggestion we would arrive at the true picture indicated above. The patient would help us in that reconstruction, encouraged by our assertion that she must have suffered from some ill treatment in her childhood. She would help us perhaps most reluctantly, because the whole reconstruction means unearthing an old resentment against the mother. During this work we would also understand another peculiarity of hers as a repetition of early reactions, that is, her tendency to cover up resentment against others by adoration. She did so with the mother; she does it later with the husband and with others too.

Thus far Freud's theoretical formulation is warranted by clinical facts. The assertions frequently made in psychoanalytical literature that reconstruction of the past can be valid, that it can often, for example, be confirmed by third persons, have been well substantiated. Nevertheless, the reconstruction we have achieved does not prove what it is meant to prove, that is, that the present is only a repetition of the past. Let us ask what the patient has gained through reconstruction. Certainly she has gained a true picture of her early difficulties. But since this is not an aim in itself we should ask further: what good does it do her to have this more realistic picture of the past?

According to the concept of repetition compulsion the answer would be, schematically, something like this: the patient realizes that her present reactions are antiquated; they are no longer warranted by reality, as they were previously; they occur because, without being aware of it, she was under a compulsion to repeat her early reactions; this knowledge will help to break the spell, for it will enable the patient to see reality as it is and to react accordingly.

That this result frequently fails to occur is no evidence against Freud's assumption. We still know so little about why some patients become well and others do not. Also the patient may continue the same type of reactions because other interrelated factors have not yet been worked through in analysis. Finally, it may be that in some patients the repetition compulsion exerts such an elemental power that it cannot be broken even by becoming aware of it.

But while therapeutic failures are not evidence against a theory, their frequency does warrant the question whether the theoretical expectations might not be wrong, or at least incomplete. Let us consider the contention that the actual neurotic reactions are antiquated, that they are not warranted by reality. Is this true? What is reality for the patient? [4] When asserting that the actual reactions are not warranted by reality, Freud means that they are not provoked by the environment. But there is another part of reality which is just as much reality, that is, the patient's own character structure, and this part of reality is entirely neglected in Freud's considerations. In other words, he does not take into consideration whether there are factors in the patient's actual personality which make it necessary for her to react in exactly the way she does.

Schematizing again, we find several factors in the situation which were relevant in engendering the reactions. On the basis of the whole unfortunate situation in childhood—in addition to the factors mentioned, several frightening instances made her afraid of being actually killed if she did not behave—she had developed

[4] *Cf.* Lawrence K. Frank, "Facing Reality in Family Life" in *Mental Hygiene* (1937).

an attitude of compulsory unobtrusiveness,[5] showing itself in modesty, in an inclination to stay in the background and, when there was any collision of opinions or interest, to think that the others were right in their demands or views and that she was wrong. Under the surface deeply repressed, diffuse and intensive demands developed. Their existence could be guessed from two observations of her present reactions: first, anxiety appeared when she wished something for herself which she could not justify on the grounds of needing it for education, health, and the like; second, she was subject to frequent attacks of fatigue which covered up an impotent rage, the latter occurring whenever certain secret demands were not fulfilled, when things were not done for her, when she was not first in any competition, when she had complied with the wishes of others or when others had not complied with her own unexpressed wishes. These demands, of the existence of which she was entirely unaware, were not only rigid but completely egocentric, that is, they were without any consideration for the needs of others. The latter characteristic was part and parcel of a generally disturbed relationship to others, which was hidden under an indiscriminate people-are-nice attitude existing on the surface.

Thus after considerable work we obtained this picture: rigid egocentric demands for herself—rage at nonfulfillment. We understood that here was a vicious circle at work, inasmuch as the rage which kept being generated increased the antagonism and distrust toward others and thereby increased the egocentricity.

[5] *Cf.* Chapter XV, Masochistic Phenomena.

As mentioned before, the rage did not appear as such but was covered by a paralyzing fatigue. It could not be expressed because she was much too afraid of others to do so, and much too much bent on being infallible. But some of the resentment did come out. It appeared whenever she could put it on a justified basis, when in her own mind the situation appeared as one in which she was unfairly treated. Even so, the resentment was not in the foreground, but was overshadowed by a diffuse self-pity. Thus her feeling of being unfairly treated enabled her to discharge resentment on a justified basis. But it gained something for her which was even more important. By feeling unfairly treated she escaped having to face her demands on others with all their implications of egoism and inconsiderateness: she could maintain a retouched picture of herself in which only the good qualities showed. Instead of having to change something in herself she could indulge in self-pity, which is valuable for one who does not feel loved and wanted by others.

Hence the reason why the patient tended to feel unfairly treated was not that she was under a compulsion to repeat past experiences, but that her actual structure made it inevitable for her to react in this way. And therefore a suggestion that her actual reactions were not warranted by reality could not be sufficiently helpful, because this is only a half truth and leaves out those dynamic factors within herself which determined the present reaction. To work through these latter factors is the most important therapeutic task. What this process involves for the patient will be discussed later on in connection with problems of therapy.

The genetic method in practice lends itself to various other erroneous conclusions which are, however, less fundamental in character than that presented in the above example. In that case the reconstruction of past reactions was valid; the memories it stimulated gave the patient a better understanding of her development. But a reconstruction or a childhood memory used as an explanation of present behavior is the less valuable the less it is substantiated, or the more it remains a mere possibility. Naturally, every analyst realizes this. Nevertheless the theoretical expectation that progress is to be gained by obtaining childhood memories constitutes a temptation to make use of unconvincing reconstructions or of vague memories which leave an unresolvable doubt as to whether they concern real experiences or merely fantasies. When the real picture of childhood is befogged, artificial attempts to penetrate through the fog represent an endeavor to explain one unknown— the actual peculiarities—by something still less known— childhood. It seems more profitable to drop such efforts and to focus on the forces which actually drive and inhibit a person; there is a reasonable chance of gradually understanding these, even without much knowledge of childhood.

Incidentally, when proceeding this way one does not learn less of childhood. In the process of obtaining a better grasp of actual goals, actual forces, actual needs, actual pretenses, the fog hovering over the past begins to lift. One does not regard the past, however, as the treasure long sought, but considers it simply as a welcome help in understanding the patient's development.

Another source of error in the genetic method is the

fact that the infantile experiences to which actual peculiarities are related are frequently too isolated to be able
to explain anything. There are attempts, for instance,
to view a whole intricate masochistic character structure
as ultimately arising from one incident in which sexual
excitement was felt through suffering. Of course, grossly
traumatic incidents may leave their direct traces, as is
indicated by some of Freud's early case reports.[6] But as
a result of the presupposition contained in the concept
of repetition compulsion an all too generous use is made
of such rare possibilities. That those isolated incidents
which are reported to be responsible for extensive later
character trends or symptoms are of a sexual nature—
such as observation of the parents' intercourse, birth of
a sibling, humiliations or threats because of masturbation—is due to the premises given in the libido theory.

The doctrine that past emotional experiences tend to
be repeated has determined in particular the doctrines
of regression and transference. The common denominator of these doctrines is that past emotional experiences
can be revived under certain conditions. The concept
of transference will be discussed separately. As to the
doctrine of regression, it is inextricably interwoven with
the libido theory.

It will be remembered that the development of the
libido is supposed to progress through certain stages,
through the oral, anal, phallic stages until it culminates
in the genital stage. In each case certain character trends
prevail. In the oral stage, for instance, there are expecta-

[6] *Cf.* Joseph Breuer and Sigmund Freud, *Studien über Hysterie*
(1909).

tions of obtaining things from others, dependency on others, envy, tendency toward identification with others in the form of figurative incorporations. Nothing much has been said about the psychic qualities co-ordinated with the "genital level," but it seems that the attainment of the "genital level" is supposed to coincide with what is regarded as the ideal adaptation to the requirements of the world around. To say of someone that he is on the "genital level" is equivalent to saying that he is not neurotic but is "normal" in the sense of the statistically average.[7]

It is consistent with this doctrine that any trends grossly deviating from the average are regarded as infantile. When a person always has such deviating peculiarities they are regarded as the expression of a fixation on some infantile level. When he develops them after having gone along previously without much friction, they are considered to be regression.

The libido stages to which a regression is made are considered specific for different types of neuroses or psychoses. Melancholia is considered to represent a regression to the oral stage, because in a case of this kind there are frequently difficulties in eating, cannibalistic dreams, fears concerning starvation or poisoning. The self-accusations which are typical of melancholia are considered the result of the "introjection" of another person toward whom accusations were present but repressed. The melancholic person, according to Freud, acts as if he had swallowed the accused person, and because of

[7] W. Trotter (*Instincts of the Herd in Peace and War*, 1915) points out the tendency in psychoanalytical literature to identify the normal with the statistical average.

his identification with the recriminated object his accusations appear as self-accusations.

Obsessional neuroses are regarded as regressions to
the anal-sadistic stage. The observations underlying this
interpretation are of such trends—frequent in obsessional neuroses—as animosity, cruelty, stubbornness,
preoccupation with cleanliness, orderliness, punctuality.

Schizophrenic psychoses are considered to be a regression to the narcissistic stage of development. This is
based on the observation that schizophrenic persons are
withdrawn from reality, are egocentric and frequently
have manifest or hidden grandiose ideas.

A regression does not always concern the whole libido
organization, but may be simply a return to old incestuous love objects. This type of regression is considered
specific in hysteria.

The factors precipitating a regression are supposed
to be frustrations of genital pursuits—direct or indirect.
More generally, a regression may be effected by any
experience which either blocks genital pursuits or renders them painful, such as disappointments or fears
concerning sexuality or love life.

The critical considerations concerning the whole
range of problems in the doctrine of regression are in
part the same as I have tried to formulate in regard to
the libido theory. And in so far as regression is but a
special form of repetition, my criticisms on this score
have been discussed above. I wish to emphasize here but
one point: it concerns the factors which are made responsible for the onset of a neurosis—if there is any
distinct onset—or, in theoretical terms, the factors which
precipitate a regression.

We know that neurotic disturbances can be precipitated by an endless variety of instances, among them instances which for the average person would not be traumatic. Thus, for instance, a severe depression was precipitated in a teacher by receiving a mild criticism from the principal; severe anxiety with functional disturbances appeared in a physician who was going to marry a woman of his own choice; diffuse disturbances appeared in a lawyer whose girl hesitated to accept his proposal of marriage.

I realize that in instances like these the patients' associations permit of interpretations along the principles of the libido theory, or of repetition compulsion. It might then be contended that for the teacher the principal's reproaches were traumatic because the principal represented for her a father image, and because his reproach connoted the repetition of an old rejection and at the same time aroused guilt feelings about having reached out in fantasy for the father. In the physician associations would show a general fear of being tied to anyone or anything, but this might be interpreted as the revival of an old fear of being subdued or as it were swallowed by the mother, combined with fears and guilt feelings concerning the return of incestuous wishes.

But in my opinion the task is to understand the complexities of the actual personality and the combination of conditions on which his equilibrium rests. Then we will understand why the particular incidents are bound to disturb the equilibrium. Thus in a person whose equilibrium depends mainly on the illusion of being infallible and being recognized as such, a slight criticism by a superior may bring about neurotic disturbances. In a person who has lived under the illusion of being irresistible, any kind of rejection may precipitate a neurosis. In a person whose equilibrium is bound up with being independent and detached from others, a neurosis may be brought about by the approach of marriage. Mostly it is a combination of several occurrences which in their entirety interfere with the successful functioning of defenses built up against anxiety. The more shaky a person's structure, the slighter an incident need be in order to disturb his equilibrium and throw him into anxieties, depressions or other neurotic symptoms.

In circles skeptical toward psychoanalysis the request is often made that analyses be published in detail so that it can be judged how the analyst arrives at his conclusions. I do not think this would be helpful in clarifying controversies. I also assume that underlying such requests is the unfounded suspicion that the patients do not really supply the material on which the interpretations are founded. In my experience one can safely credit analysts with conscientiousness, and can safely assume that the appropriate memories really do come up. The debatable question is whether the use of these memories as an explanatory principle is warranted, whether this practice does not mean thinking in a one-track or too mechanistic way. To refer again to the cases just mentioned, I believe that instead of finding in the memories the final answer one should try to understand what the immediate event—the principal's criticism, the anticipation of a close tie like marriage, the rebuff—

means in terms of the actual structure of the particular person.

Reviewing the discussion, my criticisms may appear like a controversy of "actual versus past." It would be an unjustified simplification, however, to see the problems in the light of a simple alternative. There is no doubt whatever that childhood experiences exert a decisive influence on development and, as I have said, it is one of Freud's many merits to have seen this in greater detail and with more accuracy than it had been seen before. The question since Freud is no longer whether there is an influence, but how it operates. In my opinion the influence operates in two ways.

One is that it leaves traces which can be directly traced. A spontaneous like or dislike of a person may have to do directly with early memories of similar traits in father, mother, maids, siblings. In the example cited in this chapter, the early experience of being unfairly treated had certain direct bearings on the later tendencies to feel badly treated. Adverse experiences of the kind described will make a child lose at an early age his spontaneous trust in the benevolence and justice of others. Also he will lose or never acquire a naïve certainty of being wanted. In this sense of, let us say, anticipating evil rather than good, the old experiences enter directly into adult ones.

The other and more important influence is that the sum total of childhood experiences brings about a certain character structure, or rather, starts its development. With some persons this development essentially stops at the age of five. With some it stops in adolescence, with others at around thirty, with a few it goes on until old age. This means that we cannot draw one isolated line from a later peculiarity—such as hatred of a husband which is not provoked essentially by his behavior—to a similar hatred of the mother, but that we must understand the later inimical reaction from the structure of the whole character. That the character has developed as it has is accounted for in part by the relation to the mother, but also by the combination of all other factors influential in childhood.

The past in some way or other is always contained in the present. If I should try to formulate briefly the substance of this discussion I should say that it is a question not of "actual versus past," but of developmental processes versus repetition.

CHAPTER IX

THE CONCEPT OF
TRANSFERENCE

WERE someone to ask me which of Freud's discoveries I value most highly, I should say without any hesitation: it is his finding that one can utilize for therapy the patient's emotional reactions to the analyst and to the analytical situation. It was a step bearing witness to Freud's inner independence to regard the patient's emotional responses as a useful tool, instead of merely using his attachment or suggestibility as a means of influencing him, or instead of regarding adverse reactions as a mere nuisance. I am stating this explicitly because of my impression that psychologists who have elaborated this approach of Freud's [1] fail to give Freud sufficient credit for pioneering work. It is easy enough to modify, but it takes genius to be the first to visualize the possibilities.

Freud observed that in the analytical situation the patient not only talks about his present and past troubles, but also shows emotional reactions to the analyst. These reactions are frequently irrational in character. A patient may forget entirely his purpose in coming to

[1] Such as O. Rank and C. G. Jung.

154

analysis and may find nothing important except being loved or appreciated by the analyst. He may develop altogether disproportionate fears about jeopardizing his relationship to the analyst. He may transform the situation, which in actuality is one in which the analyst helps the patient to straighten out his problems, into one of passionate struggle for the upper hand. For instance, instead of feeling relieved by some clarification of his problems, a patient may see only one fact, that the analyst has recognized something which he was unaware of, and he may react with violent anger. A patient may, contrary to his own interests, secretly pursue the purpose of defeating the analyst's endeavors.

Freud realizes that no reaction appears in the psychoanalytical situation which is not characteristic of the patient, a fact which makes it all the more desirable to understand it. Freud realizes, furthermore, that the analytical situation offers a unique opportunity of studying these reactions, not only because the patient is obliged to express his feelings and thoughts but because the psychoanalytical relationship is less intricate than others and more open to observation.

One can certainly learn a great deal from what the patient tells about his attitudes toward others, toward husband, wife, maids, principals, colleagues and the like, but while studying these one is often treading on insecure ground. The patient in general does not know his reactions or the conditions provoking them, and has a definite though hidden interest not to know them. In many patients the striving to appear right will make them inadvertently retouch in their favor records of difficulties; thus the reactions are frequently made to appear proportionate to the provocation. Or the patient relates incidents under the stress of self-recriminatory tendencies which likewise befog the issue. The analyst does not know the other persons concerned, and though he may be able to form a tentative picture of them it may be difficult to convince the patient of his own share in the conflicts.

It may be objected that these difficulties are present also in the psychoanalytical situation, that the patient's reactions to the analyst may also be unwarranted, that the analyst cannot know whether they are or not, for after all, he is in the difficult, if not impossible, situation of having to be actor and judge at the same time. There is but one answer to these objections: errors arising from these sources cannot be avoided but they are considerably diminished in the analytical situation. The analyst is more detached than others who play a role in the patient's life; because his attention is focused on understanding the patient's reactions he is kept from reacting as naïvely and as subjectively as he would otherwise. Also, as a rule, he has been analyzed himself, and hence is subject to fewer irrational emotional reactions. Finally, his knowledge that he is confronted with reactions which the patient is bound to carry into every relationship takes the personal edge from the patient's responses.

Unfortunately this immeasurably constructive perception of Freud's did not escape the influence of his mechanistic-evolutionistic thinking, and to the degree to which this influence is present the concept of transference becomes open to question. Freud believes that the patient's irrational emotional reactions represent a revival of infantile feelings, now attached to—that is, transferred to—the analyst, that feelings of love, defiance, distrust, jealousy and the like are attached to the analyst, regardless of the latter's sex, age or behavior, and regardless of what actually happens in the analysis. This is consistent with Freud's way of thinking. The feelings the patient develops toward the analyst may be of exorbitant strength. What else but infantile instinctual drives could account for such power of emotion! Therefore one of the analyst's primary interests is to recognize what role the patient ascribes to him at a particular period of the analysis: the role of the father, mother, sibling? The role of a good or bad image of the mother?

The practical implications of this approach may be illustrated by an example, even though it yields no basic point of view not already pointed out in the discussion of the repetition concept. Let us assume that a patient has fallen in love with the analyst. He lives for nothing but the one hour of analysis; he is delighted at any friendliness from the analyst and depressed at the slightest rejection or at what he feels to be a rejection. He is jealous of other patients or of the analyst's relatives. He fancies he is being singled out by the analyst. Sexual desires toward the analyst may appear in awareness or in dreams.

If the analyst follows Freud's interpretations he will suggest, on the basis of certain associations concerning the mother, that the patient may have been much more in love with his mother than he remembers, and that it is this old love which is now being reactivated. Such an interpretation may be valid in that the patient was in·

deed strongly attached to his mother as a child, and in that the present infatuation has, as it were, an impersonal character; to a lesser degree such an infatuation may have occurred toward other physicians, toward lawyers, clergymen or any of those who may have been friendly or protective toward him. The analyst is aware of the impersonal character of the infatuation and ascribes the indiscrimination to the patient's compulsion to repeat an old pattern. The patient feels relieved because he recognizes that there is something compulsory, something not genuine, in his feelings of love. But while as a result the actual infatuation diminishes, a dependence on the analyst remains.

The weakness of an interpretation of this kind is again the insufficient consideration of the actual factors in the patient's personality, in this case the factors engendering the attachment to the analyst. To mention but one possibility, the patient may be a type with prevailing masochistic trends. His security and satisfaction may depend upon fastening himself to others or, more accurately, merging with them.[2] Hence obtaining affection is for him a means of reassurance. In the patient's own mind, for many stringent reasons, this need for affection appears mostly as love and devotion. Whenever anxiety is stirred up—which is bound to happen frequently in every successful analysis—such a patient's need to hang on to the analyst is increased. Therefore whenever the patient shows a more than usual attachment to the analyst, the latter should in the first instance connect it with existing indications of anxiety or insecurity. The effect of this procedure is to open the gate

[2] *Cf.* Chapter XV, Masochistic Phenomena.

toward a recognition of the patient's anxiety and eventually to lead to an understanding of the underlying structure responsible for it. As it is mainly the patient's anxiety which makes him dependent on the analyst, interpretations of this kind counteract from the beginning the danger of dependency.[3]

That they may contribute to this dependency is the first of three main dangers involved in interpretations which see the patient's attachment in terms of infantile patterns. They leave the underlying anxiety untouched and therefore the patient's dependence on the analyst is increased. This is a serious danger because it counteracts the goal of therapy, which is or should be to help the patient to become a free and independent personality.

A second danger in attempts to explain emotional reactions toward the analyst, or toward the analytical situation, as repetitions of past feelings or past experiences is that the analysis as a whole may become unproductive. Supposing, for instance, that a patient secretly feels the whole procedure to be an unbearable humiliation to his pride. If this reaction, when recognized, is primarily connected with past feelings of humiliation, and if there is not a sufficient attempt to find out what factors in his actual structure may account for these feelings, the analysis may get out of gear and useless time may be spent with the patient subtly or grossly disparaging and defeating the analyst.

The third danger is that there may be an insufficient elaboration of the patient's actual personality structure, with all its ramifications. The individual trends actually

[3] Among others, Adolf Meyer has pointed out the difficulty in resolving the neurotic's dependency on his physician.

existing may be recognized as such even when they are primarily related to the past, because a particular sensitivity, or defiance, or pride, must first be recognized before it can be related to the past. But this procedure jeopardizes one's understanding of the ways in which the trends are interrelated, the ways in which one trend conditions others, reinforces others, collides with others, and it may lead to establishing wrong interrelations among them.

Because of the practical and theoretical importance of this point, I may illustrate it by an example. Since this example has to be grossly condensed and schematized, the purpose of citing it is not to convince the reader that the structural picture I arrive at approximates the truth more closely than that arrived at by "vertical" interpretations, but is merely to show the difference in approach and result.

A patient X, a highly gifted person, shows three prevailing trends in relation to the analyst which I shall call a, b, c: a, he is compliant and unconsciously expects in return to be protected, loved and admired by the analyst; b, he has hidden inflated notions about being an intellectual and moral genius, and is angry at the analyst as soon as these are questioned; c, he is afraid that the analyst despises him.

Analysis reveals childhood experiences a 1, b 1, c 1: a 1, the father made compliance a condition for giving X what he desired; b 1, the father held him to be a genius; c 1, the mother despised the father.

The interpretation according to Freud's concept of transference would be that in his childhood X identified himself with his mother and adopted a passive feminine role toward the father, with certain expectations of reward. As to the present structure: X has latent passive homosexual trends of which he is ashamed and because of which he is afraid of being despised. His inflated notions about himself are a protest against his feminine trends, and they serve as a compensation for his self-contempt and fear of being despised by others. This interpretation would also elucidate other peculiarities of X's. For example, his fear of tying himself to any woman would also be explained by the latent homosexuality and by the fear of being despised by women as the father was by the mother.

If one does not draw vertical lines from the trends a, b, c, to the factors a 1, b 1, c 1 in childhood, but draws horizontal lines, that is, if one tries primarily to understand how a, b and c are actually interrelated, one has to consider such questions as why X has this deep fear of contempt in spite of his good qualities and his exceptional gifts, why he has this necessity of clinging to inflated notions about himself. One would gradually recognize that X implicitly promises more than he can give. He arouses expectations of an all-embracing love, but because of fears and certain subtle sadistic trends is unwilling and incapable of fulfilling them. Similarly, he arouses expectations of great mental achievements, but because of self-indulgence and various inhibitions does not work sufficiently to fulfill them. Without wanting to or being aware of it, X has thus become a swindler who wants to obtain admiration, love and support by his implicit promises, but who never "delivers the goods."

Hence trend b: exalted notions are necessary to cover

up the swindle in his own eyes and to throw sand into the eyes of other people. Because of the subjective importance of these notions he cannot tolerate any questioning of them, and in the case of doubt has to react with intense hostility.

Trend a: the compliance has developed because X, as a result of his great expectations of others, cannot afford to arouse any antagonism, because he has to live up to the image of being a good person and must therefore do what others expect of him, because he needs affection, as a result of a haunting anxiety generated mainly on the basis of his unwitting pretenses.

Trend c: he despises himself partly for his unconscious sponging tendencies, partly for his compliance, partly for the false pretenses on which his life is built, and therefore he is afraid of being similarly despised by others.

Freud realizes that seemingly exaggerated emotional reactions occur not only in the analytical situation but may occur as well in any other close relationship. As a matter of fact, an intricate question arises when comparing the analytical situation with others: if in the former love is a feeling which is only transferred from an infantile object to the analyst, is it perhaps true that all love is transference, and if not how can we distinguish between love which is transference and love which is not? My viewpoint concerning questions like these is the same as that concerning the concept of transference itself. In the analytical relationship, as in others, it is the entire actual structure of the personality which decides whether and why an individual feels attracted to others.

Nevertheless, it remains true that in the analytical situation an attachment, or rather a dependency, occurs more regularly than in other relationships. Other emotional reactions too seem on the whole to be more frequent and more highly pitched in analysis than outside of it. Persons who otherwise seem to be well adapted may be, in analysis, openly hostile, distrustful, possessive, exacting.

These observations suggest that there may be specific factors in the analytical situation which precipitate such reactions. According to Freud, the patient in analysis behaves and feels increasingly in an "infantile" fashion, and thus Freud contends that analysis fosters regressive reactions. The obligation to associate freely, together with the analyst's interpretations and his attitude of tolerance, helps the patient to relinquish some of his conscious adult control and to permit infantile reactions to appear more freely. The unearthing of the patient's childhood experiences leads him to relive past feelings. Finally, and most important, the rule that analysis should be carried on with a certain amount of frustration of the patient, that is, the analyst's obligation to be reserved toward the patient's desires and demands, is assumed to further regression to infantile modes of feelings, in the same way as other frustrations are believed to precipitate regressions.

Since I have already discussed the concept of regression I can proceed to offer my explanation of the problem. As I see it, the special challenge of the psychoanalytical situation consists in the fact that the patient's customary defensive attitudes cannot be used effectively. They are uncovered as such, thus forcing to the foreground the repressed trends underlying these defenses. A patient who has developed an attitude of indiscriminate admiration for certain persons because, for instance, he wants to cover up competitive drives, will in the analytical situation try the same tactics toward the analyst, admiring him blindly; but soon he will have to face the underlying disparaging trends. A patient who has covered up his excessive demands on others by extreme modesty will in the analytical situation have to face the existence of his demands with all their implications. A patient afraid of being found out can in other circumstances avoid this danger by withdrawing from others, by being secretive and by rigid control—attitudes which cannot be maintained in analysis. As analysis unavoidably attacks defenses which hitherto fulfilled important functions, it is bound to stir up anxiety and arouse defensive hostility. A patient has to defend his defenses as long as they are necessary for him, and he is bound to resent the analyst as a dangerous intruder.

Freud's concept of transference has certain theoretical and practical implications. Since he interprets a patient's irrational feelings and impulses in analysis as repetitions of similar feelings once had toward parents and siblings, Freud believes that the transference reactions repeat the oedipal relationship "with a fatiguing regularity." He regards this frequency as his most convincing evidence for the regular occurrence of the Oedipus complex. This evidence, however, is the outcome of circular reasoning, because the interpretations themselves are already based on the—debatable—conviction that the Oedipus complex is a biological and hence ubiquitous phenomenon, and that past reactions are subsequently repeated.

One of the practical implications of the concept of transference concerns the analyst's attitude toward the patient. According to Freud, since the analyst plays the role of some person important in infancy, his own personality should be eliminated as much as possible; to use a term of Freud's, he should be "like a mirror." The advice to be impersonal, though issued from a debatable premise, may claim some validity. The analyst should not impose his own problems on the patient. Also, he should not become emotionally involved with the patient, because such involvement may impair his clear vision as to the patient's problems. The advice is disputable only inasmuch as it may lead to a stilted, disinterested, authoritative behavior on the part of the analyst.[4]

Fortunately the analyst's spontaneity usually prevents him from adhering too strictly to the ideal of being a mirror. Nevertheless, the ideal as such carries with it certain dangers for the analyst which are ultimately bound to reflect on the patient too. It may delude the analyst into denying to himself that he has any emotional reactions to the patient, whereas it would be more appropriate to advise that the analyst should understand his personal reactions to the patient. It is probable that in actual fact he does react to a patient's wishes to cheat him of money, to defeat his efforts, to humiliate him or to provoke him, particularly as long as these tendencies of the patient appear in disguised

[4] *Cf.* Clara Thompson, "Notes on the Psychoanalytic Significance of the Choice of an Analyst" in *Psychiatry* (1938).

forms and are not clearly recognized. It would be better for the analyst to admit to himself that he has such
reactions and to utilize them in two ways: by asking
himself whether the reactions he feels are not exactly
those the patient wants to effect, thus obtaining some
clue as to the processes going on; and as a challenge to
a better understanding of himself.

The principle that the analyst's emotional reactions
should be understood as a "counter-transference" may
be objected to on the same grounds as the concept of
transference. According to this principle, when an analyst reacts with inner irritation to a patient's tendency
to defeat his efforts, he may be identifying the patient
with his own father, and thus repeating an infantile
situation in which he felt defeated by the father. If,
however, the analyst's emotional reactions are understood in the light of his own character structure as it
is affected by the patient's actual behavior, it will be
seen that his irritation may have arisen because he has,
for example, the fantastic notion that he must be able
to cure every case and hence feels it as a personal humiliation if he does not succeed. Or, to take another frequent difficulty, as long as the analyst protects his own
excessive demands by feeling unfairly treated, he will
scarcely be able to disentangle similar twists in the
patient; he will be more likely to sympathize with the
patient's misery than to analyze the defensive elements
it serves to mask.

There is, however, this to be added: the more we
disregard the repetition aspect of transference, the more
stringent must be the analyst's own analysis. For it requires incomparably more inner freedom to see and

understand the patient's actual problems in all their ramifications than to relate these problems to infantile behavior. It is impossible, for instance, to analyze all the implications of neurotic ambition or of masochistic dependency if one has not worked out these problems in oneself.

I do not think it is of any consequence whether we keep or drop the term transference, provided we divorce it from the one-sidedness of its original meaning: the reactivation of past feelings. In a condensed formulation, my viewpoint concerning the phenomenon is this: neuroses are ultimately the expression of disturbances in human relationships; the analytical relationship is one special form of human relationships and existing disturbances are bound to appear here as they appear elsewhere; the particular conditions under which an analysis is conducted render it possible to study these disturbances here more accurately than elsewhere and to convince the patient of their existence and of the role they play. If the concept of transference is thus disentangled from the theoretical bias of the repetition compulsion, it will in time yield the results which it is intrinsically capable of producing.

CHAPTER X

CULTURE AND NEUROSES

DISCUSSIONS in the foregoing chapters have shown certain limitations in Freud's understanding of cultural factors, and the reasons for these limitations. I shall briefly recapitulate the reasons and summarize the influence which his attitude toward cultural questions has exerted on psychoanalytical theories.

We must remember first of all that the present knowledge of the extent and nature of cultural influence on personality was not available to Freud at the time he developed his psychological system. Besides, his orientation as an instinct theorist kept him from a proper evaluation of these factors. Instead of recognizing that the conflicting trends in neuroses are primarily engendered by the conditions under which we live, he regards them as instinctual trends which are only modified by the individual environment.

As a consequence Freud ascribes to biological factors the trends prevailing in the middle-class neurotic of western civilization, and hence regards them as inherent in "human nature." This type is characterized by a great potential hostility, by much more readiness and capacity for hate than for love, by emotional isolation, by a tendency to be egocentric, ready to withdraw, acquisitive, entangled in problems concerning possession and prestige. Not recognizing that all these trends are brought about ultimately by the conditions of a specific social structure, Freud ascribes the egocentricity ultimately to a narcissistic libido, the hostility to a destruction instinct, the difficulties in money matters to an anal libido, the acquisitiveness to an oral libido. It is logical then to regard the masochistic trends frequent in modern neurotic women as akin to feminine nature, or to infer that a specific behavior in present-day neurotic children represents a universal stage in human development.

Since he is convinced of the universality of the role played by allegedly instinctual drives, Freud feels entitled to explain cultural phenomena too on that basis. Capitalism is seen as an anal-erotic culture, wars are determined by an inherent destruction instinct, cultural achievements in general are sublimations of libidinal drives. Qualitative differences in different cultures are accounted for by the nature of the instinctual drives which are characteristically expressed or repressed, that is, they are considered to depend on whether expression or repression concerns mostly oral, anal, genital or destruction drives.

It is also on the basis of these presuppositions that intricate customs of primitive tribes are explained as though they were analogous to neurotic phenomena of our culture.[1] A German writer caricatures this procedure as the habit of psychoanalytical writers to regard

[1] *Cf.* E. Sapir, "Cultural Anthropology and Psychiatry" in *Journal of Abnormal and Social Psychology* (1932).

primitives as a bunch of neurotics gone savage. Polemics arising because of such ventures into sociological and anthropological fields sometimes attempt to disqualify psychoanalysis altogether by pointing to the recklessness of its generalizations in cultural matters. This is not warranted. Such generalizations merely reflect certain debatable principles of psychoanalysis, and they are far indeed from the core of what psychoanalysis has to offer.

How little weight Freud ascribes to cultural factors is evident also in his inclination to regard certain environmental influences as the incidental fate of the individual instead of recognizing the whole strength of cultural influences behind them. Thus, for example, Freud regards it as incidental that a brother in the family is preferred to the sister, whereas a preference for male children belongs to the pattern of a patriarchal society. Here the objection might be raised that for the individual analysis it is irrelevant whether the preference be regarded in one way or the other, but this is not quite so. In reality, the preference for the brother is one of many factors impressing on the female child the feeling that she is inferior or less desirable; therefore Freud's regarding the presence of a preferred brother as an incidental occurrence indicates that he does not see the entirety of factors which influence the girl.

Although it is true that childhood experiences vary not only in individual families but also with respect to each child in the same family, nevertheless most experiences are the result of the entire cultural situation and are not incidental. It would be unsafe to assume, for instance, that sibling rivalry, since it exists so generally in our culture, is a general human phenomenon;

we have to query to what degree this phenomenon is determined by the competitiveness existing in our culture. It would be miraculous indeed if the family alone were exempt from competitiveness, since it permeates all other spheres of our life.

In so far as Freud does consider the influence of cultural factors on neuroses, he does it in a one-sided way. His interest is restricted to the question as to how cultural conditions influence existing "instinctual" drives. In accord with his belief that the main external factor precipitating a neurosis is frustration, he assumes that cultural conditions bring about neuroses by imposing frustrations on the individual. He believes that culture, by enforcing restrictions on libidinal and particularly on destructive drives, is instrumental in bringing about repressions, guilt feelings and needs for self-punishment. Hence his general slant is that we have to pay for cultural benefits by dissatisfaction and unhappiness. The way out is by sublimation. But since the capacity for sublimation is limited, and since repression of "instinctual" drives is one of the essential factors in bringing about neuroses, Freud assumes a quantitative relation between the degree of repression imposed by a culture and the frequency and severity of ensuing neuroses.

The relation between culture and neuroses, however, is primarily not quantitative but qualitative.[2] What matters is the relation between the quality of cultural trends and the quality of individual conflicts. The diffi-

2 For a more extensive discussion of this relationship *cf.* Karen Horney, *The Neurotic Personality of Our Time* (1937).

culty in studying this relation is one of diverging com-petences. The sociologist can give information only on the social structure of a given culture; the analyst can give information only on the structure of a neurosis. The way to overcome the difficulty is by co-operative work.[3]

In considering the relation between culture and neu-roses only those trends matter which neuroses have in common; from the sociological viewpoint individual variations in neuroses are not relevant. We have to discard the bewildering wealth of individual differences and search for the common denominators in the con-ditions engendering individual neuroses and in the content of neurotic conflicts.

When these data become available to the sociologist he can relate them to the cultural conditions which foster the development of neuroses and are responsible for the nature of neurotic conflicts. Three main sets of factors are to be taken into account: those which repre-sent the matrix out of which a neurosis may grow; those which constitute the basic neurotic conflicts and the attempts at their solution; and those entailed in the façade which the neurotic shows to himself and others.

A neurotic development in the individual arises ulti-mately from feelings of alienation, hostility, fear and diminished self-confidence. These attitudes do not them-selves constitute a neurosis, but they are the soil out

[3] Actually much work is done nowadays in this respect by psychia-trists, sociologists and anthropologists. To mention but a few names there are among the psychiatrists, A. Healy, A. Meyer, H. S. Sullivan; among the sociologists, J. Dollard, E. Fromm, M. Horkheimer, F. B. Karpf, H. D. Lasswell; among the anthropologists, R. Benedict, J. Hal-lowell, R. Linton, S. McKeel.

of which a neurosis may grow, since it is their combination which creates a basic feeling of helplessness toward a world conceived as potentially dangerous. It is basic anxiety or basic insecurity which necessitates the rigid pursuit of certain strivings for safety and satisfaction, the contradictory nature of which constitutes the core of neuroses. Consequently, the first group of factors bearing on neuroses which is to be looked for in a culture is the circumstances which create emotional isolation, potential hostile tension between people, insecurity and fears, and a feeling of individual powerlessness.

When in the following remarks I point out some factors which are relevant in this respect, I do not mean to trespass on the sociological domain but wish mainly to illustrate a possible co-operation. Among the factors in western civilization which engender potential hostility, the fact that this culture is built on individual competitiveness probably ranks first. The economic principle of competition affects human relationships by causing one individual to fight another, by enticing one person to surpass another and by making the advantage of one the disadvantage of the other. As we know, competitiveness not only dominates our relations in occupational groups, but also pervades our social relations, our friendships, our sexual relations and the relations within the family group, thus carrying the germs of destructive rivalry, disparagement, suspicion, begrudging envy into every human relationship. Existing gross inequalities, not only in possessions but in possibilities for education, recreation, maintaining and regaining health, constitute another group of factors replete with potential hostilities. A further factor is the possibility for one group or person to exploit another.

As to factors creating insecurity, our actual insecurity in the economic and social fields should probably be named first.[4] Another powerful factor in creating personal insecurity is certainly the fears created by the general potential hostile tensions: fear of envy in case of success, fear of contempt in case of failure, fear of being abused and, on the other hand, retaliation fears for wanting to shove others aside, to disparage and exploit them. Also the emotional isolation of the individual, resulting from disturbances in interpersonal relations and the accompanying lack of solidarity, is probably a powerful element in engendering insecurity; under such conditions the individual, thrust upon his own resources, is and feels unprotected. The general feeling of insecurity is increased by the fact that for the most part neither tradition nor religion is strong enough today to give the individual a feeling of being an integral part of a more powerful unity, providing shelter and directing his strivings.

Finally, there is the question of how our culture impairs individual self-confidence. Self-confidence is an expression of an individual's factually existing strength. It is impaired by any failure which the individual ascribes to his own deficiencies, whether the failure occur in social, professional or love life. An earthquake may make us feel powerless, but it does not impair our self-confidence, because we recognize the operation of a

[4] Cf. H. Lasswell, *World Politics and Personal Insecurity* (1935); L. K. Frank, "Mental Security," in *Implications of Social Economic Goals for Education* (1937).

major force. The individual's existing limitations in choosing and attaining some goal by himself should not impair his self-confidence; but by virtue of the fact that external limitations are less visible than an earthquake, and particularly by virtue of the ideology that success is dependent only on personal efficiency, the individual tends to accredit failures to his own deficiencies. Furthermore, the individual in our culture is as a rule not prepared for the hostilities and struggles that are in store for him. He is taught that people are well-intentioned toward him, that it is a virtue to confide in others, and that to be on one's guard is almost a moral defect. This contradiction between factually existing hostile tensions and the gospel of brotherly love may also, I believe, have a decisive influence on lowering self-confidence.

The second set of factors to be considered is those inhibitions, needs and strivings which constitute the neurotic conflicts. When studying neuroses in our culture we find that in spite of great differences in the symptomatic picture, the basic problems are strikingly alike in all of them. I do not refer to similarities in what Freud considers to be instinctual drives, but to similarities in actually existing conflicts, such as conflicts between a ruthless ambition and a compulsory need for affection, between wishes to keep apart from others and wishes to possess someone entirely, between an extreme emphasis on self-sufficiency and parasitic desires, between a compulsion to be unobtrusive and wanting to be a hero or a genius.

The sociologist, after recognizing the individual conflicts, has to look for conflicting cultural trends which might be responsible for the individual ones. Since the neurotic conflicts concern incompatible strivings for safety and satisfaction, he would have to search particularly for contradictory cultural ways of obtaining safety and satisfaction. The neurotic development of boundless ambition, for instance, as a means of safety, revenge, self-expression, is unthinkable in a culture which does not know individual competitiveness and which offers no rewards for outstanding individual achievements. This holds true also with regard to neurotic strivings for prestige and possessions. To hold on to a person as a means of reassurance would scarcely be possible in a culture which definitely discourages attitudes of dependency. Suffering and helplessness will probably not be resorted to as a solution for neurotic dilemmas in a culture in which suffering and helplessness mean social disgrace or, as in Samuel Butler's *Erewhon,* are met with punishment.

The most obvious influence of cultural factors on neuroses is to be seen in the image the neurotic is anxious to present to himself and others. This image is determined mainly by his fear of disapproval and his craving for distinction. Consequently it consists of those qualities which in our culture are rewarded with approval and distinction, such as unselfishness, love for others, generosity, honesty, self-control, moderation, rationality, good judgment. Without the cultural ideology of unselfishness, for instance, the neurotic would not feel compelled to keep up an appearance of not wanting anything for himself, not only hiding his egocentricity but also suppressing his natural desires for happiness.

Thus the problem of the influence of cultural conditions in creating neurotic conflicts is far more complex than Freud sees it. It involves no less than a thorough analysis of a given culture from such points of view as these: In what ways and to what extent are interpersonal hostilities created in a given culture? How great is the personal insecurity of the individual and what factors contribute toward making him insecure? What factors impair the individual's inherent self-confidence? What social prohibitions and tabus exist and what is their influence in bringing about inhibitions and fears? What ideologies are effective and what goals or rationalizations do they provide? What needs and strivings are created, encouraged or discouraged by the given conditions?

The types of problems which recur in neuroses are not essentially different from those of the healthy individual in our culture. He too has contradictory tendencies in regard to competition and affection, egocentricity and solidarity, self-aggrandizement and inferiority feelings, egoism and altruism. The difference is that in the neurotic these contradictory tendencies reach a higher peak, that the trends on both sides of the conflicts are more imperative, as a result of his greater amount of underlying anxiety, so he is unable to find any satisfactory solution.

The question remains why certain persons become neurotic while others, living under similar conditions, are able to cope with the existing difficulties. This question resembles one that is often asked concerning siblings of the same family: why is it that one among them acquires a severe neurosis while the others are but lightly affected? In such a question there is an implicit premise that psychic conditions for different individuals are essentially alike, and this premise leads to the seeking of an explanation in the constitutional differences of the various siblings. Although constitutional differences are certainly relevant to the general development, the type of reasoning leading to this conclusion is nevertheless erroneous, for the premise it rests upon is false. Only the general psychic atmosphere is the same for all the siblings, and in one way or another they will all be affected by it. In detail, however, the experiences of one child may be entirely different from those of another child in the same family. As a matter of fact, there may be an endless variety of important differences, the nature and influence of which may sometimes be revealed only by a careful analysis. These may be differences in the relationship to the parents, in the degree a child is wanted, in the parents' preference for one or the other child, in the siblings' behavior toward one another, and many others. The child who is hit to a lesser degree may be able to cope with the existing difficulties, while the child who is hit harder may develop conflicts in which he becomes hopelessly caught: that is, he may become neurotic.

A similar answer can be given to the question as to why only some persons become neurotic, and not all, when they all live under the same difficult cultural conditions. The persons who succumb to a neurosis are those who have been more severely hit by the existing difficulties, particularly in their childhood.

A great frequency of neuroses and psychoses in a given culture is one of the indicators showing that something is seriously wrong with the conditions under which people live. It shows that the psychic difficulties engendered by the cultural conditions are greater than the average capacity of people to cope with them.

Thus far the psychiatrist's interest in cultural influences, though important in many ways, has but a limited bearing on his practical dealing with patients. It helps him to see neuroses in a proper frame of reference, to understand why one patient after another struggles with essentially similar problems, why his patients' problems are similar to his own. Some of the personal sting for the patient is removed when the analyst can help him to realize that fate has not been especially unfair to him alone, but that ultimately he shares his fate with his fellow beings. Also the patient is relieved of individual guilt feelings if the analyst leads him to recognize the social nature of such tabus as those on masturbation, incest, death wishes or protests against parental authority. The analyst who struggles with the problem of competition is encouraged to tackle his personal problems on that basis when he realizes that in one way or another it is a problem for all of us.[5]

There is one way, however, in which an awareness of cultural implications is of specific importance for therapy: its implications for the question of what constitutes psychic health. Psychiatrists who are not culture-conscious tend to believe this question to be a purely medical one. This interpretation may suffice as long as the psychiatrist is concerned only with gross symptoms,

[5] The instinct theory brings about in other ways a reassurance as to universality: there the analyst points out the universality of certain instinctual drives.

such as phobias, obsessions, depressions, and their cure. The goal of psychoanalytical therapy is, however, more ambitious. It is not only to remove the symptoms but to effect such a change in the personality that the symptoms cannot recur. This is done by the analysis of the character. But in dealing with character trends the analyst has no simple measuring rod as to what is healthy or not. Then, inadvertently, the medical criterion is replaced by a social evaluation, that is, a criterion of "normality," which means the statistically average in a given culture or in a given part of the population.[6] It is this implicit evaluation that determines which problems will be tackled and which not. By implicit I mean that the analyst is unaware of using any evaluation.

Those analysts not aware of cultural implications would, in good faith, refute the above statement. They would point out that they do not evaluate at all, that it is none of their business to have any judgment of values, that they simply tackle the problems which the patient offers. But in this they overlook the fact that the patient has certain problems which he does not offer at all, or makes only timid attempts to offer—and this for the same reason which prevents the analyst from recognizing them: the patient too considers certain of his peculiarities as "normal" because they coincide with the average.

For instance, when a woman uses all her energy to further her husband professionally, when she is capable of and successful in taking all sorts of steps for him

[6] W. Trotter, *Instincts of the Herd in Peace and War* (1915).

while her own talents and career remain in the background, an analyst may see nothing problematic in this attitude because it appears to be "normal." Nor may the woman herself feel or recognize that there is a problem. Of course a problem does not necessarily exist here. The husband may be much more gifted than the wife. She may love him so much that her best capacities are unfolded in just the kind of devoted friendship she gives to him, and that her best chances for her own happiness lie in doing so. But in other patients this may not be so. I have in mind, for instance, a patient who was more gifted than her husband. The relationship to the husband was as disturbed as a human relationship can be. One of her deepest problems was her total incapacity to do anything for herself. But because it was hidden behind a "normal" feminine attitude this problem had always been overlooked.

Another of the problems which is rarely seen as such by the analyst and never offered by the patient is the patient's incapacity to form a judgment concerning a person, a cause, an institution, a theory; this uncertainty is overlooked because it is "normal" for the average liberal-minded individual.[7] Like the previous example, this peculiarity does not necessarily constitute a perplexity for every patient. But sometimes the patient's decisive fears may lurk behind just such a façade of indiscriminate tolerance. The individual may be excessively afraid of arousing any hostility or of provoking any alienation by taking a critical stand, may dread any step toward inner independence. In that case, a failure

[7] *Cf.* Erich Fromm, "Die gesellschaftliche Bedingtheit der psychoanalytischen Therapie" in *Zeitschrift für Sozialforschung* (1935).

to see that his lack of discernment is a problem to be analyzed will leave his deepest difficulties untouched.

Naturally the analyst's insufficient culture-consciousness may appear also in grosser forms which because of their conspicuous inadequacy need no discussion. Thus, for instance, the analyst may feel it necessary to tackle a patient's revolutionary strivings while the patient's adherence to conservative standards is not touched upon; in the same way he may see a problem in the patient's being critical of psychoanalytical theories, but overlook the problem that may lie in their acceptance.

Thus an unawareness of existing cultural evaluations combines with certain theoretical biases which have been discussed previously to promote a one-sided selection of the material offered by the patient. In psychoanalytical therapy then—as in education—the goal inadvertently becomes adaptation to the "normal"; only in matters of sexuality—because a good sexual regime is deemed an essential factor in psychic health—does the analyst become conscious of goals which are independent of currently accepted practices. Instead, one should distinguish, with Trotter, between psychic normality and psychic health, and understand by the latter a state of inner freedom in which "the full capacities are available for use." [8]

[8] *Cf.* W. Trotter, *op. cit.*

CHAPTER XI

THE "EGO" AND THE "ID"

THE concept of the "ego" is replete with inconsisten-
cies and contradictions. When Freud in one of his re-
cent papers [1] asserts that neurotic conflicts are between
the "ego" and the instincts, it would seem that the
"ego" is understood as different from and opposed to
instinctual strivings. If that be so, it is difficult to see
what concretely this "ego" consists of.

Originally the "ego" comprised all that was not
libido. It was the non-sexual part of ourselves serving
the sheer needs of self-preservation. With the introduction of narcissism, however, the majority of phenomena
previously relegated to the "ego" became libidinal in
nature: concern about ourselves, strivings toward self-
aggrandizement, toward prestige, self-esteem, ideals, creative abilities.[2] Later on, with the introduction of the
"super-ego," moral goals, inner norms regulating our
behavior and feelings, also became instinctual in nature
(the "super-ego" being a mixture of narcissistic libido,

[1] Sigmund Freud, "Analysis Terminable and Interminable" in *International Journal of Psychoanalysis* (1937).

[2] Sigmund Freud, "Narcissism: An Introduction" in *Collected Papers,*
Vol. IV (1914).

destruction instinct and derivatives of previous sexual attachments). Hence Freud's reference to the "ego" and the instincts as a pair of opposites lacks lucidity.

It is only by collecting data from various writings of Freud's that we can achieve an approximate notion as to which phenomena he relegates to the "ego." It seems to entail the following groups of factors: the narcissistic phenomena; desexualized derivatives of "instincts" (qualities developed, for instance, through sublimatior or reaction-formation); instinctual drives (for instance, sexual desires of a non-incestuous character) which have undergone such changes as to have become acceptable to the individual—which is probably equivalent to their being socially acceptable.[3]

Hence Freud's "ego" is not the opposite pole to instincts, because it is itself instinctual in nature. It is rather, as he has declared in some writings, the organized part of the "id," the latter being the sum total of crude, unmodified instinctual needs.[4]

The essential characteristic of the "ego" is weakness. All sources of energy rest in the "id"; the "ego" lives on borrowed forces.[5] Its preferences and dislikes, its goals, its decisions are determined by the "id" and the "super-ego"; it must take care that the instinctual drives do not collide too dangerously with the "super-ego" or the external world. It has, as Freud describes it, a three-fold dependency—on the "id," on the "super-ego" and

[3] Although in general Freud considers the "super-ego" to be a special part of the "ego," in some papers he stresses the conflict between the two.

[4] Sigmund Freud, *Group Psychology and the Analysis of the Ego* (1922).

[5] Sigmund Freud, *The Ego and the Id* (1935).

on the external world—acting, as it were, as an intermediary. It wants to enjoy the satisfactions the "id" is striving for but tends to submit also to the prohibitions of the "super-ego." Its weakness is similar to that of an individual who has no resources of his own and wants to benefit from one party without spoiling anything with regard to the opposite party.

In evaluating this concept of the "ego" I arrive at the same conclusion as that for almost every doctrine propounded by Freud: underlying observations of great keenness and depth are robbed of their constructive value because of their integration into an unconstructive theoretical system. From a clinical standpoint one may indeed say much in favor of the concept. Chronic neurotics give the impression of having no say in their lives. They are driven by emotional forces which they do not know and over which they have no control. They cannot but act and react in rigid ways, often in contrast to their intellectual judgment. Their attitude toward others is determined not by conscious wishes and conscious values but by unconscious factors of imperative character. This is most conspicuous with the compulsion neurosis but is roughly true for all severe neuroses, not to speak of psychoses. Freud's metaphor of the rider who, though thinking he guides the horse, is taken where it wants to go, appears to be a good description of the neurotic "ego."

Such observations in neuroses do not, however, permit the conclusion that the "ego" in general is merely a modified part of the instincts. This is not conclusive even for neuroses. Assuming that to a large extent a neurotic's pity for others is transformed sadism or externalized self-pity, this does not prove that some part of sympathy for others is not "genuine." [6] Or assuming that a patient's admiration for his analyst is determined largely by his unconscious expectations of miracles which the analyst may perform for him, or by unconscious endeavors to exclude any form of rivalry, this does not prove that he may not also have a "genuine" appreciation for the analyst's capacities or for his personality. Consider a situation in which A has an opportunity to injure an adversary B by making disparaging remarks about him. A can refrain from doing so because of any number of unconscious emotional reasons: he may be afraid of B's retaliation; he may have to keep up the appearance of righteousness in his own eyes; he may simply cater to the good opinion of others by appearing to be above malice. All this does not prove, however, that he might not also abstain from making remarks because he would feel it beneath his dignity, that he might not consciously decide that this kind of revenge is too cheap or too insidious. It would lead too far afield to consider here the question of the extent to which the content of moral qualities is itself conditioned by cultural factors. In my opinion, however, there may be "genuineness" which can be dissolved neither by Freud's resort to instincts nor by the relativists' resort to social valuations and conditioning.

The same may be said of the mentally healthy individual. The fact that he too may deceive himself about his motivations does not prove that he does so always.

[6] "Genuine" in this context means that the feelings—or judgments—in question do not permit further analysis into allegedly instinctual components; it combines the meaning of elemental and spontaneous.

Since he is less anxiety-ridden and hence less subject to the power of unconscious drives than the neurotic, Freud's conclusions for him are all the less warranted. Thus in his concept of the "ego" Freud denies—and on the basis of the libido theory must deny—that there are any judgments or feelings which are not dissolvable into more elemental "instinctual" units. In general his concept means that on theoretical grounds any judgments about people or causes must be regarded as rationalizations of "deeper" emotional motivations, that any critical stand toward a theory must be viewed as an ultimately emotional resistance. It means that theoretically there is no liking or disliking of people, no sympathy, no generosity,[7] no feeling of justice, no devotion to a cause, which is not in the last analysis essentially determined by libidinal or destructive drives.

The denial that mental faculties may exist in their own right fosters insecurity of judgment; for example, it may lead analyzed people not to take a stand toward anything without making the reservation that probably their judgment is merely an expression of unconscious preferences or dislikes. It may also encourage the illusion that a superior knowledge of human nature consists in detecting ulterior motives in every judgment or feeling—of others!—and thereby contribute to a smug know-it-all attitude.

Another consequence is that it promotes uncertainty about feelings and thus involves the danger of render-

[7] In the paper mentioned above Freud declares, when speaking of observations that generous people may surprise us by some isolated trend of miserliness, "they show that *every* praiseworthy and valuable quality is based on compensation and overcompensation" (italics mine).

ing them shallow. A more or less conscious awareness of "it is only because" will easily jeopardize the spontaneity and the depth of emotional experiences. Hence the frequent impression that although an analyzed individual is better adapted he has become "less of a real person," or as one might say, less alive.

The observations of such effects as these is sometimes used to perpetuate the time-honored fallacy that too much awareness makes a person futilely "introspective." What accounts for such "introspectiveness," however, is not the greater awareness as such, but the implicit belief in the omnipresence of motivations which are generally regarded as inferior. Freud himself regards them as inferior in value, though he wishes to consider them from the viewpoint of science and emphasize that they are as far beyond moral evaluation as is the instinct compelling a salmon to swim upstream during the time of ovulation. As often happens, the zest in pursuing a new finding which is valid may lead to carrying it to a point where it loses its validity. Freud has taught us to make a skeptical scrutiny of our motivations; he has demonstrated the far-reaching influence of unconscious egocentric and anti-social drives. But it is merely dogmatic to assert, for instance, that a judgment cannot be simply the expression of what one holds to be right or wrong, that one cannot be devoted to a cause because one is convinced of its value, that friendliness cannot be a direct expression of good human relationships.

It is often regretted in psychoanalytical literature that we know little about the "ego" in comparison with our extensive knowledge concerning the "id." This deficiency is attributed to the historical development of psychoanalysis, which led first to an elaborate study of the "id." The hope is expressed that just as elaborate a knowledge of the "ego" will follow in time, but this hope is likely to be disappointed. The theory of instincts, as propounded by Freud, leaves no more scope, no more life to the "ego" than is indicated above. Only by abandoning the theory of instincts can we learn something about the "ego," but then it will be a different phenomenon from the one Freud has in mind.

It will be seen then that an "ego" approximating Freud's description is not inherent in human nature but is a specifically neurotic phenomenon. Nor is it inherent in the constitution of the individual who later develops a neurosis. It is in itself the result of a complex process, the result of an alienation from self. This alienation from self, or as I have called it on other occasions,[8] the stunting of the spontaneous individual self, is one of the crucial factors which not only is at the root of a neurotic development but also prevents an individual from outgrowing his neurosis. If he were not alienated from himself it would not be possible for the neurotic to be driven by his neurotic trends toward aims which are essentially alien to him. Furthermore, if he had not lost his capacity for evaluating himself or others he could not possibly feel as dependent on others as he actually does, because in the last analysis neurotic dependency of whatever kind is based on the fact that the individual has lost his center of gravity in himself and shifted it to the outside world.

[8] *Cf.* Chapter V, The Concept of Narcissism, Chapter XIII, The Concept of the "Super-Ego," Chapter XV, Masochistic Phenomena, Chapter XVI, Psychoanalytical Therapy.

When we abandon Freud's concept of the "ego" a
new possibility for psychoanalytical therapy opens up.
As long as the "ego" is considered to be by its very
nature merely a servant and a supervisor of the "id,"
it cannot be itself an object of therapy. Therapeutic
expectations must then be restricted to bringing about
a better adaptation of the "untamed passions" to "reason." If, however, this "ego," with its weakness, is
regarded as an essential part of the neurosis, then changing it must become a task of therapy. The analyst then
must deliberately work toward the ultimate goal of
having the patient retrieve his spontaneity and his faculty of judgment, or in James' term, his "spiritual self."

In accordance with his assumption of an "ego"-"id"-
"super-ego" anatomy of the personality Freud arrives at
certain formulations concerning the nature of conflicts
and the nature of anxiety in neuroses. He distinguishes
three types of conflicts: those between the individual
and the environment, which though ultimately responsible for the other two kinds of conflicts are not specific
for neuroses; those between the "ego" and the "id,"
resulting in the danger of the "ego" being overwhelmed
by the magnitude of instinctual drives; those between
the "ego" and the "super-ego," resulting in fear of the
"super-ego." These contentions will be discussed in
successive chapters.[9]

Discarding terminology and theoretical details,
Freud's concept of neurotic conflicts is roughly as follows: man collides inevitably with the environment
because of his instinctual heritage; the conflict between

[9] *Cf.* Chapter XII, Anxiety, and Chapter XIII, The Concept of the
"Super-Ego."

the individual and the outside world is carried on later within the individual himself as a conflict between his untamed passions and his reason or his moral standards.

One cannot escape the impression that this concept follows on a scientific level the Christian ideology of a conflict between good and evil, between moral and immoral, between man's animal nature and his reason. That in itself entails no criticism. The question is only whether neurotic conflicts are actually of this nature. The conclusions drawn from my observations of neuroses lead me to assume roughly the following standpoint: man does not collide with his environment as inevitably as Freud assumes; if there is such a collision it is not because of his instincts but because the environment inspires fears and hostilities. The neurotic trends which he develops as a consequence, though in some ways they provide a means of coping with the environment, in other ways enhance his conflicts with it. Therefore, in my judgment, conflicts with the outside world are not only at the bottom of neuroses but remain an essential part of neurotic difficulties.

Moreover, I do not consider it feasible to localize neurotic conflicts in a schematic way, as Freud does. Actually they may spring from manifold sources.[10] There may be, for example, a conflict between two incompatible neurotic trends, such as a conflict between a desire for dictatorial power and a need for dependence on others. An individual neurotic trend may bear a conflict in itself, as the need to appear perfect contains

[10] Franz Alexander was the first to point out the existence of different kinds of neurotic conflicts (cf. his "The Relation of Structural and Instinctual Conflicts" in Psychoanalytic Quarterly, 1933).

both a tendency toward compliance and a tendency toward defiance. A need to present an infallible façade will conflict with all trends not fitting into the façade. Since the nature of conflicts and the role they play in the neurotic's character and in his life are implicitly or explicitly dealt with throughout this book, I need not go into further detail here. I shall discuss presently the ways in which the different slants on neurotic conflicts lead to a different understanding of anxiety in neuroses.

CHAPTER XII

ANXIETY

TO those who, like Freud, tend to explain psychic manifestations ultimately on an organic basis, anxiety is a
challenging problem because of its close relation to
physiological processes.

Anxiety, it is true, often appears simultaneously with
physiological symptoms such as palpitations, perspiration, diarrhea, quick breathing. These physical con-
comitants may appear with or without awareness of
anxiety. Before an examination, for instance, a patient
may have diarrhea and be fully aware of having anxiety.
But also there may be palpitations or a frequent urge
to urinate, without any awareness of anxiety, and only
later a recognition that anxiety must have been present.
Though physical expressions of emotion are particularly conspicuous in anxiety they are not, however,
characteristic of anxiety alone. In depressions there is
a slowing up of physical and mental processes; acute
joy has the effect of changing the tension of the tissues
or of making the gait lighter; acute rage may make us
tremble and may cause an afflux of blood to the head.
Another fact often pointed out to show the relation of
anxiety to physiological factors is that anxiety may be

produced by chemicals. This too, however, is not true for anxiety alone. Chemicals may also produce elation or sleep, and their effect constitutes no psychological problem. The psychological problem can only be this: what are the psychic conditions for such states as anxiety, sleep, elation?

Anxiety is an emotional response to danger, as is fear. What characterizes anxiety in contradistinction to fear is, first, a quality of diffuseness and uncertainty. Even if there is a concrete danger, as in an earthquake, it has something of the horror of the unknown. The same quality is present in neurotic anxiety, regardless of whether the danger is undefined or whether it has crystallized into something concrete as, for instance, a phobia of high places.

Second, what is menaced by a danger provoking anxiety is, as pointed out by Goldstein,[1] something belonging to the essence or the core of the personality. As there is wide variation in what different individuals feel to be their vital values, there is also variation in what they feel as a vital menace. Though there are certain values which are almost universally felt to be of vital importance, such as life, freedom, children, it depends entirely on the conditions under which a person lives and on the structure of his personality what for him specifically represents an essential value— whether that would be, for instance, his body, his possessions, his reputation, his convictions, his work, his love relationships. As we shall see presently, recognition

[1] Kurt Goldstein, "Zum Problem der Angst" in *Allgemeine ärztliche Zeitschrift für Psychotherapie*, Vol. II.

of this condition for anxiety represents a constructive lead for understanding anxiety in neuroses.

Third, as Freud emphasizes rightly, anxiety in contra-distinction to fear is characterized by a feeling of help-lessness toward the danger. The helplessness may be conditioned by external factors, as in the case of an earthquake, or by internal factors such as weakness, cowardice, lack of initiative. Thus the same situation may provoke either fear or anxiety depending on the individual's capacity or willingness to tackle the danger. To illustrate by a story a patient told me: one night the patient heard noises in an adjoining room which sounded as if burglars were trying to break in. She reacted with palpitations, perspiration and a feeling of anxiety. After a while she got up and went into her eldest daughter's room. The daughter too was afraid but she determined to take active steps toward the danger and go into the room where the intruders were at work. By doing so she managed to chase away the burglars. The mother felt helpless toward the danger, the daughter did not; the mother had *anxiety,* the daughter had *fear.*

Thus a satisfactory account of any type of anxiety should answer three questions: What is endangered? What is the source of danger? What accounts for the helplessness toward the danger?

The puzzle in neurotic anxiety is the apparent ab-sence of a danger provoking the anxiety, or at any rate the disproportion between apparent danger and inten-sity of anxiety. One has the impression that the dangers the neurotic fears are merely imaginary. Yet neurotic

anxiety can be at least as intense as an anxiety provoked by any obvious danger situation. It was Freud
who led the way to an understanding of this bewilder·
ing issue. He asserted that, regardless of contradictory
surface impressions, the danger feared in neurotic anxiety is just as real as in objective anxiety. The difference
is that in the former the danger is constituted by subjective factors.

Pursuing the nature of the subjective factors involved,
Freud, with his usual consistency, relates neurotic anxiety to instinctual sources. Briefly, the source of danger
is, according to Freud, the magnitude of instinctual tension or the punitive power of the "super-ego"; the
object of danger is the "ego"; the helplessness is constituted by the "ego's" weakness and dependency on the
"id" and the "super-ego."

As the fear of the "super-ego" will be discussed in
connection with the "super-ego" concept, I shall deal
here mainly with Freud's view of what he calls neurotic anxiety in its stricter sense, which is the "ego's"
fear of being overwhelmed by the instinctual claims of
the "id." This theory rests ultimately on the same
mechanistic concept as does Freud's doctrine of instinc·
tual satisfaction: satisfaction is the result of a decrease
of instinctual tension; anxiety is the result of its increase. The tension engendered by pent-up repressed
drives is the real danger feared in neurotic anxiety:
when a child feels anxiety because he has been left
alone by his mother it is because he unconsciously
anticipates a damming up of libidinal drives as a consequence of their frustration.

Freud finds support for this mechanistic concept in

such observations as that a patient may be relieved of anxiety when he becomes capable of expressing hitherto repressed hostility directed against the analyst: in Freud's view it is the pent-up hostility which has caused the anxiety, and it is the discharge which has dissipated it. Freud recognizes that the relief may be due to the fact that the analyst has not responded to the hostility with reproaches or anger, but he has not seen that this explanation is sufficient to rob his mechanistic concept of the only evidence it has. That this conclusion was not drawn is again evidence of the extent to which theoretical bias has impeded psychological progress.

Though it is quite true that the fear of reproaches or retaliation may precipitate anxiety, this alone is not a sufficient explanation. Why is the neurotic so afraid of such consequences? If we accept the premise that anxiety is a response to a threat to a vital value we should examine, without Freud's theoretical preconceptions, what it is that the patient feels to be endangered by his hostility.

The answer is not the same for every patient. If he is of a type with prevailing masochistic trends [2] he will feel as dependent on the analyst as he has hitherto felt on his mother, his principal, his wife; he will feel that he cannot possibly live without the analyst, that the analyst has the magic power either to destroy him or to fulfill all his expectations. His personality structure being what it is, his feeling of safety in life depends on this subjection. Thus the preservation of the relationship is for him a matter of life and death. For other stringent reasons lying in himself this type of patient

[2] *Cf.* Chapter XV, Masochistic Phenomena.

feels that any hostility on his part will conjure up the danger of being deserted. Hence any emergence of hostile impulses must provoke anxiety.

If, however, he is of a type with a prevailing need to appear perfect [3] his safety rests on measuring up to his particular standards or to what he feels is expected of him. If his image of perfection is essentially constituted, for example, by rationality, impassivity and gentleness, then the prospect of an emotional outbreak of hostility is sufficient to provoke anxiety because it conjures up the danger of condemnation, which is as vital a menace to the perfectionistic type as is desertion to the masochistic type.

Other observations of anxiety in neuroses invariably conform with the same general principle. For a person of the narcissistic type, whose safety rests on being appreciated and admired, the vital danger is that of losing caste. In him anxiety may appear if he finds himself in an environment that does not recognize him, as observable in many a refugee who in his homeland was held in high regard. If the individual's safety rests on merging with others anxiety may arise if he is alone. If a person's safety rests on being unobtrusive, anxiety may emerge if he is in the limelight.

In view of these data, the formulation appears warranted that what is endangered in the neurotic's anxiety is his particular neurotic trends, that is, those trends on the pursuit of which his safety rests.

This interpretation of what is endangered in neurotic anxiety makes it easy to answer the question as to the sources of danger. The answer is a general one: any-

[3] *Cf.* Chapter XIII, The Concept of the "Super-Ego."

thing may provoke anxiety which is likely to jeopardize the individual's specific protective pursuits, his specific neurotic trends. If we understand a person's main means of gaining security we can predict at what provocations he is likely to feel anxiety.

The source of danger may be in the external circumstances, as in the case of the refugee who suddenly loses the prestige he needs for his feeling of security. Similarly, a woman who is masochistically dependent on her husband may feel anxiety if there is a danger of losing the husband through external conditions, whether through illness, through his leaving the country or through another woman.

The understanding of anxiety in neuroses is complicated by the fact that sources of danger also may be in the neurotic himself. Any factor within himself—a normal feeling, a reactive hostility, an inhibition, a contradictory neurotic trend—may be a source of danger if it is likely to jeopardize a safety device.

This anxiety may be provoked in a neurotic by a trivial error or a normal feeling or impulse. It may arise in a person whose safety rests on infallibility, for example, from a mistake or error in judgment of a kind that may happen to anyone, such as forgetting names or a failure to consider all possibilities in a travel arrangement. Similarly, in a person bent on presenting a façade of unselfishness, a legitimate modest wish for himself may provoke anxiety; in one whose safety rests on aloofness anxiety may develop at an emergence of love or affection.

There is little doubt that among the internal factors which are felt as a menace, emerging hostility ranks first. The reasons are twofold. Hostile reactions of various kinds are particularly frequent in neuroses because every neurosis, regardless of its special nature, renders a person weak and vulnerable. More frequently than the healthy person he feels rejected, abused, humiliated, and therefore he reacts more frequently with anger, defensive attacks, envy, derogatory or sadistic impulses. The other reason is that in one or another form his fear of people is so great that—unless reckless hostile aggression represents for him a means of safety, which is comparatively rare—he cannot easily afford to antagonize them. But the frequency of emerging hostility as the endangering factor should not tempt us to conclude that hostility per se provokes anxiety. As is implicit in the foregoing discussion, we must always ask precisely what is endangered by hostility.

An inhibition does not in itself provoke anxiety, but it may do so if it jeopardizes some vital value. Thus if an officer must give an order to change the ship's course, in order to avoid immediate collision, and at that moment his hand or voice fails to function, he would be thrown into a panic which is exactly comparable to the neurotic's anxiety. An inhibition about making decisions, for example, is not in itself conducive to anxiety, but it will tend to that result if it cannot be overcome in a crucial moment.

Finally, a neurotic trend may be endangered by the existence of a contradictory trend. Thus a drive toward independence may give rise to anxiety if it endangers a dependent relationship which is equally necessary for purposes of security, and, in the same way, a drive toward a masochistic dependency may provoke anxiety if the individual's safety rests primarily on a feeling of independence. As there are plenty of conflicting trends in every neurosis there is infinite opportunity for one trend to jeopardize another.

We have to consider, however, that the mere existence of contradictory trends does not account for the development of anxiety. There are many possibilities for dealing with contradictory trends. A trend may be repressed so radically as not to interfere with any other; it may be relegated to fantasy; compromise solutions may be found, such as passive resistance, which is a compromise solution between defiance and compliance; a trend may simply inhibit another trend, as a compulsory need for unobtrusiveness may inhibit a concurrent compulsory ambition. Such various solutions can create an equilibrium, shaky though it may be. It is only when the equilibrium is disturbed, and a safety device is thereby more or less acutely endangered, that anxiety arises.

It may help to clarify my concept of anxiety in neuroses if we compare it with that of Freud. According to Freud the source of danger is in the "id" and "super-ego," as I have mentioned, which already may be said to coincide roughly with what I call neurotic trends. According to my concept the source of danger is non-specific; it may consist of either internal or external factors; the internal factor provoking anxiety is not necessarily a drive or impulse, as Freud contends, but it may be an inhibition. A neurotic trend too may be a source of danger, but if so it is for the same reason as in the case of the other provocative factors: because it endangers a safety device of vital importance.

According to my concept, the neurotic trends are not as such the source of danger but are the thing endangered, inasmuch as safety rests on their unhampered operation. Anxiety emerges as soon as they fail to operate. Another slant on the difference is that what is endangered is not the "ego," as Freud contends, but the individual's security, inasmuch as his security rests on the functioning of his neurotic trends.

My difference from Freud concerning anxiety in neuroses boils down ultimately to the difference presented in the discussions of the libido theory and the "superego." What Freud regards as instinctual drives or their derivatives are, in my judgment, trends developed for the sake of safety. They are conditioned by an underlying "basic anxiety." [4] Thus, according to my interpretation of neuroses, we must distinguish two types of anxiety: the basic anxiety, which is the response to a *potential* danger, and the manifest anxiety, which is the response to a *manifest* danger. The term manifest does not in this context mean conscious. Every type of anxiety, whether potential or manifest, may be repressed for various reasons; [5] anxiety may manifest itself only in dreams, in concomitant physical symptoms, in a general restlessness, without being felt consciously.

The difference between the two types of anxiety can be illustrated by a picture. Let us assume that a person is traveling in an unknown country which he knows is full of dangers: hostile aborigines, dangerous animals, scarcity of food. As long as he has his gun and his food

[4] *Cf.* Chapter III, The Libido Theory.

[5] As a matter of fact, the different attitudes which persons assume toward their anxiety deserve close observation because they reveal significant characteristics.

supply he will be aware of potential dangers, but he will not have manifest anxiety because he feels that he has means of protecting himself. But if his munitions and food supply are damaged or stolen the danger becomes manifest. Then—provided life is an essential value for him—he will have manifest anxiety.

The basic anxiety is itself a neurotic manifestation. It results largely from a conflict between existing dependency on the parents and rebellion against them. Hostility toward them has to be repressed because of the dependency. As I have elaborated in an earlier publication,[6] repression of hostility helps to render a person defenseless because it makes him lose sight of the danger which he should fight. If he represses his hostility it means that he is no longer aware that some individual represents a menace to him; hence he is likely to be submissive, compliant, friendly in situations in which he should be on his guard. This defenselessness, in combination with the fear of retaliation, which remains in spite of its repression, is one of the powerful factors accounting for the neurotic's basic feeling of helplessness in a potentially hostile world.[7]

It remains to discuss the third question relevant to an understanding of anxiety: the individual's helplessness toward the danger. Freud holds that the cause of this helplessness is the weakness of the "ego," condi-

[6] Karen Horney, *The Neurotic Personality of Our Time* (1937), ch. 4.

[7] The difference between neurotic basic anxiety and the general human phenomenon of *Urangst* lies in the fact that *Urangst* is the expression of existing human helplessness in the face of existing dangers—illness, destitution, death, powers of nature, enemies—while in basic anxiety the helplessness is largely provoked by repressed hostility, and what is felt as the source of dangers is primarily the anticipated hostility of others.

tioned by its dependency on the "id" and the "super-ego." According to my view the helplessness is to some extent implicit in the basic anxiety. Another reason for it is that the neurotic's situation is a precarious one. His rigid adherence to his safety devices protects him in some ways, but renders him defenseless in others. He is like a rope dancer whose ability to keep balanced protects him from a fall caused by losing his equilibrium but leaves him helpless toward other possible dangers. Finally, helplessness is implicit in the compulsory nature of neurotic drives. The main internal factors precipitating anxiety in neuroses have also an imperative character because they are imbedded in the rigid neurotic structure. It is not in the neurotic's power to refrain from reacting with hostility to certain provocations, or even to diminish this reaction, no matter how much it endangers his safety. It is not in his power to dispense even temporarily with, for example, his inertia, no matter how acutely he thereby endangers his ambitious pursuits which are likewise imperative. The neurotic's frequent complaint of feeling caught is entirely warranted. By far the greatest part of manifest anxiety is the result of his being helplessly caught in a dilemma both sides of which are imperative.

The alteration in the concept of anxiety necessarily alters also the therapeutic approach. An analyst following Freud's concept will respond to the patient's anxiety with a search for repressed drives. When anxiety arises during the psychoanalytic treatment he would raise in his own mind such questions as whether the patient has

repressed any hostile impulses toward the analyst, or
whether he has sexual desires he is not aware of. Furthermore—in so far as the analyst's thoughts are directed
by theoretical presuppositions—he would expect to find
a huge quantity of these affects and, finding himself embarrassed in accounting for these quantities in the actual situation, would ultimately resort to the notion that
the amount of desire or hostility represents an unbroken
infantile affect which was once repressed but is now revived and transferred to him.

According to my interpretation of anxiety an analyst
confronted with the problem of the patient's anxiety
should explain to the patient, at the appropriate time,
that anxiety is frequently the result of being in some
acute dilemma without being aware of it, thereby en-
couraging him to search for the nature of the dilemma.
To return to our first example of a patient who shows
an emerging hostility toward the analyst, the latter, after
understanding the reasons for the hostile reaction,
should tell the patient that the unearthing of this hostility, though it relieves the patient, does not solve completely the problem of his anxiety; that one may feel
hostile without having anxiety; that if anxiety has en-
sued he probably felt that something important was endangered by the hostility. The pursuit of this question—
if successful—would reveal the neurotic trend which was
endangered by the hostility.

This approach, according to my experience, makes it
possible not only to deal in a shorter time with the
patient's anxiety but also to learn important data as to
the patient's character structure. Freud has rightly said

that dream analysis is the *via regia* to understanding the patient's unconscious processes, and the same may be said of the analysis of manifest anxiety. A correct analysis of an anxiety situation is one of the main roads to an understanding of the patient's conflicts.

CHAPTER XIII

THE CONCEPT OF THE "SUPER-EGO"

THE main observations underlying Freud's concept of the "super-ego" are as follows: certain neurotic types seem to adhere to particularly rigid and high moral standards; the motivating force in their lives is not a wish for happiness but a passionate drive toward rectitude and perfection; they are ruled by a series of "shoulds" and "musts"—they must do a perfect job, be competent in divergent fields, have perfect judgment, be a model husband, a model daughter, a model hostess, and the like.

Their compulsory moral goals are relentless. No allowance is made for circumstances over which they have no control, whether these be internal or external. They feel they should be able to control every anxiety, no matter how deep it is, should never be hurt, should never make any mistake. If they do not measure up to their moral demands, anxiety or guilt feelings may ensue. Patients who are in the clutches of these demands scold themselves not only for failures to measure up to them in the present but also for failures in the past.

Though they have grown up under unfavorable conditions they feel they should not have been influenced by
these conditions; they should have been strong enough
to endure any maltreatment without such emotional reactions as fears, compliance, resentment. This unreasonable amount of taking responsibility is easily attributed
wrongly to guilt feelings dating back to childhood.

The categorical character of the demands is evident
also in the fact that they tend to be applied indiscriminately; the individual may feel obliged to like everyone, regardless of objectionable qualities, and will find
fault with himself if he is not capable of doing so. A
patient, for instance, talked about a woman who, from
the incidents related, was hard, egocentric, inconsiderate, begrudging; then the patient proceeded to "analyze" herself as to the reasons for her dislike. I inter-
rupted, asking her why she felt compelled to like the
woman, as it seemed to me that there were ample reasons for disliking this particular person; to this my patient responded with great relief, realizing at that moment that liking everyone, regardless of the value of the
person's qualities, had been an unwritten law of hers.

Another aspect of the imperative nature of these
standards is what Freud calls their "ego-alien" character.
What he means by this term is that the individual seems
to have no say in the matter of the self-imposed rules:
whether he likes them, whether he believes in their
value, enters as little into the picture as his capacity to
apply them with discrimination. They exist unquestioned, inexorable, and have to be obeyed. Any deviation from them has to be carefully justified in the in-

dividual's conscious mind, or it is followed by guilt feelings, inferiority feelings or anxiety.

An individual may be aware that compulsory moral goals exist, may say, for instance, that he is a "perfectionist." Or he may not say so—because his very insistence on perfection will not allow him to admit any irrational drives for perfection—but may talk incessantly about how he should be able never to feel hurt, how he should be able to control every emotion or cope with every situation. Or he may be naïvely convinced that by temperament he is "good," conscientious, rational. Finally, he may be entirely unaware of having any such goals, not to speak of their compulsory character. In short, the degree to which a person is aware of these standards varies.

On the whole, here as elsewhere, the question whether or not a drive is conscious is too general to lead to as revealing results as might be expected. A person may be aware of being ambitious but be unaware of the hold the ambition has on him or of its destructive character. He may be aware of having anxiety now and then, but may not know to what extent his whole pattern of life is determined by anxiety. Similarly, the simple statement that a person is or is not aware of the need for moral perfection does not signify much. It is not too difficult to elicit awareness of its existence. What matters is for analyst and patient to recognize the extent and the nature of the influence which these needs have on the individual's relationships to others and to himself, and to recognize also those factors which render it necessary for the individual to maintain his rigid standards. Proceeding along these two lines means hard work because it is in these problems that the struggle with all sorts of unconscious factors begins.

The question may be asked how it is possible, if a patient is rarely aware of the existence of his standards and never aware of their strength and influence, for the analyst to conclude that these demands are present and effective. There are three main types of data.

First, there is the observation that a person may invariably have a rigid kind of behavior even though it may not be called for either by the situation or by his interests. For instance, he may invariably and indiscriminately do things for others, lend them money, get jobs for them, do their errands, while just as invariably he is incapable of doing things for himself.

Second is the observation that certain kinds of anxiety, inferiority feelings or self-accusations emerge as reactions to actual or possible deviations from existing compulsory standards. For instance, a medical student starting to do laboratory work feels stupid because he cannot at once make blood counts quickly and accurately; a person who is invariably generous to others has a fit of anxiety when he wants to make a trip or take a comfortable apartment, though both of these would be well within his means; a person reacts to a reproach for an error in judgment with abysmally deep feelings of unworthiness, though it concerns a matter about which different opinions may be held.

Finally there is the observation that a person often feels that others are condemning him or expecting unreasonable achievements from him, while in reality they are neither reproachful nor exacting. In such cases it may be concluded that the individual has stringent reasons for assuming that these attitudes exist; his assumption may indicate, for instance, a projection of his own exacting and condemning attitude toward himself.

I consider these data to be correct. To have seen this phenomenon and its importance for the understanding and therapy of neuroses is one of many witnesses to Freud's power of observation. The question is how to explain it.

On the basis of his theory of instincts Freud could not but assume that such a powerful force as the neurotic need for perfection is instinctual in nature. He regards it as a combination of instincts or their derivatives. According to Freud, it is a composite of narcissistic, masochistic and particularly destruction drives; it is also a residue of the Oedipus complex, in so far as it represents incorporated parent images whose forbiddings have to be obeyed. I shall not discuss these possibilities here because in previous chapters I have stated the reasons why I hold the theoretical issues involved to be debatable. Only this much: Freud's concept of the "super-ego" is consistent with the libido theory and the theory of the death instinct; if we accept these theories we have also to accept his views on the "super-ego."

Reviewing Freud's writings on the subject we find it to be his main contention that the "super-ego" is an inner agency of a primarily forbidding character. It is like a secret police department, unerringly detecting any trends of forbidden impulses, particularly of an aggressive kind, and punishing the individual inexorably if any are present. As the "super-ego" seems to arouse anxiety and guilt feelings, Freud concludes that it must be endowed with a power to destroy. The neurotic need for perfection is thus seen as a consequence of the "super-ego's" tyrannical power. The individual has to attain perfection willy-nilly, in order to comply with the "super-ego" and to avoid punishment. To elucidate this point: Freud explicitly rejects the usual view concerning the relation between self-imposed restrictions and ideals; usually, the restrictions are regarded as a consequence of existing moral goals, but Freud regards the moral goals as a consequence of sadistic infringements. "The ordinary view sees the situation the other way round: the standard set up by the ego-ideal seems to be the motive for the suppression of aggressiveness." [1] The sadism which the individual thus directs against himself derives its energy from the sadism which would otherwise be discharged toward others. Instead of hating, tormenting, accusing others, he hates, torments, accuses himself.

Freud offers two kinds of observations as evidence for these contentions. One is that types obsessed by the need for perfection render themselves miserable; briefly, they suffocate under the restricting demands. The other is, in Freud's terms, the fact that "the more a man checks his aggressive tendencies toward others the more tyrannical, that is, aggressive he becomes in his ego-ideal." [2]

The first observation is undoubtedly true, but it permits of other interpretations. The second is debatable. It is true that persons of this type may appear to be generous toward others while they do not grant themselves any enjoyment, that they may anxiously refrain from criticizing or hurting others while they castigate

[1] Sigmund Freud, *The Ego and the Id* (1935).
[2] Sigmund Freud, *ibid.*

themselves with self-recriminations. But this observation, apart from the fact that it too can be interpreted differently, does not warrant generalization. There are many contradictory data: neurotics who even on the surface are just as exacting toward others as toward themselves, just as contemptuous of others as they are of themselves, just as ready to condemn others as they are to condemn themselves. What about all the cruelties, for example, which are committed in the name of moral or religious demands?

If the neurotic need for perfection is not the result of a postulated forbidding agency, then what is its meaning? Freud's interpretations, although debatable, nevertheless entail a constructive lead; this is their implication that the strivings for perfection lack genuineness. If I may use a slang expression, there is something fishy about the moral pursuits. Alexander has elaborated this aspect in pointing out that the neurotic's pursuit of moral goals is too formalistic and that it has a pharisaic, hypocritical character.[3]

Those who seem to be driven by a relentless need for perfection only go through the motions of exercising the virtues they pretend to have.[4] When anyone who

[3] Franz Alexander, *Psychoanalysis of the Total Personality* (1935).

[4] The most famous expression of the difference between a formalistic fulfillment of the law and a wholehearted one is in the first letter of Paul to the Corinthians: "Though I speak with the tongues of men and of angels, and have not charity, I am become as sounding brass, or a tinkling cymbal. And though I have the gift of prophecy, and understand all mysteries, and all knowledge; and though I have all faith, so that I could remove mountains, and have not charity, I am nothing. And though I bestow all my goods to feed the poor, and though I give my body to be burned, and have not charity, it profiteth me nothing" (I Corinthians XIII 1-3).

seriously wants to achieve something notices within himself obstacles to his goal he is willing to go to the root of the evil so that he may eventually overcome it; for instance, if he finds himself irritable at times, without any good reason, he will first try to control his irritability, and if that is ineffectual he will make constructive efforts to find out what trends within his personality are responsible for it and will try to change them if possible. Not so the neurotic type we are speaking of. He will start by minimizing his irritability or by putting it on a justified basis. These ways failing, he will scold himself mercilessly for his attitude. He will try hard to control it. Not succeeding in controlling it, he will scold himself for his insufficient self-control. But there his efforts stop. It will never occur to him that something can be wrong with him which engenders irritability. Hence nothing ever changes, and this play repeats itself endlessly.

When he is analyzed he will realize the futility of his efforts, though reluctantly. He may politely and intellectually follow the analyst's suggestions that the irritations are only bubbles coming to the surface. But as soon as the analyst puts his finger on one of the deeper disturbances he will react with a mixture of concealed irritation and diffuse anxiety, and soon will argue most cleverly that the analyst is wrong, that at least he is exaggerating grossly; and he may end by again condemning his failure to control his irritations. This reaction may repeat itself for each deeper problem that is touched upon, and no matter how gingerly it is done.

Thus not only do these types lack the incentive to probe, to go to the roots of a disturbance, to really change, but they are positively opposed to it. They have no wish to be analyzed, but loathe it. If it were not for certain gross symptoms such as phobias, hypochondriac fears and the like, they would never come to analysis, no matter how great their character difficulties actually are. When they do come for treatment they want to have their symptoms removed without their personality being touched.

The conclusion I draw from these observations is that the type in question is driven not by a need for an "ever-increasing perfection," as Freud assumes, but by a need to maintain the *appearance* of perfection. Appearance in whose eyes? The first impression is that this type must primarily appear right to himself. He may castigate himself indeed for shortcomings, regardless of whether or not they are noticed by others. He is ostensibly comparatively independent of people. It is this impression that gave rise to Freud's belief that the "super-ego," though originally arising from infantile love, hatred and fear, eventually became an autonomous intrapsychic representation of moral prohibitions.

It is true that these types show a marked trend toward independence as appears clearly when they are compared with types having prevailingly masochistic trends. But it is an independence born of defiance rather than of inner strength, and for this very reason it is largely spurious. Actually they are extremely dependent on others—in their own specific way. Their feelings, thoughts and actions are determined by what they feel is expected of them, whether they react to such expectations with compliance or defiance. Also they are dependent on others' opinion about them. Here again the dependency is specific; it is imperative for them that their infallibility be recognized. Any dissension makes them feel uneasy because it implies for them that their righteousness is not beyond doubt. The façade of rightness which they are anxious to present is hence a pretense for the benefit of others as well as themselves. When in the following I speak of the need to appear perfect, it is a simplified expression for the need to appear perfect in one's own eyes as well as in those of others.

This characteristic of pretense appears also, and often more blatantly, in those compulsory needs for perfection which concern not moral issues but merely egocentric goals, such as having to know everything, a phenomenon which is frequent among intellectuals of our time and can be observed easily. When such a type is confronted with a question he cannot answer, he will pretend to know it at any price, even though an admission of ignorance would in no way reflect on his intellectual prestige. Or he will juggle merely formalistically with scientific terms, methods and theories.

The whole concept of the "super-ego" is fundamentally changed if we regard the individual's efforts as directed toward a "pretense" of perfection and infallibility, which for some reason it is necessary to maintain. The "super-ego" is then no longer a special agency within the "ego" but it is a special need of the individual. It is not the advocate of moral perfection, but expresses the neurotic's need to keep up appearances of perfection.

To some extent everyone living in an organized community must keep up appearances. To some extent every one of us has imbibed the standards of the environment. To some extent we are all dependent on the regard others have for us.[5] What happens, however, in the type we are considering is—allowing a little exaggeration—that a human being turns altogether into a façade. It simply does not matter what he himself wants, likes, dislikes, values. The only thing which matters is to measure up to expectations and standards and to fulfill duties.

The compulsion to appear perfect may pertain to whatever is valued in a given culture: orderliness, cleanliness, punctuality, conscientiousness, efficiency, intellectual or artistic achievements, rationality, generosity, tolerance, unselfishness. The kind of perfection which a particular individual will emphasize depends on various factors, such as: his inherent capacities; the persons or qualities which have impressed him favorably in childhood; the environmental inadequacies which he suffered as a child and which made him determined to do better; his actual possibilities to excel; the kind of anxieties against which he has to protect himself by being perfect.

How are we to understand such a stringent need to appear perfect?

As to its genesis, Freud has given us a general lead in pointing out that the tendency starts in childhood and that it has something to do with the prohibitions of

[5] Among others, W. James and C. G. Jung have emphasized this fact when pointing out that everyone has a "social self" (James) or a "persona" (Jung).

the parents and with the suppressed resentment against them.[6] It seems to be a simplification, however, to regard the prohibitions of the "super-ego" as almost direct remnants of the tabus imposed by the parents. As in any other neurotic tendency, what accounts for its development is not one or another individual feature in childhood, but the sum total of the entire situation. The attitude of perfectionism grows from essentially the same basis as do the narcissistic trends. Since that basis has been discussed in reference to narcissism it suffices here merely to recapitulate. As the result of many adverse influences the child finds himself in a distressing situation. His own individual self is stunted through his being forced to conform with his parents' expectations. He loses thereby the capacity for initiative of his own, wishes of his own, goals of his own, judgments of his own. On the other hand, he is alienated from people and is afraid of them. As mentioned before, there are several ways out of this fundamental calamity: narcissistic, masochistic or perfectionistic trends may develop.

The childhood history of a patient with pronounced perfectionistic trends often shows that he had self-righteous parents who exercised unquestioned authoritative sway over the children, an authority that may have referred primarily to standards or primarily to a personal autocratic regime. Often too the child suffered much unfair treatment, such as the parents' preference for other siblings or reproaches for things for which not he but the parents or another sibling were to blame. Although such unfair treatment may not have exceeded the average, it nevertheless created more than average

[6] Melanie Klein was the first to see this latter connection.

resentment and indignation, because of the disparity between the actual treatment and the parents' pretenses of infallibility. Accusations arising on these grounds could not be expressed because the child was too uncertain of his acceptability.

As a result of these conditions the child ceases to have a center of gravity in himself but shifts it entirely to the authorities. This process goes on gradually and unconsciously. It is as if the child decided that father or mother is always right. The measurements for what is good or bad, desirable or undesirable, enjoyable or unenjoyable, likable or not, are taken outside the individual himself, and remain outside. He has no longer a judgment of his own.

By adopting this course he saves himself from knowing that he has ducked under, has made external standards his own, and thus he secures the semblance of independence. Its meaning may be paraphrased as: I do all that I am supposed to do and therefore I buy myself off from any obligation and acquire the right to be left alone. By adhering to external standards the individual also acquires a certain firmness which hides his existing weakness, a firmness analogous to that which a corset provides for an individual whose backbone is injured. His standards tell him what he should want, what is right or wrong, and therefore he gives the deceptive impression of having a strong character. Both of these gains distinguish him from the masochistic person, who is openly dependent on others and whose too great softness is not concealed by a rigid armor of rules.

Furthermore, by his overconformity to standards or

to expectations he puts himself beyond reproach and attack and thereby eliminates conflicts with the environ-ment; his compulsory inner standards regulate his hu-man relationships.[7]

Finally, by his adherence to standards he gains a feel-ing of superiority. This satisfaction is similar to that gained by self-inflation, but with this difference: a nar-cissistic person may enjoy being so wonderful and enjoy the admiration he receives for it; in the righteous per-son vindictiveness toward others prevails. Even the guilt feelings which arise so easily are felt as a virtue because they prove to the individual his high sensitivity toward moral requirements. Thus if the analyst points out to a patient how exaggerated his self-recriminations are, the patient—consciously or unconsciously—will make the mental reservation that he is so much finer than the analyst that the latter, with his "lower" measurements, cannot possibly understand him. This attitude entails a mostly unconscious sadistic satisfaction: to prick and crush others by one's very superiority. The sadistic im-pulses may be expressed merely in derogatory thoughts concerning the mistakes and shortcomings of others. But the impulse is to tell others how stupid, worthless and contemptible they are and to make them feel like dust; the impulse is to strike them with righteous indignation from the height of one's own infallibility.[8] By being "holier than thou" the individual acquires the right to look down on others and thereby to inflict the same in-

[7] Cf. Ernest Jones, "Love and Morality: A Study in Character Types" in International Journal of Psychoanalysis (January 1937).

[8] Compare the character of the canon in Paul Vincent Carroll's play, Shadow and Substance.

jury upon others as his parents inflicted upon him. Nietzsche, in *The Dawn of Day*, has described this kind of moral superiority under the heading, "Refined Cruelty as Virtue":

"Here we have a morality which is based entirely upon our thirst for distinction—do not therefore entertain too high an opinion of it! Indeed, we may well ask what kind of an impulse it is, and what is its fundamental significance? It is sought, by our appearance, to grieve our neighbor, to arouse his envy, and to awaken his feelings of impotence and degradation; we endeavor to make him taste the bitterness of his fate by dropping a little of *our* honey on his tongue, and, while conferring this supposed benefit on him, looking sharply and triumphantly into his eyes.

"Behold such a man, now become humble, and perfect in his humility and seek those for whom, through his humility, he has for a long time been preparing a torture; for you are sure to find them! Here is another man who shows mercy toward animals, and is admired for doing so—but there are certain people on whom he wishes to vent his cruelty by this very means. Look at that great artist: the pleasure he enjoyed beforehand in conceiving the envy of the rivals he had outstripped, refused to let his powers lie dormant until he became a great man—how many bitter moments in the souls of other men has he asked for as payment for his own greatness! The nun's chastity: with what threatening eyes she looks into the faces of other women who live differently from her! what a vindictive joy shines in those eyes! The theme is short, and its variations, though they might well be innumerable, could not easily become tiresome—for it is still too paradoxical a novelty, and almost a painful one, to affirm that the morality of distinction is nothing, at bottom, but joy in refined cruelty."

The impulse of this type to triumph vindictively over others arises from many sources. Such a person has but scant possibilities of deriving satisfaction from either human relationships or from work. Both love and work turn into imposed duties against which he rebels inwardly. Spontaneous positive feelings for others are choked, reasons for resentment are plenty. But the specific source from which sadistic impulses are incessantly generated is his feeling that his life is not his own, that he always must live up to outside expectations. Not knowing that he himself has relegated his will and his standards to others, he suffocates under the yoke of obligations. Hence his desire to triumph over others in the only way he can do it, which is through excelling in righteousness and in virtues.

Thus the reverse side of such an individual's smooth façade is an inner rebellion against everything that is expected of him. The simple fact that an activity or feeling belongs to the category of what he is supposed to do or feel is sufficient to arouse his defiance. In extreme cases there are but few activities which escape this category, such as reading mystery stories or eating candies; then these may be the only things done without inner resistance. In every other matter such a person may unwittingly obstruct what is expected of him or what he feels is expected of him. The result is often listlessness and inertia. Individual activities, as well as life as a whole, become drab and unappealing for a person who, though not aware of it, is not a free agent, who does not move by his own motive force, whose actions and feelings are prescribed.

Because of its practical importance, a special consequence of this unwitting obstruction of expectations shall be pointed out separately: the inhibitions in work. Even though a piece of work may be originated by the person's own initiative it will soon fall under the category of an obligation that must be fulfilled and hence will precipitate a passive resistance against doing it. Thus frequently the individual finds himself in a conflict between a hectic drive toward accomplishing something perfect and an unwillingness to work at all. The results of this conflict vary according to the strength of the factors involved on both sides. It may lead to a more or less complete inertia. Periods of hectic work and inertia may alternate in one and the same person. It may render work inordinately strenuous. The strain is all the greater the more a work surpasses menial routine tasks, because every undertaking must be unassailably right and the possibility of committing an error arouses anxiety. Hence excuses are sought and found to give up work entirely or to relegate responsibility for work to others.

This double tendency of compliance and defiance also accounts for one of the difficulties in therapy. The fact that the analyst expects the individual to express his thoughts and feelings, to gain insights about himself, eventually to change something within himself, arouses his utmost defiance against the procedure. As a consequence this type of patient is outwardly docile but inwardly set on obstructing every effort of the analyst.

This basic structure may give rise to two different kinds of anxiety. One of them has been described by Freud. It is the anxiety which he designates as fear of the punitive power of the "super-ego." In simple terms it is the anxiety that may arise because of making any mistake, of recognizing any shortcoming or of anticipating any failure.

In the light of my interpretation this anxiety arises from the existing disparity between façade and back-ground. It is mainly a fear of being unmasked. This fear, though it may be attached to something special, such as masturbation, is the neurotic's all-pervading, diffuse fear that one day he will be unmasked as a swindler, that one day the others will detect that he is not really generous or altruistic but is really egocentric and egoistic, or that he is really interested not in his work but only in his own glory. In an intelligent person this fear may provoke an apprehensiveness regarding any discussion because some point might be made, some question raised, which he might not be able to refute or to answer instantly—and thus his bluff of "knowing it all" would be called. Here are friends who are fond of him; but better not become intimate with them, because they might become disappointed in him. His employer thinks well of him and offers him a more responsible position; but better not accept it, because it might be found out that he is not so very efficient after all.

The fear of being found out in all his pretenses, though these are made in good faith, makes a person of this type distrustful and apprehensive toward analysis, for it explicitly wants "to find out." His fear may flare up in acute anxiety; it may be conscious; it may show in a general shyness; it may go with an apparent frankness. The fear of being unmasked is the source of much intangible misery. It contributes, for instance, to the painful feeling of not being wanted, which in this context is the feeling "no one would like me as I am." It is one of the main sources of exclusiveness and loneliness.

The fear of being unmasked is all the greater because of the sadistic impulses involved in the need to appear perfect. If one has lifted oneself on a high pedestal from which to jeer at others' shortcomings, then to make a mistake provokes the danger of being exposed to ridicule, contempt and humiliation.

The other kind of anxiety involved in this structure arises when the person becomes aware of having or pursuing wishes of his own, wishes which he cannot justify as necessary for health, education, altruism and the like. A woman, for example, who was invariably overmodest in what she demanded for herself had an attack of anxiety when going to a first-class hotel, though the expenditures involved in no way exceeded her means, and though friends and relatives would have regarded it as silly if she had not gone there. The same patient would feel distinct anxiety when in analysis the question of her own claims on life was touched.

There are several ways of understanding this kind of anxiety. One may regard the modesty as a reaction-formation to greediness, and regard the anxiety arising at the emergence of any legitimate wish as a fear of losing control over the greediness. Interpretations of this kind, however, do not prove to be satisfactory. To be sure, these patients do have spells of greediness, but in my opinion they are secondary reactions to a general suppression of all personal wishes.

Or one may hold that the appearance of "unselfishness" is as imperative for the patient as the appearance of tolerance, rationality and the like. Then the anxiety arising on discovering "selfish" wishes would be explainable as fear of the pretenses being unmasked. This explanation, though right, is according to my experience insufficient, that is, it does not enable the patient to feel free to have wishes of his own.

It was only after seeing the structure of this type in the way I have presented it that I realized a possibility of reaching a deeper understanding of this kind of anxiety. In analysis such a person often believes that the analyst expects a certain behavior of him and will censor him if he does not comply. This tendency is usually described as a projection of the "super-ego" to the analyst. Therefore the patient is told that it is his own demands on himself which he projects to the analyst. According to my experience this interpretation is incomplete. The patient does not only project his own demands; also he has a definite interest in regarding the analyst as the captain steering his boat. Without rules he would feel lost, like a ship drifting without directive. Thus it is not only that he fears being found out but also that his security is so rooted in his subjection to rules and to what is expected of him that he would not know how to act without them.

Once when I was persuading a patient that it was not I who expected her to sacrifice everything for the analysis but that for some reason she herself had built up that assumption, she became angry at me and told me that I had better distribute leaflets to the patients telling them how to behave in analysis. We discussed her having lost her own initiative (as was suggested by a dream) and her own wishes, so that she could not be herself. Though the notion of being herself appealed to her as something she desired more than anything else in life, she had an anxiety dream the following night that a flood came up and endangered her records. There was no fear for herself but only for the records. The records for her symbolized perfection. To have them up-to-date and flawless was a matter of life and death. The meaning of the dream was: if I am myself, if I give vent to my feelings (the flood), then my façade of perfection is endangered.

We tend to think naïvely—as did the patient—that it is wholly desirable to be oneself. To be sure it is precious. But if the safety of a person's entire life has been built upon not being himself, then it is appalling to discover that there is a human being behind the façade. One cannot be at once a marionette and a spontaneous human being. Only after overcoming the anxiety that arises from this discrepancy can one find the security which lies in retrieving the center of gravity in oneself.

The viewpoints presented here shed a different light on the dynamics of repression, both on the force which represses and on the factors which are repressed. Freud assumes that, apart from the direct fear of people, fear of the "super-ego" is the force which brings about repression. I believe that this slant on the repressing factors is too narrow. Any drive, need, feeling can be repressed if it endangers another drive, need, feeling, which for the individual is of vital importance. A destructive ambition can be repressed because of the necessity to keep up an altruistic façade. But a destructive ambition also may be repressed because, for reasons of safety, the individual must hang on to others in a masochistic way. The "super-ego," however it be understood, is thus relevant in provoking repression but according to my views it is but one important factor among others.[9]

As to the power of the "super-ego" which enables it to engender repressions, Freud ascribes it mainly to the self-destruction instinct. In my opinion the phenomenon is as powerful as it is mainly for the reason that it constitutes a mighty bulwark against underlying anxiety. Therefore, like other neurotic trends, it has to be maintained at any price.

Freud believes that it is instinctual drives which, because of their anti-social character, succumb to repression by the "super-ego." If for the sake of clarity I may express it in naïve moral terms, it is in Freud's opinion the bad, the evil in man that is repressed. This doctrine undoubtedly contains one of Freud's striking discoveries. But I should like to suggest a more flexible formulation: what is repressed depends on the kind of façade an individual feels forced to present; everything is repressed which does not fit into the façade. A person, for instance, may feel free to indulge in obscene thoughts and actions or to have death wishes against many people, but may repress any wish for personal gain. The difference I suggest in formulation has no great practical importance, however. The façade will roughly coincide with what is regarded as "good," and hence what is repressed on its behalf will mostly coincide with what is regarded as "bad" or "inferior."

[9] Cf. Franz Alexander's significant paper on "The Relation of Structural and Instinctual Conflicts" in Psychoanalytic Quarterly (1933).

There is, however, another more significant difference concerning the factors which are repressed. Briefly, the necessity to maintain a certain façade leads not only to repressing "bad," anti-social, egocentric, "instinctual" drives, but also to repressing the most valuable, the most alive factors in a human being, such as spontaneous wishes, spontaneous feelings, individual judgment and the like. Freud has seen this fact but not its significance. He has seen, for example, that people may repress not only greediness but also their legitimate wishes. But he has explained this by pointing out that it is not in our power to delineate the extent of a repression: while what was meant to be repressed was only greediness, legitimate wishes are carried away with it. To be sure, this may happen; but there also exists a repression of valuable qualities as such. They must be repressed because they would endanger the façade.

Thus, in summary, the neurotic's need to appear perfect leads to repressing, first, everything that does not fit into his particular façade and, second, everything that would render it impossible for him to maintain that façade.

In view of the painful consequences engendered by the need to appear perfect it is understandable why Freud contended that the "super-ego" is an essentially anti-self agency. But according to my point of view what seems to be aggression against the self is an unavoidable result, as long as an individual feels it imperative to be infallible.

Freud regards the "super-ego" as the inner representative of moral demands and particularly of moral prohibitions. Because of this opinion he feels entitled to draw the generalization that the "super-ego" is in essence identical with the normal phenomenon of conscience and ideals, only more exacting than these. According to Freud, both are essentially a discharge of cruelty against the self.[10]

With the different interpretation that I have elaborated there still remains some similarity between normal morals and the neurotic need to appear perfect. It is true that the moral standards of many persons mean nothing more than keeping up the appearance of morality. But it would be a dogmatic statement not consistent with facts to assert that moral norms in general are nothing but that. Leaving apart the philosophical intricacies involved in the definition of ideals, one may say that they represent the standard of feelings or behavior which the individual himself recognizes as valuable and obligatory to him. They are not ego-alien but are an integral part of the self. To them the "super-ego" has but a superficial resemblance. It would not be quite correct to say that the content of the need to appear perfect coincides only incidentally with the culturally approved moral values: the perfectionistic aims would not fulfill their various functions if they did not coincide with the approved standards. But they only ape the gestures of moral norms. They are, as it were, a counterfeiting of moral values.

The pseudo-moral aims, far from being identical with moral norms and ideals, prevent the latter from developing. The type we have been discussing has adopted

[10] "But even the ordinary normal morality has a harshly restraining, cruelly prohibiting quality" (Sigmund Freud, *The Ego and the Id*).

his standards under the stress of fear for the sake of peace. He complies with them formalistically but with inner opposition. For example, he is superficially friendly to people but feels this attitude—unconsciously —as a burdensome imposition. Only after his friendliness has lost its compulsory character can he start to consider whether perhaps he himself would like to be friendly to others.

There are indeed moral problems involved in the neurotic need for perfection, but they are not the ones with which the patient is apparently struggling nor those which he pretends to have. The real moral issues lie in the insincerity, the haughtiness and the refined cruelty which are inseparable from the structure that has been described. The patient is not responsible for these traits; he could not help their developing. But in analysis he has to face them, not because it is the analyst's business to improve his morals, but because he suffers from them: they interfere with a good relationship with others and with himself and they prevent his best possible development. Though this part of the analysis is particularly painful and upsetting to the patient, it is also the one which may give the most intense relief. William James has said that to give up pretensions is as blessed a relief as to have them gratified; judging from observations in analysis the relief resulting from giving them up seems to be the greater of the two.

CHAPTER XIV

NEUROTIC GUILT FEELINGS

ORIGINALLY no outstanding role was ascribed to guilt feelings in neuroses. In so far as they were considered, they were related to libidinal impulses or to fantasies of pre-genital or incestuous character. But rarely was the claim raised, as by Marcinowski, that all neuroses are guilt neuroses. It is only since the formulation of the "super-ego" concept that attention has been focused on guilt feelings and that they have eventually come to be regarded as a crucial element in the dynamics of neuroses. As a matter of fact, the emphasis on guilt feelings, especially the theory of unconscious guilt feelings and the concept of masochism, are but other aspects of the "super-ego" concept. If I deal with them separately it is because otherwise certain problems which I deem important would not receive due consideration.

In some cases guilt feelings may be expressed as such, and may overshadow the whole picture. Then they may either appear in general feelings of unworthiness or be attached to special actions, impulses, thoughts, fantasies concerning incest, masturbation, death wishes concerning beloved persons and the like. Clinically, however, what led to the belief that guilt feelings play a universal and central role in neuroses was not so much these comparatively infrequent direct expressions as the much more frequent indirect expressions. Of the many manifestations which are suggestive of underlying guilt feelings I shall mention a few that are particularly significant.

In the first place, certain neurotic types indulge in subtle and gross self-recriminations which concern anything and everything: hurting other people's feelings, being mean, dishonest, stingy, wanting to destroy everyone, being lazy, weak, unpunctual. The recriminations are usually connected with an inclination to take the blame for any adverse happenings, ranging from the murder of a mandarin in China to having caught a cold. When a person of such a type falls ill he blames himself for not having taken care of his health, for not having dressed properly, for not having gone to the physician in time, or for having exposed himself to the infection. If a friend has not called for some time his first reaction is to ponder over the possibility that he has hurt the friend's feelings. If there is a misunderstanding about appointments he feels that this was certainly his own fault, that he had not listened carefully.

Sometimes these self-recriminations appear in an endless pondering over what he should have said, done, or omitted doing, going so far as to exclude any other activities or to cause insomnia. It would be futile even to begin describing the content of such pondering: he may think for hours about what he has said, what the other person has said, what he might have said, what effect his words had; about whether he closed the gas jet and whether someone might have come to harm by its being left open; about whether someone might have fallen because of an orange peel lying on the sidewalk which he failed to pick up.

In my estimation the frequency of self-recriminations is still greater than is usually assumed, because they may hide behind what looks like merely the individual's wish to recognize his motivations. In these cases the neurotic will not be openly self-condemnatory in any way, but will seemingly only "analyze" himself. He may wonder, for instance, whether he had not started a certain affair in order to prove his attractiveness; whether with some remark he did not want to hurt the other person; or whether it is not plain laziness that keeps him from doing any work. It may be difficult at times to distinguish whether all this is an honest questioning of motivations, born of a wish for eventual improvement, or whether it is merely a form of self-recrimination subtly adapted to the psychoanalytic method.

Another group of manifestations which are likewise suggestive of existing guilt feelings takes the form of a hypersensitivity to any disapproval by others or of a fear of being found out. Neurotics having this fear may be constantly afraid that people will become disappointed on better acquaintance with them. In the psychoanalytic situation they may retain important information. They feel toward the psychoanalytic process as a criminal feels toward a trial at court; consequently they are always on the defensive without knowing, however, exactly what kind of detection they dread. In order to banish or to invalidate any possible reproach they may be extremely careful not to make any mistakes and to conform to the letter of the law.

Finally, there are neurotics who seem to invite adverse happenings. Their behavior may be so provocative that they are constantly mistreated. They may seem to incur accidents easily, may often fall ill, lose money—and they may feel actually more at ease when they do than when they do not. These manifestations too are assumed to indicate deep guilt feelings, or rather a need to atone for them by suffering.

It seemed reasonable to conclude from all these tendencies the existence of guilt feelings. Self-recriminations seem to be a rather direct expression of guilt feelings; certainly hypersensitivity to any criticism or any questioning of motivations is often the result of an offense which it is feared will be detected (a maid who has stolen something will interpret any harmless question with regard to the whereabouts of an object as a doubt of her honesty); to take a cross upon oneself for one's sins is a usage of venerable standing. Therefore it seemed reasonable to assume an abundance of guilt feelings in neurotics surpassing those in the average person.

This assumption, however, constituted a problem: why should neurotics feel so guilty? They did not seem to be worse than other people. The answer Freud gave to this question is implicit in the "super-ego" concept. Neurotics are not worse than others but because of their severe hypermoral "super-ego" they feel guilty more easily than others do. Thus according to Freud's formulation guilt feelings are the expression of the tension existing between the "super-ego" and the "ego."

But here another difficulty arose. While some patients readily accepted suggestions concerning their guilt feelings, others refused to do so.[1] The way out of this dilemma was the theory of unconscious guilt feelings: without knowing it the patient may suffer from deep unconscious guilt feelings; he has to atone for them with unhappiness and neurotic illness. His fear of the "super-ego" is so great that he prefers staying ill to recognizing that he feels guilty and why he feels so.

It is true that a feeling of guilt can be repressed. But it is not enough to accept the existence of unconscious guilt feelings as a final explanation of the manifestations which those feelings are believed to produce. The theory of unconscious guilt feelings is not concerned with the content of such feelings, with their why and when and how. It merely decrees, on circumstantial evidence as it were, that here must be guilt feelings of which the individual is unaware. This leaves the analysis without value for therapy and leaves the theory unsubstantiated.

It would clarify the issue—here as in other problems —to agree on the meaning of the term and not use it for other purposes. In psychoanalytical literature the term guilt feeling is used sometimes to indicate the response to an unconscious guilt; sometimes it is used

[1] "But as far as the patient is concerned this sense of guilt is dumb; it does not tell him he is guilty; he does not feel guilty, he simply feels ill. This sense of guilt expresses itself only as a resistance to recovery which it is extremely difficult to overcome. It is also particularly difficult to convince the patient that this motive lies behind his continuing to be ill; he holds fast to the more obvious explanation that treatment by analysis is not the right remedy for his case" (Sigmund Freud, *The Ego and the Id*).

synonymously with the need for punishment.[2] In common language, the term is used nowadays frequently
and loosely, so that we often wonder whether a person
really feels guilty when he says he does.

What is meant by "really feeling guilty"? I should
say that in any situation guilt is constituted by the violation of moral demands or prohibitions valid in the
given culture, and that a feeling of guilt is the expression of a painful belief that such a violation has been
made. But one person feels guilty for not helping a
friend in an emergency or for having extramarital relations, and another one does not, though the existing
norm is the same for both. So we must add that in
guilt feelings the painful belief concerns the violation
of a norm which the individual himself recognizes as
such.

The feeling of guilt may or may not be a genuine
feeling. An important criterion as to the genuineness
of guilt feelings is whether they are accompanied by a
serious wish to make amends or to do better. Whether
this wish exists depends as a rule not only on the
importance attached to the violated norm but also on
the benefit derived from the violation. These considerations remain applicable whether the offense be one of
action or of feelings, of impulses or of fantasies.

It is certainly true that a neurotic may have guilt
feelings. To the extent that his standards contain genuine elements his response to their actual or imagined

2 H. Nunberg has rightly questioned this identification of guilt feelings with a need for punishment, though for other reasons ("The
Sense of Guilt and the Need for Punishment" in *International Journal
of Psychoanalysis,* 1926).

violation may be a genuine feeling of guilt. But his standards, as we have seen, are at least in part only a façade designed to serve a particular purpose. To the extent that they are spurious his response to a violation of that façade has nothing to do with a feeling of guilt, as defined above, but is merely counterfeit. Thus it cannot be assumed that a failure to comply with the stringent moral demands of the "super-ego" produces genuine guilt feelings, nor can it be concluded from the appearance of guilt feelings that the source is a real guilt.

If we do not accept the contention that the neurotic manifestations we have described are the result of un-conscious guilt feelings, what is their actual content and significance? Some aspects of this problem have already been indicated in the discussion on the "super-ego." But as certain others have to be added I shall repeat them here.

Hypersensitivity to anything resembling a criticism or a questioning of motivations results predominantly from a disparity between the façade of perfection and the existing shortcomings or deficiencies. Since the façade has to be maintained, any questioning of its solidity is necessarily frightening and irritating. In addi-tion, the perfectionistic standards and the attempts to attain them are linked up with the person's pride. It is a false pride, substituting for real self-esteem. But whether false or genuine, the person himself feels proud of his standards and superior to others because of them. Therefore he reacts also in another way to criticism: by feeling humiliated. This reaction is of practical impor-tance in therapy, for although some patients express it,

others keep it under cover or repress it. Inasmuch as
their image of perfection implies rationality they feel
they should not be hurt by suggestions made by the
analyst since they come to analysis for the explicit purpose of hearing them. If these feelings of hidden humiliation are not uncovered in time, the analysis may go
on the rocks because of them. The tendency to fall ill
or to remain ill will be discussed in connection with
the masochistic phenomena.

Self-recriminations as a rule are complicated in structure. There is not any one single answer as to their
meaning, and those who insist on getting simple answers to psychological questions will necessarily go
astray. To begin with, self-recriminations are an unavoidable consequence of the categorical character of
the need to appear perfect. Two simple analogies from
everyday life may illustrate: if for any reason it is important for a person to win a game of ping-pong, he
will be angry at himself for making an awkward play;
if for any reason it is important for him to make a good
impression at an interview, he will be angry at himself
for having forgotten to mention a point which would
have put him in a good light, and may scold himself
afterwards and say how silly it was of him not to have
talked about that point. We have but to apply this
description to the neurotic self-recriminations. There,
as we have seen, the need to appear perfect is for many
reasons imperative. For the neurotic individual any
failure to maintain the semblance of perfection means
defeat and danger. Therefore he must necessarily be
angry at himself for any move, whether in thought,

feelings or actions, which to him means failing to be perfect.

This process is described by Freud as "turning against oneself," which implies being hostile toward oneself as a whole. Actually, however, the individual is angry at himself only for something special. In general we may say that he recriminates himself for having endangered a goal the attainment of which is important, even indispensable. As will be remembered, this formulation is akin to that of neurotic anxiety, and anxiety may indeed arise in such situations. We might speculate on whether the self-recriminations are not themselves an attempt to cope with an emerging anxiety.

A second implication of self-recriminations is closely interrelated with the first one. Perfectionistic persons, as has been said, are deeply afraid of anyone recognizing that their façade is only a façade; hence their madding fear of criticism and reproaches. In this regard their self-recriminations are an attempt to anticipate reproaches and, by raising them themselves, to prevent others from making them—even more, to appease others by demonstrating their apparent severity toward themselves and to elicit reassurance. The analogy with normal psychology is obvious. A child afraid of being blamed for having made an inkblot may appear inconsolable about it, expecting thereby to appease the teacher and to elicit consoling remarks such as that it is after all not a crime to have made an inkblot. In a child this may be a conscious strategy. Also the neurotic who recriminates himself makes a strategical move, though he is unaware that he does so: if someone takes his self-recriminations at their face value he will immediately take the defensive; furthermore, this very person who accuses himself so abundantly is furious if others criticize him in the slightest way, and resents it as an unfair deal.

In this context it should be recalled that self-recriminations are not the only strategy of warding off reproaches. There is also the opposite one of turning the tables and taking the offensive, a strategy which follows the old maxim that attack is the best way of defense.[3] This is a more direct method, as it reveals the tendency which in self-recriminations is concealed, that is, the tendency to deny vigorously the existence of any shortcomings. It is also the more effective defense. But only those neurotics can use it who are not afraid of attacking others.

This fear of reproaching others is usually present, however. In fact it is another factor instrumental in engendering self-reproaches. The mechanism is to take the blame on oneself because of the fear of accusing others. It plays a significant role in neuroses because of the intensity of the reproaches against others which a neurotic usually harbors and the intensity of his fear of accusing them.

Reasons for accusatory feelings toward others are manifold and divergent. The neurotic has good reason for feeling bitter against his parents or other persons of his early environment. As to the present, the neurotic part of his accusations arises from his particular character structure. We cannot do it justice here because

[3] Why Anna Freud describes this simple process as an identification with the attacker is not comprehensible (Anna Freud, *Das Ich und die Abwehrmechanismen*, 1936).

that would mean reviewing all the possibilities of neurotic entanglements and then understanding in detail
how accusations are bound to arise. Therefore it must
suffice merely to sketch a few reasons: excessive, though
unrecognized, expectations of others, and a feeling of
being unfairly treated if they are not fulfilled; dependency on others—easily feeling enslaved and resenting it; self-inflation or an appearance of righteousness—
feeling misunderstood, depreciated, unjustly criticized;
necessity to appear infallible; warding off insight into
one's shortcomings by blaming others; altruistic façade
—easily feeling abused and imposed upon, and the like.

Similarly, there are often many stringent reasons for
repressing accusatory feelings. To begin with, the neurotic is afraid of people. In one way or another he is
inordinately dependent on others, whether on their protection, their help or their opinion. In so far as he must
present a rational front he is prevented from feeling or
venting any grievance which is not entirely justified.
Thus a situation frequently arises in which bitter reproaches against others are piled up. Because they are
kept from discharge they become an explosive force and
thus represent a source of danger for the individual. He
has to exert increasing efforts to keep them in abeyance.
It is here that self-recriminations enter as a means of
checking them. The individual makes himself feel that
others are not to be blamed at all, that it is only himself who is to be blamed.[4] In my judgment this is the
dynamics of the process which Freud describes as identi-

[4] The anxious need to withhold any criticism from others contributes
to the incapacity to evaluate others critically, and thus helps to increase
a feeling of helplessness toward them.

fication with the person against whom one feels accusations.[5]

The practice of shifting reproaches from others to oneself is often based on the philosophy that someone has to be blamed whenever anything adverse happens. Usually, if not always, persons who build up a colossal apparatus to maintain the semblance of perfection are highly apprehensive of impending disaster. They feel as if they were living under a suspended sword which may fall down at any moment, although they may not be aware of these fears. They have a fundamental incapacity to face life's ups and downs in a matter of fact way. They cannot reconcile themselves to the fact that life is not calculable like a mathematical task, that it is to some extent like an adventure or like a gamble, subject to good and ill luck, full of unpredictable difficulties and risks, unforeseen and unforeseeable perplexities. As a means of reassurance they cling to the belief that life is calculable and controllable. Hence they believe it is the fault of someone if something goes wrong, for this makes it possible to avoid the unpleasant and frightening realization that life is incalculable and uncontrollable. If such persons are for any reason stopped from reproaching others they will take on themselves the blame for adverse happenings.

The range of problems which may be hidden behind apparent guilt feelings is not exhausted by the factors I have mentioned; for instance, self-minimizing tendencies, arising out of various sources, may easily be

---

5 *Cf.* Sigmund Freud, "Mourning and Melancholia" in *Collected Papers*, Vol. IV (1917); Karl Abraham, *Versuch einer Entwicklungsgeschichte der Libido* (1924).

taken for a feeling of unworthiness born of a feeling of guilt. But it is not so much my intention to give an exhaustive presentation of the underlying dynamics as to illustrate the one point that not all manifestations suggestive of guilt feelings are actually to be interpreted in that way: there may be a counterfeit feeling of guilt, and no guilt; and there may be a response—such as fear, humiliation, anger, determination to ward off criticism, inability to reproach others, need to fix somewhere the blame for adverse happenings—which has nothing to do with remorse and is interpreted in that way only because of theoretical preconceptions.

My difference from Freud in regard to the "super-ego" and guilt feelings entails a different approach to therapy. Freud regards unconscious guilt feelings as an obstacle to a cure of severe neuroses, as elaborated in his theory of the negative therapeutic reaction.[6] According to my interpretation the difficulty in leading the patient to acquire a real insight into his problems lies in the seemingly impenetrable front he offers because of his compulsory need to appear perfect. He comes to psychoanalysis as a last resort, but he comes with the conviction that at bottom he is all right, that he is normal, that he is not really ill. He resents any kind of interpretation which questions his motivations or which shows him that there are problems, and at best he follows only intellectually. He is so bound to appear infallible that he has to deny any deficiency or even

[6] Sigmund Freud, New Introductory Lectures on Psychoanalysis (1933), "The Economic Problem in Masochism" in Collected Papers, Vol. II (1924), Beyond the Pleasure Principle (1920), and The Ego and the Id (1935).

any problem existing in himself. With a certainty approximating that of a real instinct his neurotic self-recriminations avoid what are actually the weak points. In fact their very function is to prevent him from facing any real deficiencies. They are a perfunctory concession to the existing goals, a mere means of reassurance that he is not so bad after all and that his very qualms of conscience make him better than others. They are a face-saving device, for if a person really wishes to improve and sees a possibility of doing so, he will not waste time on self-recriminations; at any rate, he will not feel that enough is accomplished by accusing himself; he will make constructive efforts toward understanding and changing. The neurotic, however, does nothing but scold himself.

Thus what is necessary is first to show him that he demands the impossible of himself, then to make him realize the formalistic nature of his aims and his achievements. The disparity between his façade of perfection and his actual trends has to be revealed. He has to acquire a feeling that there is a problem in the stringency of his perfectionistic needs. All the consequences of these needs have to be worked through carefully. His actual reactions to the analyst's questioning him, wanting to find out something about him, have to be analyzed. He has to understand the factors which created the need and those which maintain it. He has to understand the function it serves. He has to see, finally, the real moral issue involved. This approach is more difficult than the usual one but it allows a less pessimistic view than Freud's concerning the possibilities of therapy.

CHAPTER XV

MASOCHISTIC PHENOMENA

MASOCHISM is usually defined as a striving for sexual satisfaction through suffering. This definition contains three postulates: that masochism is essentially a sexual phenomenon; that it is essentially a striving for satisfaction; and that it is essentially a wish to suffer.

The data for the first contention are the well-known facts that children may become sexually excited by being beaten, that in masochistic perversion sexual satisfaction is arrived at by being humiliated, enslaved or physically ill-treated, that in masochistic fantasies the imagination of similar situations leads to masturbation. The bulk of masochistic phenomena, however, is not apparently sexual in nature, nor are there any data to show an ultimate sexual origin. Data are substituted for by the contention, based on the libido theory, that masochistic character trends or attitudes toward others represent some kind of transformation of masochistic sexual drives. Thus it would be contended, for example, that the satisfaction a woman gains from playing the martyr role, though not manifestly sexual in nature, is nevertheless a derivative from an ultimate sexual source.

Another hypothesis concerns so-called "moral masochism," that is, the "ego's" eagerness to incur failures or accidents or to lash itself with self-reproaches for the sake of reconciling the "super-ego." Freud suggests that "moral masochism" too is ultimately a sexual phenomenon. He contends that while a need for punishment serves as a reassurance against the fear of the "super-ego," it is at the same time a modified sexual masochistic subjection of the "ego" to the "super-ego," the latter representing an incorporated parent image. All these theories are debatable because they operate from premises which I consider erroneous. As the premises have been discussed, the contentions need not be considered further.

Other authors put less emphasis on the sexual satisfaction in masochistic phenomena, but retain the premise that in order to understand masochism one must define it in terms of a striving for satisfaction. The reasoning on which this premise is founded is the belief that strivings which are as irresistible and difficult to combat as the masochistic strivings are necessarily determined by an ultimate goal promising satisfaction.[1] Thus Franz Alexander [2] suggests that persons who are willing to take suffering upon themselves do so not only because they want to ward off punishment threatening from the "super-ego," but also because they believe that by paying the penalty of suffering they may live out certain forbidden impulses. Fritz Wittels [3] suggests that

[1] *Cf.* Chapter III, The Libido Theory.

[2] Franz Alexander, *Psychoanalysis of the Total Personality* (1935).

[3] Fritz Wittels, "The Mystery of Masochism" in the *Psychoanalytic Review* (1937).

"the masochist wishes to prove the futility of one part of his person in order to live the more secure in the important other part. He derives pleasure from the pain felt by the other figure." I myself have propounded an hypothesis [4] that all masochistic strivings are ultimately directed toward satisfaction, namely, toward the goal of oblivion, of getting rid of self with all its conflicts and all its limitations. The masochistic phenomena which we find in neuroses would then represent a pathological modification of the dionysian tendencies [5] which seem to be spread throughout the world.

The question remains, however, whether it is strivings for this kind of satisfaction which ultimately determine the masochistic phenomena. Could one, in short, define masochism as essentially a striving toward the relinquishment of self? While such strivings are distinctly observable in some cases, in others they are not apparent. If the definition of masochism as a striving for oblivion is to be maintained, we should need for its support the further hypothesis that this striving is operative also when it is not apparent. Assumptions of this kind are frequently made; they are, for instance, the cornerstone of the postulate that all masochistic phenomena are ultimately sexual in nature. And it certainly happens that we chase after some phantoms of satisfaction without being aware of it. But it is precarious to operate with such assumptions without having data for them.

As I shall try to show in the following considerations,

[4] Karen Horney, *The Neurotic Personality of Our Time* (1937).
[5] Friedrich Nietzsche, *Die Geburt der Tragödie;* Ruth Benedict, *Patterns of Culture* (1934).

it would be more constructive if we desisted from approaching the problem of masochism with the preconceived idea that it is essentially a striving for satisfaction. As a matter of fact, Freud himself is not quite rigid concerning this assumption. He has contended that masochism is the result of a fusion of the death instinct with sexual drives, the function of this fusion being to protect the individual from self-destruction. Although this hypothesis is not on safe ground because of the speculative character of the death instinct, it is noteworthy because it introduces into the discussion of masochism the idea of a protective function.

The third contention implicit in the usual definition of masochism—regarding it essentially as a wish to suffer—coincides with popular opinion. It is evidenced in such sayings as that such and such a person is not happy unless he has something to worry about, unless he feels victimized, or the like. In psychiatry this premise entails the danger of accounting for the difficulties of curing certain neuroses by relating them to the patient's wish to remain ill, instead of relating them to inadequacies of our present psychological knowledge.

As pointed out before, the basic fallacy in this contention is the neglect of the fact that the stringency of a striving can be determined by its faculty of allaying anxiety. We shall see presently that masochistic strivings too represent to a great extent a special way of gaining safety.

The term masochistic is used to denote a certain quality in character trends without, however, a concise notion as to the nature of this quality. Actually masochistic character trends entail two main tendencies.

One is a tendency toward self-minimizing. Most frequently the individual is not aware of this tendency but only of its result, which is to feel unattractive, insignificant, inefficient, stupid, worthless. In contrast to narcissistic trends, which I have described as a tendency toward self-inflation, this masochistic trend is one toward self-deflation. While a narcissistic person [6] tends to exaggerate to himself and others his good qualities and capacities, the masochistic person tends to exaggerate his insufficiencies. The narcissistic person tends to feel that he can easily master any task, the perfectionistic person tends to feel he must be able to cope with any situation, but the masochistic person tends to react with a helpless "I can't." The narcissistic person craves to be the center of attention, the perfectionistic person is seclusive, harboring a secret feeling of superiority given him by his standards, but the masochistic person tends to be inconspicuous and to cringe into a corner.

The other main tendency is toward personal dependency. The masochistic dependency on others is different from that of the narcissistic or the perfectionistic person. The narcissistic person is dependent on others because he needs their attention and admiration. The perfectionistic person, though overconcerned with preserving his independence, is actually dependent on others too because his security rests on an automatic

[6] When I speak of narcissistic, masochistic or perfectionistic persons I mean the phrase as a simplified expression for one in whom narcissistic, masochistic or perfectionistic tendencies prevail.

conformance with what he believes others expect of him. But he is anxious to hide from himself the fact and the extent of his dependency, and any revelation of it, as in analysis, is felt as a blow to his pride and his security. In both these types dependency is the unwanted result of the particular character structure. For the masochistic person, on the other hand, dependency is actually a life condition. He feels that he is as incapable of living without the presence, benevolence, love, friendship of another person as he is incapable of living without oxygen.

Let us, for the sake of simplicity, call the person on whom the masochistic type is dependent, his partner, whether he be parent, lover, sister, husband, friend, physician; [7] the "partner" may be not an individual but a group, such as fellow members of the family or of a religious sect.

The masochistic person feels he cannot do anything on his own, and expects to receive everything from the partner: love, success, prestige, care, protection. Without ever realizing it, and mostly in contrast to his conscious modesty and humility, his expectations are parasitic in character. His reasons for clinging to another person are so stringent that he may exclude from awareness the fact that the partner is not and never will be the appropriate person to fulfill his expectations; he does not want to recognize limitations that are implicit in a

[7] F. Kuenkel pointed out the importance of a *Beziehungsperson* for the neurotic, but he considered this a general characteristic of neuroses instead of relating it specifically to masochism. E. Fromm calls this type of relationship a symbiotic one and regards it as a basic trend in the masochistic character structure.

certain relationship. Therefore he is insatiable for any sign of affection [8] or interest. Usually he has the same kind of attitude toward fate in general: he feels a helpless toy in the hands of fate or he feels doomed and cannot visualize any possibilities for taking his fate into his own hands.

These basic masochistic trends grow on essentially the same soil as the narcissistic and perfectionistic trends. To summarize briefly: through a combination of adverse influences a child's spontaneous assertion of his individual initiative, feelings, wishes, opinions, is warped and he feels the world around him to be potentially hostile; under such difficult conditions he must find possibilities of coping with life safely and thus he develops what I have called neurotic trends. We have seen that self-inflation is one such trend, that overconformity to standards is another. I believe that the development of masochistic trends, as described above, is a further one. The security offered by any of these ways is real. The pseudo-adaptation of the perfectionistic person, for instance, actually eliminates manifest conflicts with people and gives him some feeling of firmness. We shall try to understand now in what fashion masochistic trends too provide reassurance.

To have friends or relatives on whom one can rely is reassuring for anyone. The reassurance sought in masochistic dependency is, in principle, of the same kind. Its peculiarity results from the fact that it is built up on different presuppositions. The Victorian girl who grew up in a sheltered environment also was dependent

[8] *Cf.* Karen Horney, *op. cit.*, chapter on "The Neurotic Need for Affection."

on others. But the world on which she was dependent was friendly as a rule. To have a leaning and receptive attitude toward a generous, benevolent and protective world is neither painful nor conducive to conflict.

In neuroses, however, the world is considered as more or less unreliable, cold, begrudging, vindictive; and to feel helpless and dependent on such a potentially hostile world is equal to feeling defenseless in the midst of danger. The masochistic way of coping with this situation is to thrust oneself on the mercy of someone. By submerging his own individuality entirely and by merging with the partner the masochistic person gains a certain reassurance. His reassurance is to be compared with that achieved by a small endangered nation which surrenders its rights and its independence to a powerful and aggressive nation and thereby wins protection. One of the differences is that the small nation knows it does not take this step because of its love for the bigger nation, while in the neurotic's mind the process often takes on the appearance of loyalty, devotion or great love. But actually the masochistic person is incapable of love, nor does he believe that the partner or anyone else can love him. What appears under the flag of devotion is actually a sheer clinging to the partner for the sake of allaying anxiety. Hence the precarious nature of this kind of security, and the never-vanishing fear of being deserted. Any friendly gesture on the part of the partner brings reassurance, but any kind of interest that the partner may have for other people or for his own work, any failure to satisfy the permanent hunger for signs of positive interest, may at once conjure up the danger of desertion and thereby engender anxiety.

The kind of security that may be achieved by self-belittling is the security of unobtrusiveness. Again it should be emphasized that security can really be found by making oneself insignificant, unattractive and inconspicuous, just as it can really be found by impressing others with one's glorious qualities. A person seeking this security of unobtrusiveness behaves like a mouse that prefers staying in its hole because it is afraid that a cat would eat it if it were to come out. The resulting feeling toward life can be described as that of a stowaway who has to remain unnoticed and who has no rights of his own.

The presence of such an attitude is suggested by the rigidity with which the person clings to a behavior pattern of unobtrusiveness, and its compulsory character is suggested in the fact that anxiety appears when such a regime is abandoned. For instance, if such a person is offered a more favorable position than the one he holds, he becomes alarmed. Or a person who in his own mind diminishes his capacities may become frightened when he wishes to assert his opinion in a discussion; even when making a valuable contribution he expresses it in an apologetic way. Often in their childhood or adolescence these individuals were afraid to wear any elaborate clothes, prettier than those worn by friends, because they would feel conspicuous. They can neither conceive that anyone can feel hurt by them nor be fond of them nor appreciate them; because despite evidence to the contrary, they hold on to their conviction that they "do not matter." They are likely to feel embarrassed and uneasy at any well-deserved praise for a job done well; they themselves tend to diminish its value, thus depriving themselves of the satisfaction to be gained out of the achievement. Anxiety arising on this score is often an important feature in inhibitions concerning work. Creative work, for instance, may become painful because it always implies asserting oneself with one's particular views or feelings. The task can then be done only if some other person is at hand to give constant reassurance.

That anxiety arising from the "mouse-hole" attitude does not appear as often as would be proportionate to the frequency of the attitude is due to the fact that life is automatically arranged in a fashion to prevent anxiety from arising, or to the fact that reactions of retreat occur automatically. Opportunities are not seized, or are not even noticed; second-rate positions which are beneath existing possibilities and capacities are held on to, under some pretext or other; there is not even an awareness of claims that could and should be made; contacts with people who are really liked or who could be helpful are avoided. Success, if it occurs in spite of all these difficulties, is emotionally not experienced as such. A new idea conceived, a work well done, is immediately devaluated in the person's own mind. He buys a Ford rather than a Lincoln, though he would prefer the latter and though he is financially able to have it.

The neurotic is mostly unaware of the fact that he is subject to a tendency toward unobtrusiveness; as a rule he feels only the results. He may consciously adopt a defensive attitude and believe that he hates being conspicuous or that he does not care for success. Or he

may simply regret that he is weak, insignificant, unattractive. Or, most frequently, he may have a general
notion of having inferiority feelings. These feelings are
the result rather than the cause of his tendency to recoil
from self-assertion.

All these trends implying the existence of a weak and
helpless attitude toward life are familiar phenomena,
but they are usually attributed to other sources. They
are described in psychoanalytical literature as results of
passive homosexual trends, of guilt feelings or of a wish
to be a child—all of these interpretations in my opinion
befogging the issue. As to the wish to be a child, the
masochistic trends may indeed be expressed in these
terms; there may be in dreams a fantasy of returning to
the womb or of being carried in the mother's arms. But
it is unjustifiable to interpret such manifestations as a
wish to be a child, for the neurotic "wishes" as little to
be a child as he "wishes" to be helpless; it is the stress
of anxiety which forces him to adopt the tactics he does.
A dream of being an infant is not proof of a wish to
be an infant but is the expression of a wish to be protected, not to have to stand on one's own feet, not to
have responsibilities—a wish which is appealing because
a feeling of helplessness has developed.

Thus far we have seen the masochistic trends as a
specific way of allaying anxiety and of coping with the
difficulties of life, particularly with its dangers or what
are felt as such. It is a way, though, which in itself spells
conflict. To begin with, the neurotic invariably despises
himself for his weakness. Here is a distinct difference
from the culturally patterned helplessness and dependency. The Victorian girl, for instance, could be quite

content with her dependency; it did not detract from her happiness nor did it undermine her self-confidence. On the contrary, a certain frailty and attitude of help-less leaning were desirable feminine qualities. For the masochistic person, however, there is no cultural pattern to give prestige for such an attitude. Furthermore, what the neurotic wants is not helplessness, though it pro-vides him with a valuable strategical means of achieving whatever he desires, but unobtrusiveness and depend-ency; and even that he wants only for the feeling of safety he gains by it. The weakness is an unavoidable and unwanted result of the course adopted. It is all the more unwanted because—as has been pointed out—it is dangerous to be weak in the midst of a potentially hostile world. Both this danger and the disapproval which others feel for his weakness contrive to make it contemptible to the neurotic.

Thus the weakness is a source of almost incessant irritation or even of powerless rage, which may be precipitated by an infinite variety of occasions occurring daily. Both the occasions and the subsequent irritations are often perceived but dimly. But a person of this type does not fail to register deep down that here he has not stood up for his opinion, has not dared to express his wishes, has yielded where he felt like refusing, has noticed much too late that someone has been insidiously mean to him. Here he has been conciliatory and apolo-getic where he should have been assertive, here he has missed an opportunity, here he has avoided a difficult situation by falling ill.

This constant suffering through his own weakness is one cause among others which leads to an indiscriminate

adoration of strength. Any person who dares to be
openly aggressive or assertive is certain of at least secret
adoration, regardless of the value ascribed to him. A
person who dares to lie or to bluff inspires an under-
current of adoration as much as does the person who
shows courage for the sake of a good cause.

Another consequence of this inner calamity is an
abundant growth of grandiose notions. In his fantasy
the masochistic person can tell his employer and his
wife what he thinks of them, in his fantasies he is the
most successful Don Juan of all time, in his fantasies
he makes inventions and writes books. These fantasies
have the value of consolation but also they sharpen the
existing contrast within him.

Relationships built upon masochistic dependency are
replete with hostility toward the partner. I shall mention but three main sources of this hostility. One is the
expectations the neurotic has of the partner. Since he
is himself without energy, initiative and courage, he
secretly expects everything from the partner, ranging
from care, help, relief of risks and responsibilities, to
maintenance, prestige and glory. At bottom—and this is
always deeply repressed—he wants to feed on the partner's life. These expectations cannot possibly be fulfilled
because no partner who wants to preserve his individuality and his individual life can possibly live up to what
is expected of him. The hostile reactions to disappointment would not assume the proportions they often do
if the neurotic were aware of the extent of his demands
on the partner; in that case he would merely be angry
for not obtaining all that he wants to obtain. It is to
his interest, however, not to play with open cards, and

thus he has to appear as the modest or innocent little boy or girl. The process which in reality is a simple egotistic reaction of anger becomes distorted in his own mind. It is not he who is egocentric and inconsiderate in his expectations, but he is the one who is neglected, fooled, abused by the partner. Hence the unwarranted anger reactions turn into a vicious kind of moral indignation.

Furthermore, though the masochistic person for safety's sake cannot budge an inch from his conviction that he "does not matter," he is hypersensitive to the slightest sign of disregard or neglect on the part of others and reacts to it with intense anger, which for many reasons is barred from expression. Even if true friendliness is offered to him, it does not register because anyone who "does not matter" to himself cannot possibly perceive that he matters to anyone else. The bitterness toward others thus generated is one of the main factors responsible for sharpening the conflict between needing others and hating them.

The third main source of hostility is more deeply hidden. Because the masochistic person cannot possibly stand any distance between himself and the partner, not to speak of separation, he actually feels enslaved. He feels that he has to accept the terms of the partner, no matter what they are. But since he hates his own dependency, resenting it as a humiliation, he is bound to rebel inwardly against any partner, no matter how considerate. He feels that the latter is dominating him, that he is caught like a fly in the spider's web, the partner being the spider. In a marriage, since wife and husband often have a similar structure, it may happen that both complain thus of being dominated in an unbearable fashion.

Part of the hostility thus generated may be discharged in occasional explosions. On the whole, however, the masochistic person's hostility toward the partner constitutes a constant, unrelieved danger, because he needs the partner and is bound to be afraid of alienating him.

At any more acute rise of hostility anxiety may ensue. But an increase in anxiety increases in turn the need to hang on to the partner. The vicious circles thus operating make a separation increasingly difficult and painful. The conflict inherent in the human relationships of the masochistic person is thus ultimately a conflict between dependency and hostility.

The above basic trends in the masochistic structure necessarily have a bearing on all spheres of life. To the extent that they exist they determine the way in which a person pursues his wishes, expresses his hostility, avoids difficulties. They determine also the way he deals with other neurotic needs in himself, such as a need to control others or a need to appear perfect. Finally, they determine the kind of satisfaction which is accessible to him and thereby they influence his sexual life. When in the following I discuss the specific masochistic features in these various spheres I shall select but a few characteristic features, because the intention of this chapter is not a study of masochism but is to convey a general impression of the fundamentals of masochistic phenomena.

Certain wishes of the masochistic person may be expressed directly, though there are varying degrees and conditions under which this can be done. The specific masochistic way of expressing wishes, however, consists in the person impressing on others how great his need is because of his bad condition. An insurance man, for instance, instead of praising the value of the insurance, implores the prospective customer to take the insurance from him on the ground that he needs the commission very badly; a good musician, when applying for work, instead of giving an impression of his skill, stresses his need to earn money. More acutely, the specific form of expressing wishes appears as a desperate cry for help, implying something like "I am so miserable and desperate—help me," or "I am entirely lost if you do not help me," or "I have no one in the world but you— you must be kind to me," or "I cannot possibly do it— you have to do it for me," or "You have done me so much harm you are responsible for all my misery—you must do something for me." The person to whom this is addressed is put under a stringent moral obligation. The more detached psychiatric observer will make a mental note that the patient inadvertently exaggerates his misery and needs for the strategical purpose of getting what he wants. That is quite right as far as it goes; the patient is displaying the typical masochistic strategy of getting something by a display of misery and helplessness.

The question remains, however, why he uses just this particular strategy. It may be effective at times, but as most case histories show, the effect wears off after a while; the persons around him become tired of this type of entreaty and sooner or later take his misery for granted and are no longer spurred to action. The masochistic person may still attain his end if he reinforces his attacks as, for instance, by threats to commit suicide; but that too wears off in time. Therefore we cannot regard his attitude merely as a strategy. In order to understand it more fully we have to realize that the masochistic person is deeply convinced, consciously or unconsciously, that the world around him is hard and begrudging and that there is no such thing as spontaneous kindness. Hence he feels that only by exerting strong pressure can he get what he wants. Furthermore, he basically feels that he has no right to demand anything for himself, and thus in his own mind his wishes must be justified. In this calamity the solution he finds is to use his existing helplessness and distress as a means of exerting pressure as well as of justifying his demands. Without knowing it, he lets himself slide into a deeper feeling of misery and helplessness than already exists, and then subjectively he feels entitled to demand help. Whether this process is carried out more or less amiably or pugnaciously depends on many factors, but in principle the elements in this "masochistic cry for help" seem to be always alike.

The manner in which hostility is expressed varies with the structure of a personality. The type whose predominant need is to appear perfect wants to prick or to hurt others by his moral or intellectual superiority and by his infallibility. The specifically masochistic way of expressing hostility is by suffering, helplessness, by the person representing himself as victimized and harmed, by spitefully letting himself go to pieces—in anthropological terms, killing himself on the offender's doorstep. His hostility may appear also in fantasies of cruelty, particularly in the form of humiliations heaped upon those by whom he has felt offended.

The hostility of the masochistic type is not altogether merely defensive. It often has a sadistic character. A person is sadistic when he derives satisfaction from his power of making others helpless or making them suffer.[9] The sadistic impulse springs from the vindictiveness of a weak and suppressed individual, of a slave, as it were, who craves to feel that he too can subject others to his wishes and make them cringe under whatever he inflicts on them. The masochistic person in his basic structure has all the preconditions which foster the development of sadistic trends in the sense defined above: he is weak for many reasons, he is or feels humiliated and suppressed, and in his heart he makes others responsible for his suffering.

A little theoretical divergence is in place here. Freud always postulated an interrelation between sadistic and masochistic trends. His original suggestion was to regard masochism as a turned-in sadism, thus contending that the primary satisfaction is in making others suffer and that secondarily the same impulse may be turned toward oneself. Freud's later view on masochism does not alter this contention because also when masochism is regarded as a fusion of the sexual and the destruction instincts, its clinical manifestations—and that is all we are

[9] This definition is incomplete because a similar satisfaction may be gained when disasters or acts of cruelty are only witnessed or heard of. Nevertheless here too is the element of enjoying a superiority over those who are subjected to accidents, acts of cruelty, humiliations and the like. The element of power in sadism was pointed out by the Marquis de Sade himself. It was emphasized by Nietzsche in all his writings. It has been stressed lately by Erich Fromm in his lectures on the psychology of authority.

interested in—remain a turning of sadistic impulses from the outside toward the self. The new theory, however, by way of speculation, adds the possibility that masochism is nevertheless earlier than sadism (primary masochism). While I do not agree with the theoretical implications of the latter suggestion, I do agree with it from the clinical standpoint. The basic masochistic structure is a fertile soil for sadistic trends. One should hesitate, however, to generalize the statement, because sadistic trends are in no way characteristic of the masochistic type alone. Any individual who is weak and suppressed for other than neurotic reasons may develop them too.

To shrink from tackling difficulties is certainly not in itself masochistic. The specifically masochistic elements lie in what the person feels to be a difficulty and particularly in the ways he chooses to avoid it. Because of his compulsory unobtrusiveness and dependency, with all their implications, molehills often appear to him as mountains, particularly when he is supposed to do something for himself, or when he is faced with responsibilities and risks. Some types may simply shun every effort and may react, for instance, with deadly fatigue at the mere prospect of greater work, such as Christmas shopping or moving. The masochistic person's typical reaction to difficulties is an immediate response of "I can't," sometimes clad in the form of a fear that the necessary effort would harm him.

His characteristic way of avoiding difficulties is by procrastination and particularly by falling ill. When an unpleasant and frightening task awaits him, such as an examination or an argument with his employer, the prospect of which is terrifying, he may fall ill or may wish at least to have an accident. When it is necessary that he go to a physician, or that he make definite business arrangements, he procrastinates, shoves the existing problems out of his mind. An intricate family situation has to be straightened out, for instance. Were he to sit down and tackle it actively he would see ways of solving it and then would have it off his mind. Instead he never thinks distinctly of the existing calamity; he harbors an indistinct and muddled hope that it will straighten itself out in due time, and as a consequence he feels it looming overhead as a vague and huge menace. This shirking of all difficulties reinforces his feeling of weakness, and makes him weaker in actual fact, because he misses the strength he would acquire in fighting them through.

The basic masochistic structure determines also the ways in which the individual deals with other neurotic trends which may be combined with his masochistic trends. I shall point out briefly some of the possible interrelations.

The masochistic structure, as already mentioned, cannot be regarded separately from tendencies toward grandiose notions about oneself.[10] They belong to that structure, representing mostly a means of saving oneself from being submerged in self-contempt. They usually remain entirely in fantasy, absorbing a good proportion of time and energy.

It is a different picture, however, when there exists at

10 This statement is not reversible; self-inflation may occur without masochistic trends, or at least without their being significant in the personality; cf. Chapter V, The Concept of Narcissism.

the same time a neurotic ambition which renders it unbearable not to achieve great and unique things in reality. In that case there is a sharp dilemma because the ambition urges the individual toward success while the need for unobtrusiveness makes him afraid of success. The specifically masochistic way of coping with it is to put the blame for a lack of achievement on others—persons or circumstances—and to seek an alibi in illness or in pretended insufficiencies. A woman may blame her failure on the fact that she is a woman. Or a failure to do creative work may be blamed on the exigencies of daily life. A girl wanting to be a great actress but afraid of undertaking it put her reluctance to go on the stage on the basis of her being too small in stature. Another woman ascribed her failure to make a great career on the stage to the envy of others. Others accredit their failures to their poor family background or to friends and relatives who interfere with their plans or who have not given them sufficient support.

Patients of this type may consciously harbor the wish for a chronic illness such as tuberculosis. Usually they are unaware that the prospect of illness has some fascination for them. But one can hardly escape this conclusion when one sees how such a person avidly seizes upon the slightest possibility of illness: how any heart-pounding conjures up the conviction of a heart disease, any temporary frequency of urination, that of diabetes, any stomach-ache that of appendicitis. This interest is often one of the elements involved in hypochondriac fears, the fears then being a reaction to the prospect of illness which is so vividly present in imagination. The positive interest which such a person has in being ill makes it difficult to convince him that nothing is the matter with his heart, lungs, stomach. As every physician knows by experience, such a patient may, in spite of his fears, resent a statement that he is all right. Needless to say, this is not the whole explanation of hypochondriac fears, but is only one of the factors which may be operating in them.

Finally, the neurotic disturbances themselves may be used as an alibi, a fact which may retard the cure. A person of this type feels that in the event of a cure he would lose any good excuse for not putting his capacities to the test of actual work. He is afraid of that test for several reasons. One is that because of his self-minimizing tendencies he essentially doubts that he can achieve anything; another is that any real striving for achievement seems to him to be "sticking his neck out"; also, he realizes dimly that the prospect of real work and success does not appeal to him. In comparison with the glamorous goals to be attained in fantasy without any effort at all there is too little glamour in doing some respectable piece of work requiring many strenuous and consistent efforts. Hence he will often prefer to let his ambitious goals remain in fantasy and to retain his neurotic troubles as an alibi. In psychoanalysis this is often interpreted as an unwillingness to become well, because of a need for punishment, for instance. Such an interpretation is untenable. The patient may, for instance, feel temporarily well if he is in a sanitarium or a resort, with no responsibilities, obligations or expectations on the part of others or himself. It is more correct to say that these patients, while wanting to get well, nevertheless shrink from the prospect, inasmuch as being well means also taking an active stand toward life and losing any excuse for not realizing actively some of their ambitions.

Masochistic trends can also be combined with an imperative need for power and control. I can be brief about this because it is common knowledge that the way the masochistic person exerts control is by his very suffering and helplessness. His family and friends may submit to his wishes because they are afraid that if they do not there will be an upheaval of some kind: despair, depression, helplessness, functional disorders and the like. It should be added, however, that relatives usually regard his behavior as mere strategy. It is the merit of Alfred Adler [11] to have pointed out the importance of unconscious strategical maneuvers, but it is one of his many superficialities to consider such explanations sufficient. One has to understand the whole structure in order to grasp why it is indispensable for a neurotic to attain a certain goal and why only certain ways to reach it are accessible to him.

A last combination to be mentioned here is the combination of masochistic trends with a compulsory need to appear perfect. The self-recriminations connected with this need Freud contends to be rooted in a masochistic subjection to the punitive power of the "super-ego." As I have already shown, these tendencies are not in themselves masochistic but are determined by other factors in the character structure.[12] They may appear, however, in a person in whom masochistic trends prevail; in that case they are not merely self-recriminations,

[11] Alfred Adler, *Understanding Human Nature* (1927).
[12] *Cf.* Chapter XIV, Neurotic Guilt Feelings.

but take the form of a tendency to wallow in guilt feelings and to resort to suffering in order to atone for them. A non-neurotic dealing with guilt feelings consists in facing one's shortcomings squarely and in trying to overcome them. This way requires, however, an amount of inner activity which is alien to the masochistic type.

Of course in attempting to atone by suffering the masochistic person follows a cultural pattern. To placate the gods through sacrifice is a widely spread religious usage. In our culture there is the Christian belief in suffering as a means of atonement; there is the criminal law inflicting suffering as a punishment for offenses; and education has only recently relinquished this principle. The masochistic person makes use of such patterns because they fit into his structure. The striking feature in his readiness to accept suffering as a punishment, or to lash himself with self-reproaches, lies in its utter futility; the reason is that this readiness to accept punishment does not concern genuine guilt feelings, but serves his compulsory need to appear perfect and is ultimately an attempt to re-establish his image of perfection.

Finally, the basic masochistic structure determines also the kinds of satisfaction attainable. Satisfactory masochistic experiences can be sexual or non-sexual, the former consisting in masochistic fantasies and perversions, the latter in wallowing in misery and worthlessness.

In order to understand the puzzling fact that suffering may entail satisfaction, we have to realize first that almost all the ways which otherwise yield satisfaction are closed to the masochistic type. Any kind of constructive self-assertive activity is usually avoided completely, and if undertaken involves sufficient anxiety to mar any satisfaction otherwise to be gained from it. The possibilities for gratifying experiences which are thus eliminated comprise not only any kind of leadership and pioneering work but also any independent work or consistent planned efforts aiming at some goal. Furthermore, because of the compulsory unobtrusiveness, there can be no enjoyment of recognition or success. Finally, the masochistic person is incapable of putting all his energies voluntarily into the service of a cause. Although he has to hang on to a "partner" or to a group because he cannot stand on his own he is much too apprehensive, distrustful and egocentric to give himself voluntarily and wholeheartedly to anything or anyone.

Both his incapacity to give active spontaneous affection to others and his incapacity to surrender are bound to cause a basic impairment of his love life. Others are indispensable to him for the fulfillment of certain needs but he cannot afford to have spontaneous feelings for them concerning their interests, their needs, their happiness, their development; and he can give himself in love to others no more than he can give himself to a cause. Thus the satisfactions otherwise to be had in love and sexuality are also warped.

The kind of satisfaction which is accessible is therefore greatly restricted. In fact, satisfaction can be obtained only along the same ways through which safety is found. These ways, as we have seen, are characterized by dependency and unobtrusiveness. But here we en-

counter a problem, because dependency and unobtrusiveness alone do not bring about satisfaction. Observation shows that satisfaction is experienced when
these attitudes are carried to extremes. In a sexual
masochistic fantasy or perversion the masochistic person is not simply dependent on the partner, but he is
clay in his hands, is raped, is enslaved, humiliated, tor-
tured. Similarly, unobtrusiveness may afford him satisfaction if it is carried to such extremes as losing himself
entirely in "love" or in a sacrifice, losing his identity,
losing his dignity, submerging his individuality in self-
deprecation.

Why is it necessary to go to such extremes in the
search for satisfaction? The dependency on the partner,
while it is a sort of life condition for the masochistic
type, cannot yield much satisfaction because it is laden
with conflicts and painful experiences. Let me restate
explicitly, in order to combat a common misunderstanding, that the conflicts and painful experiences are
neither secretly wanted nor enjoyed, but are unavoidable and are as painful to the masochistic person as they
would be to anyone else. The kind of experiences which
are bound to render masochistic relationships unhappy
have been mentioned in the discussion of the basic
structure. To repeat some of them: the masochistic type
despises himself for being dependent; because of his
excessive expectations of his partner he is bound to
become disappointed and resentful; he is bound to
feel frequently unfairly treated.

Therefore only by eliminating conflicts and narcotiz-
ing the pains involved can satisfaction be derived from
such a relationship. Conflicts can be eliminated and

psychic pain lulled in several ways. In the masochistic person the conflict on the score of dependency is, in general terms, one between weakness and strength, between merging and self-assertion, between self-contempt and pride. His particular way of resolving this conflict is to thrust aside, in perversions and fantasies, his striving toward strength, pride, dignity, self-respect, and to abandon himself completely to his leanings toward weakness and dependency. When he has thus become a helpless tool in his partner's hands, when he has thus submerged himself in abjection, he can have a satisfactory sexual experience. The specific masochistic way of lulling psychic pains is to intensify them and wholly surrender to them. By the person's wallowing in humiliation his pain of self-contempt is narcotized and may then be turned into a gratifying experience.

That an unbearable pain can be alleviated and turned into something pleasurable by submerging the self in a feeling of misery is shown by many observations. A patient capable of good self-observation will confirm it spontaneously. He may feel a slight, a reproach, a failure, as merely painful, but then he may let himself slide into a feeling of abject misery. He is dimly aware that he exaggerates and that he could pull himself out of his misery, but fundamentally he knows too that he does not want to do so because there is an irresistible attraction in thus abandoning himself to grief. When the masochistic trends are combined with a compulsory need to appear perfect, a deviation from the image of perfection is dealt with in a similar way. A realization of a mistake is merely painful, but by intensifying this feeling and wallowing in self-accusations and feelings of unworthiness the masochistic person may narcotize the pain and derive satisfaction from an orgy of self-degradation. This, then, would be a non-sexual masochistic satisfaction.

How can pain be alleviated by its intensification? I have previously described the principle operating in this process and shall cite it here verbatim. Speaking of the seemingly voluntary increases in suffering, I have said: "In such suffering there are no apparent advantages to be gained, no audience that might be impressed, no sympathy to be won, no secret triumph in asserting his will over others. Nevertheless, there is a gain for the neurotic, but of a different kind. Incurring a failure in love, a defeat in competition, having to realize a definite weakness or shortcoming of his own is unbearable for one who has such high-flown notions of his uniqueness. Thus when he dwindles to nothing in his own estimation, the categories of success and failure, superiority and inferiority cease to exist; by exaggerating his pain, by losing himself in a general feeling of misery or unworthiness, the aggravating experience loses some of its reality, the sting of the special pain is lulled, narcotized. The principle operating in this process is a dialectic one, containing the philosophical truth that at a certain point quantity is converted into quality. Concretely, it means that though suffering is painful, abandoning one's self to excessive suffering may serve as an opiate against pain." [13]

The kind of satisfaction obtained in these ways consists in abandoning oneself to and losing oneself in something. I do not know whether it allows of further

[13] Karen Horney. *op. cit.*, ch. 14.

analysis. We can, however, divest it of its mystery by relating it to familiar experiences, such as sexual abandon, religious ecstasy, losing oneself in some great feeling, whether it be produced by nature, music or enthusiasm for a cause. Nietzsche has called it the dionysian trend, and believes it to be one of the fundamental human possibilities for satisfaction. Ruth Benedict [14] and other anthropologists have shown it to operate in many cultural patterns. That in the masochistic person it appears in the form of abandonment to dependency, misery and self-deprecation is due to his basic structure, which does not allow of any other form of satisfaction.

Returning to the questions raised at the beginning— whether masochism is a particular kind of sexual striving, whether it can be defined as a search for satisfaction in general or for satisfaction in suffering in particular—I arrive at the conclusion that all these strivings represent but certain aspects of the phenomenon and not its core. Its core is the attempt of an intimidated and isolated individual to cope with life and its dangers by dependency and unobtrusiveness. The character structure resulting from these basic strivings is what determines the ways in which wishes are asserted, in which hostilities are expressed, in which failures are justified and in which other neurotic strivings existing simultaneously are dealt with. Also it determines the kind of satisfaction that is sought and the way in which it is found. The particular sexual satisfaction in masochistic perversions and fantasies is likewise determined by the basic structure. To put the issue polemically, masoch-

[14] Ruth Benedict, *Patterns of Culture* (1934).

istic perversion does not explain the masochistic character, but the character explains the perversion. The masochistic person enjoys suffering as little as others do, but his suffering is the result of his character structure. The satisfactions he occasionally finds are not in suffering but in ecstatic abandon to misery and self-degradation.

Therefore in therapy the task is to unravel the basic masochistic character trends, to follow them in all their ramifications and to discover their conflicts with opposite trends.

CHAPTER XVI

PSYCHOANALYTIC THERAPY

PSYCHOANALYTIC therapy, in so far as it is not intuitive or directed by plain common sense, is influenced by theoretical concepts. To a great extent these concepts determine which factors are observed and which factors are deemed important in creating, maintaining and curing a neurosis, and determine also what is regarded as the therapeutic goal. New ways in theory necessarily condition new ways in therapy. Here more than in other chapters I regret that the frame of this book does not allow me to go into greater detail and that I have to omit many relevant problems altogether. The questions I shall discuss will be more or less restricted to the work to be done in analysis, the curative factors, the therapeutic goal, the difficulties involved for patient and analyst, the psychic factors which drive the patient to overcome his disturbances.

In order to understand these factors let us briefly summarize what essentially constitutes a neurosis. The combination of many adverse environmental influences [1]

[1] I do not discuss the influence of constitutional factors, partly because they are not relevant for psychoanalytic therapy but mostly because we know too little about them.

produces disturbances in the child's relation to self and others. The immediate effect is what I have called the basic anxiety, which is a collective term for a feeling of intrinsic weakness and helplessness toward a world perceived as potentially hostile and dangerous. The basic anxiety renders it necessary to search for ways in which to cope with life safely. The ways that are chosen are those which under the given conditions are accessible. These ways, which I call the neurotic trends, acquire a compulsory character because the individual feels that only by following them rigidly can he assert himself in life and avoid potential dangers. The hold which the neurotic trends have on him is further strengthened by the fact that they serve as his only means of attaining satisfaction as well as safety, other possibilities of attaining satisfaction being closed to him because they are too replete with anxiety. Furthermore, the neurotic trends provide an expression for the resentment which he harbors toward the world.

While the neurotic trends have thus a definite value for the individual they also invariably have far-reaching unfavorable consequences for his further development.

The security they offer is always precarious; the individual is easily subject to anxiety as soon as they fail to operate. They make him rigid, all the more so since further protective means often have to be built up to allay new anxieties. Invariably he becomes entangled in contradictory strivings; these may develop from the beginning, or a rigid drive in one direction may call forth an opposite drive, or a neurotic trend may bear a con-

flict in itself.[2] The presence of such incompatible strivings adds to the ample possibilities for the generation
of anxiety, for their very incompatibility implies the
danger that one of them will jeopardize the other.
Hence on the whole the neurotic trends render a person
still more insecure.

Moreover, the neurotic trends further alienate the
individual from himself. This fact, along with the rigidity of his structure, essentially impairs his productivity.
He may be able to work, but one live source of creativeness which is in his real spontaneous self necessarily
becomes choked. Also, he becomes discontented, for his
possibilities of satisfaction are limited, and the satisfactions themselves are usually merely temporary and
partial.

Finally, the neurotic trends, although their function
is to provide a basis on which to deal with others, contribute to a further impairment of human relationships.
The main reasons for this are that they help to increase
dependency on others, and that they precipitate various
kinds of hostile reactions.

The character structure which thus develops is the
kernel of neuroses. Despite infinite variations it always
contains certain general characteristics: compulsory
strivings, conflicting trends, a propensity to develop
manifest anxiety, impairment in the relation to self and

[2] A typical example of the first kind is the development of a neurotic
ambition simultaneously with a neurotic need for affection; an example
of the second kind is the masochistic tendency toward unobtrusiveness,
calling forth propensities toward self-inflation; an example of the third
kind is the conflicting tendencies toward compliance and defiance
which are at the root of the need to appear perfect.

others, marked discrepancy between potentialities and actual attainments.

The so-called symptoms of neuroses, which are usually regarded as the criteria for their classification, are not essential constituents. Neurotic symptoms such as phobias, depressions, fatigue and the like may not develop at all. But if they develop they are an outgrowth of the neurotic character structure and can be understood only on that basis. As a matter of fact, the only distinction between "symptoms" and neurotic character difficulties is that the latter obviously pertain to the structure of the personality while the former are not obviously connected with the character but appear to be, as it were, an extra-territorial growth. A neurotic's timidity is an obvious outcome of his character trends; his phobia of high places is not. Nevertheless, the latter is merely an expression of the former, for in his phobia of high places his various fears have merely been shifted to and focused on one special factor.

In the light of this interpretation of neuroses two kinds of therapeutic approach appear to be erroneous. One is the attempt to arrive at a direct understanding of the symptomatic picture without first having a grasp of the particular character structure. In mere situation neuroses it is possible sometimes to tackle directly the symptom that has emerged by relating it to the actual conflict. But in chronic neuroses we understand at the beginning little if anything of the symptomatic picture because it is the ultimate result of all existing neurotic entanglements. We do not know, for instance, why one patient has a syphilidophobia, another recurring eating spells, a third hypochondriac fears. The analyst should know that the symptoms cannot be directly understood, and why. As a rule, any attempt to make an immediate interpretation of the symptoms proves to be a failure, and means at least a waste of time. It is better to keep them in the background of one's mind and to take them up later on when an understanding of character trends sheds light upon them.

The patient, as a rule, is not content with this procedure. He naturally wants to have his symptoms explained at once, and resents what he feels to be an unnecessary delay. Often a deeper reason for his resentment is that he does not want anyone to intrude into the secrecies of his personality. The analyst does best to explain frankly the reasons for his procedure and to analyze the patient's reactions to it.

The other erroneous way is to relate the patient's actual peculiarities directly to certain childhood experiences and to establish a quick causal connection between two series of factors. In therapy Freud is primarily interested in tracing actual difficulties back to instinctual sources and infantile experiences, and this procedure is consistent with the instinctivistic and genetic character of his psychology.

In accordance with this principle Freud has two objectives in therapy. If—allowing for the inaccuracy involved—we consider what Freud calls instinctual drives and "super-ego" equivalent to what I call neurotic trends, Freud's first objective is to recognize the existence of neurotic trends. He would, for example, conclude from the existence of self-recriminations and self-imposed restrictions that the patient has a severe "super-ego" (need to appear perfect). His next objective is to relate these trends to infantile sources and to explain them on that basis. Concerning the "super-ego" he would be primarily interested in recognizing the kind of parental prohibitions which are still operating in the patient, and in unearthing the oedipal relations (sexual ties, hostilities, identifications) which he believes to be ultimately responsible for the phenomenon.

According to my slant on neuroses, the main neurotic disturbances are the consequences of the neurotic trends. Hence my main objective in therapy is, after having recognized the neurotic trends, to discover in detail the functions they serve and the consequences they have on the patient's personality and on his life. Taking again as an example the need to appear perfect, I would be interested primarily in understanding what this trend accomplishes for the individual (eliminating conflicts with others and making him feel superior to others), and also what consequences the trend has on his character and his life. The latter investigation would make it possible to understand, for example, how such a person anxiously conforms with expectations and standards to the extent of becoming a mere automaton, and yet subversively defies them; how this double play results in listlessness and inertia; how he is proud of his apparent independence, yet actually is entirely dependent on the expectations and opinions of others; how he resents everything that is expected of him, yet feels lost without such expectations to guide him; how he is terrified lest anyone should discover the flimsiness of his moral strivings and the duplicity which has pervaded his life; how this in turn has made him seclusive and hypersensitive to criticism.

I differ from Freud in that, after recognition of the neurotic trends, while he primarily investigates their genesis I primarily investigate their actual functions and their consequences. The intention in both procedures is the same: to diminish the holds the neurotic trends have on the person. Freud believes that by recognizing the infantile nature of his trends the patient will automatically realize that they do not fit into his adult personality and will therefore be able to master them. The sources of error involved in this contention have been discussed. I believe that all the obstacles which Freud holds responsible for therapeutic failures—such as depth of unconscious guilt feelings, narcissistic inaccessibility, unchangeability of biological drives—are really due to the erroneous premises on which his therapy is built.

My contention is that by working through the consequences the patient's anxiety is so much lessened, and his relation to self and others so much improved, that he can dispense with the neurotic trends. Their development was necessitated by the child's hostile and apprehensive attitude toward the world. If analysis of the consequences, that is, analysis of the actual neurotic structure, helps the individual to become discriminately friendly toward others instead of indiscriminately hostile, if his anxieties are considerably diminished, if he gains in inner strength and inner activity, he no longer needs his safety devices, but can deal with the difficulties of life according to his judgment.

It is not always the analyst who suggests to the patient that he search for causes in his childhood; often the patient spontaneously offers genetic material. In so far as he offers data relevant to his development this tendency is constructive. But in so far as he unconsciously uses these data to establish a quick causal connection the tendency is evasive in character. More often than not he hopes thereby to avoid facing trends which actually exist within him. The patient has an understandable interest in not realizing either the incompatibility of such trends or the price he pays for them: up to the time of analysis both his safety and his expectations of satisfaction rested on the pursuit of these strivings. He would prefer to preserve a muddled hope that his drives are not so imperative and not so incompatible as they seem, that he can have his cake and eat it, that nothing has to be changed. Therefore he has good reasons to resist when the analyst insists on working through the actual implications.

As soon as the patient himself is able to realize that his genetic endeavors lead to a dead-end, it is best to interfere actively and to point out that even though the experiences he recalls may have a bearing on the actual trend, they do not explain why the trend is maintained today; it should be explained to him that it is usually more profitable to postpone curiosity as to causation and study first the consequences which the particular trend entails for his character and for his life.

The emphasis I lay on the analysis of the actual character structure does not imply that data concerning childhood should be neglected. In fact, the procedure I have described—a procedure which desists from artificial reconstructions—even leads to a clearer understanding of childhood difficulties. In my experience, regardless of whether I work with the old or with the modified technique, it is comparatively rare that entirely forgotten memories creep up. More frequently falsifications of memories are corrected, and incidents which were regarded as irrelevant are given significance. The resultant understanding which the patient gradually acquires of his particular course of development helps to restore him to himself. Furthermore, through understanding himself he becomes reconciled to his parents or to their memory; he understands that they too were caught in conflicts and could not help harming him. What is more important, when he no longer suffers from the harm done him, or at least sees a way of overcoming it, old resentments are mitigated.

The tools with which the analyst operates during this procedure are to a large extent those which Freud has taught us to use: free associations and interpretations, as a means of lifting unconscious processes into awareness; a detailed study of the relationships between patient and analyst, as a means of recognizing the nature of the patient's relationships to others. In this regard my differences from Freud concern basically two groups of factors.

One is the kind of interpretations given. The character of interpretations depends on the factors which one deems to be essential.[3] Since I have discussed the differences on this score throughout the book this point need only be mentioned here.

The other group concerns factors which are less tangible and hence more difficult to formulate. They are implicit in the analyst's way of handling the procedure·

[3] *Cf.* Fay B. Karpf, "Dynamic Relationship Therapy" in *Social Work Technique* (1937).

his activity or passivity, his attitude to the patient, his making or refraining from value judgments, the attitudes he encourages and discourages in the patient. Some of these points have been discussed, others have been implied in the foregoing chapters. The outstanding considerations may here be briefly summarized.

According to Freud the analyst should play a comparatively passive role. Freud's advice is that the analyst should listen to the patient's associations with an "evenly-hovering attention," avoiding deliberate attentiveness to certain details and avoiding conscious exertion.[4]

Naturally, even in Freud's view, the analyst cannot be altogether passive. He exerts an active influence on the patient's associations by the interpretations he gives. When, for instance, the analyst tends to make reconstructions of the past, the patient is thereby implicitly directed to search in the past. Also, every analyst will actively interfere when he notices that the patient persistently avoids certain topics. Nevertheless, the ideal, in Freud's view, is that the analyst be guided by the patient and merely interpret the material when he sees fit to do so. That in this procedure he also influences the patient is, as it were, an effect which though desirable is only reluctantly admitted.

[4] ". . . he must bend his own unconscious like a receptive organ towards the emerging unconscious of the patient, be as the receiver of the telephone to the disc. As the receiver transmutes the electric vibrations induced by the sound-waves back again into sound-waves, so is the physician's unconscious mind able to reconstruct the patient's unconscious, which has directed his associations, from the communications derived from it" (Sigmund Freud, "Recommendations for Physicians on the Psycho-analytic Method of Treatment" in *Collected Papers*, Vol. II, 1924).

My view, on the other hand, is that the analyst should deliberately conduct the analysis. This statement, however, like Freud's emphasis on passivity, is to be taken with a grain of salt, because it is always the patient who indicates the general line by showing, through his associations, the problems which are uppermost in his mind. Also, according to my view, there will be many hours in which the analyst does nothing but interpret. Interpretation may imply many things: clarifying the problems which the patient, because he is unaware of their existence, presents in involved and disguised forms; pointing out existing contradictions; making suggestions as to possible solutions for a problem on the basis of insights already achieved concerning the patient's structure, and the like. These are hours in which the patient follows a profitable path. But as soon as I believe that the patient is running into a blind alley I would not hesitate to interfere most actively and to suggest another way, though of course I would analyze why he prefers to proceed along a certain line, and would present the reasons why I prefer that he try to search in another direction.

As an example let us assume that a patient has realized that it is imperative for him to be right. He has realized this sufficiently to begin to wonder about it and to ask why it is so important. My method would be to point out deliberately that as a rule one does not get very far with an immediate search for reasons, that it is more profitable to recognize first in detail all the consequences this attitude has for him and to understand what functions it fulfills. Of course the analyst takes more risk and more responsibility this way. Responsibility, however, rests on the analyst anyhow, and the risk of making wrong suggestions and thereby losing time is, according to experience, less than the risk entailed in non-interference. When I feel uncertain about a suggestion made to the patient I point out its tentative character. If then my suggestion is not to the point, the fact that the patient feels that I too am searching for a solution may elicit his active collaboration in correcting or qualifying my suggestion.

The analyst should exercise a more deliberate influence not only on the direction of the patient's associations but also on those psychic forces which may help him eventually to overcome his neurosis. The work the patient has to accomplish is most strenuous and most painful. It implies no less than relinquishing or greatly modifying all the strivings for safety and satisfaction which have hitherto prevailed. It implies relinquishing illusions about himself which in his eyes have made him significant. It implies putting his entire relations to others and to himself on a different basis. What drives the patient to do this hard work? Patients come for analytical help because of different motivations and with different expectations. Most frequently they want to get rid of manifest neurotic disturbances. Sometimes they wish to be better able to cope with certain situations. Sometimes they feel arrested in their development and wish to overcome a dead point. Very rarely do they come with the outright hope for more happiness. The strength and constructive value of these motivations vary in each patient, but all of them can be actively used in effecting a cure.

One has to realize, however, that these driving forces

are not entirely what they seem.[5] The patient wants to achieve his ends on his own terms. He may wish to be freed of suffering without his personality being touched. His wish for greater efficiency or for a better develop‐ment of his talents is almost always determined largely by an expectation that analysis will help to maintain more perfectly his appearance of infallibility and su‐periority. Even his quest for happiness, in itself the most effective of all motivations, cannot be taken at its face value, because the happiness the patient has in mind secretly entails the fulfillment of all his contra‐dictory neurotic wishes. During the analysis, however, all of these motivations are reinforced. This occurs in a very successful analysis without the analyst paying spe‐cial attention to it. But since their reinforcement, or we might say their mobilization, is of paramount impor‐tance for effecting a cure, it is desirable for the analyst to know what factors bring this about, and to conduct the analysis in such a way as to make these factors op‐erative.

In analysis the wish to become free from suffering gains in strength, because, even though the patient's symptoms may decrease, he gradually realizes how much intangible suffering and how many handicaps his neu‐rosis entails. A painstaking elaboration of all the conse‐quences of the neurotic trends helps the patient to rec‐ognize them and to acquire a constructive discontent‐ment with himself.

Also, his desire to improve his personality is put on a more solid basis as soon as his pretenses are removed.

[5] *Cf.* H. Nunberg, "Über den Genesungswunsch" in *Internationale Zeitschrift für Psychoanalyse* (1925).

Perfectionistic drives, for example, are replaced by a genuine wish to develop inherent potentialities, regardless of whether these concern special gifts or general human faculties, such as the faculty for friendship and love, the faculty to do a good job and enjoy it for its own sake.

Most important of all, the quest for happiness becomes stronger. Most patients have known merely the partial satisfaction attainable within the boundaries set by their anxieties; they have never experienced true happiness nor have they dared to reach out for it. One reason for this is that the neurotic has been altogether engrossed in his pursuit of safety and has felt content when merely free of haunting anxiety, depressions, migraine and the like. Also, in many cases, he has felt bound to maintain, in his own as in others' eyes, the appearance of misunderstood "unselfishness"; hence despite his actual egocentricity he has not dared to have outright wishes for himself. Or it may be that he has expected happiness to shine upon him like sunrays from the sky without his own active contribution. Deeper than all of these reasons and probably their ultimate cause, the individual has been a puffed-up balloon, a marionette, a success hunter, a stowaway, but never himself. And it seems that a precondition for happiness is to have the center of gravity within oneself.

There are several ways in which analysis reinforces the desire for happiness. By removing the patient's anxieties analysis frees energies and wishes for something more positive in life than mere riskless safety. Also it unmasks the "unselfishness" as a pretense maintained because of fears and a thirst for distinction. The analysis of this part of the façade deserves special attention because it is especially here that a wish for happiness may be liberated. Furthermore, analysis helps the patient to realize gradually that he is following the wrong path in expecting happiness to come to him from without, that the enjoyment of happiness is a faculty to be acquired from within. It is of no use merely to tell this to him, because he knows it anyhow as an age-old and undisputed truth, and because it would remain for him an abstract fact without bearing on reality. The way it gains life and reality in analysis is through psychoanalytic means. For instance, a patient who desires happiness through love and companionship realizes in analysis that for him "love" unconsciously signifies merely a relationship in which he will obtain everything he wants from a partner and have him at his beck and call, that he expects to receive "unconditional love" while he keeps his inner self entirely apart and remains wrapped up in himself. By becoming aware of the nature of his demands, by becoming aware of the intrinsic impossibility of their ever being fulfilled, and particularly by becoming aware of what consequences these demands and his reactions to their frustrations have actually had on his relationships, he realizes eventually that he need not despair of obtaining happiness through love but can obtain it if only he works sufficiently at regaining his own inner activity. Finally, the more a patient can dispense with his neurotic trends the more he becomes his own spontaneous self and can be trusted to take care of his quest for happiness himself.

There is still another possibility of mobilizing and reinforcing the patient's desire to change. Even if he is familiar with psychoanalysis the patient almost invariably harbors the illusion that being analyzed means only becoming aware of certain unpleasant things in himself, particularly those lying in the past, and that such awareness, as if by magic, will set him right with the world. If he considers at all the fact that analysis aims at a change in his personality, he expects the change to happen automatically. I shall not embark upon the philosophical question as to the relationship between an insight into some undesirable trend and a will impulse to change that trend. At any rate, the patient unwittingly distinguishes between awareness and change, because of subjective reasons which are readily understandable. In principle he accepts the necessity for becoming aware of repressed trends—though in detail, naturally, he fights every step in this direction—but he refuses to accept the necessity for change. None of this is clearly thought out, but he may be greatly shocked when the analyst confronts him with the necessity for an eventual change.

While some analysts point out this necessity to the patient, others in some way share the patient's attitude. An incident which occurred when I was supervising an analysis by a colleague may serve as an illustration. The patient had reproached the colleague for wanting to make him over, to change him, at which the colleague retorted that that was not his intention, that he merely wanted to uncover certain psychic facts. I asked the colleague whether he was convinced of the truth of his answer. He admitted that it was not quite true, but he felt that it was not right to wish the patient to change.

This question involves a seeming contradiction. Every analyst is proud to hear from others that a patient of his has changed immensely, yet he would hesitate to admit or to express to the patient a deliberate wish to effect a change in the patient's personality. He is prone to insist that all he does or wants to do is to lift unconscious processes into awareness, that what the patient does with his better knowledge of himself is the patient's own business. This contradiction is accounted for by theoretical reasons. There is, first, the general ideal that the analyst is a scientist whose only task is to observe, to collect data and to present these data. There is, furthermore, the doctrine of the limited functions of the "ego." At best it is accredited with a synthetic function [6] operating automatically but with a will power of its own, because all energies are supposed to arise from instinctual sources. Theoretically the analyst does not believe that we can will something because our judgment tells us it is the right or sensible thing to do if we wish to attain certain things. Hence he refrains from deliberately mobilizing will power in a constructive direction.[7]

It would not be correct, though, to say that Freud does not recognize at all the role which the patient's will power plays in therapy. He does so indirectly when he asserts that repression has to be replaced by judg-

[6] Cf. H. Nunberg, "Die synthetische Funktion des Ichs" in Internationale Zeitschrift für Psychoanalyse (1930).

[7] Otto Rank, in his Will Therapy (1936), rightly criticizes the disregard of this faculty in psychoanalysis. Will power, however, is too formalistic a principle to form the theoretical basis of therapy. The essential points remain those of content: from what bonds and to what ends energies are liberated.

ment, or that we work with the patient's intelligence, which implies that the patient's intelligent judgment sets off a will impulse toward a change. Every analyst factually relies on such impulses operating in the patient. When, for instance, he can demonstrate to the patient the existence of an "infantile" trend, like greediness or obstinacy, and its harmful implications, he certainly mobilizes a will impulse toward overcoming this trend. The question is only whether it is not preferable to be aware of doing so and to do it deliberately.

The psychoanalytic way of mobilizing will power is to bring certain connections or motivations to the patient's awareness and thereby enable him to judge and to decide. To what extent this result occurs depends on the depth of the insight gained. In psychoanalytic literature a distinction is made between a "merely" intellectual and an emotional insight. Freud states explicitly that the intellectual insight is too weak to enable patients to make a decision.[8] It is true that there is a difference in value when a patient only concludes the existence of an early experience and when he feels it emotionally, when he merely talks of death wishes and when he really feels them. But while this distinction has its merits, it does insufficient justice to the intellectual in-

[8] "If the patient is to fight the normal conflict that our analysis has revealed against the suppressions, he requires a tremendous impetus to influence the desirable decision which will lead him back to health. Otherwise, he might decide for a repetition of the former issue and allow those factors which have been admitted to consciousness to slip back again into suppression. The deciding vote in this conflict is not given by his intellectual penetration—which is neither strong nor free enough for such an achievement—but only by his relation to the physician" (Sigmund Freud, *A General Introduction to Psychoanalysis*, 1920).

sight. In this context "intellectual" has inadvertently acquired the connotation of "superficial."

An intellectual insight can be a powerful motor, provided it carries sufficient conviction. The quality of insight I have in mind is illustrated by an experience which probably every analyst has had. The patient at some time is aware of having certain trends, for instance, sadistic ones, and really feels them. But several weeks later they appear to him as an entirely new discovery. What has happened? It was not the emotional quality that was lacking. We could say rather that the insight into the sadistic trends did not carry any weight because it remained isolated. In order for it to be integrated the following steps are necessary: knowledge of disguised manifestations of sadistic trends and of their intensity; knowledge of what situations provoke them and of their consequences, such as anxiety, inhibitions, guilt feelings, disturbances in relationships to others. Only an insight of this scope and precision is strong enough to engage all the patient's available energies for a determination to change.

What is achieved through eliciting the patient's wish to change is similar to some extent to what a physician achieves by telling a diabetes patient that in order to overcome his illness he has to adhere to a certain diet. The physician too mobilizes energies by giving the patient an insight into the consequences which indiscriminate eating would have for him, his constitution being what it is. The difference is that the analyst's task is incomparably more difficult. The internist knows exactly what ails the patient and what the latter must avoid or must do in order to get rid of the illness. But neither the analyst nor his patient realizes what trends cause what disturbances; both of them, in addition to being engaged in an incessant struggle with the patient's fears and sensitivities, have to wind their way through a bewildering network of rationalizations and seemingly strange emotional reactions, in order finally to get hold of some connection illuminating the way.

A determination to change, though immeasurably valuable, is not, however, the equivalent of an ability to do so. In order for the patient to be able to give up his neurotic trends, those factors in his structure which made the trends necessary have to be worked through. Hence the psychoanalytic way of using this newly mobilized energy is to direct it toward further analysis.

The patient may take this further step spontaneously. He may, for instance, make more accurate observations concerning the conditions which provoke sadistic impulses, and be eager to analyze these conditions. Others, however, who are still compelled to eradicate every unpleasant trend at once, may exert efforts to control the sadistic impulses immediately, and when failing to do so become disappointed. In this case I would explain to the patient that his attempts to control the sadistic trends cannot possibly succeed as long as inwardly he still feels weak, downtrodden, easily humiliated, that as long as he feels that way he is bound to feel tempted to triumph vindictively over others, and that therefore if he wishes to overcome the sadistic trends he must analyze the psychic sources which generate them. The more an analyst is aware of this further work still to be done, the more he is able to spare a patient futile disappointment, and the more he can direct his efforts into rewarding channels.

Freud's doctrine is that moral problems, or value judgments, are beyond the interest and competence of psychoanalysis. Applied to therapy, this means that the analyst has to practice tolerance. This attitude is in accordance with the claim of psychoanalysis that it is a science, and also it reflects the principle of laissez-faire which characterized a certain phase of the liberal era. As a matter of fact, refraining from value judgments, not daring to take the responsibility for making them, is a widely spread characteristic of modern liberal man.[9] The analyst's imperturbable tolerance is regarded as one of the indispensable conditions which enable the patient to become aware of and eventually express repressed impulses and reactions.

The first question which arises on this score is whether it is possible to attain such tolerance. Is it possible for the analyst to be a mirror to the extent of excluding his own valuations? We have seen, in discussing the cultural implications of neuroses, that this is an ideal which cannot be carried through in reality. Since neuroses involve questions of human behavior and human motivations, social and traditional evaluations inadvertently determine the problems tackled and the goal aimed at. Freud himself does not adhere strictly to his ideal. He leaves no doubt in the patient's mind as to his own position concerning, for instance, the value

[9] The sociological foundation of the psychoanalytical concept of tolerance has been presented by Erich Fromm in "Die gesellschaftliche Bedingtheit der psychoanalytischen Therapie," *Zeitschrift für Sozialforschung* (1935).

of the sexual morality which is current in present society, or as to his belief that sincerity toward oneself is a valuable goal. As a matter of fact, when he calls psychoanalysis a re-education Freud contradicts his own ideal, succumbing to the illusion that education is conceivable without at least implicit moral measuring rods and goals.

Since the analyst has value judgments, even though he may not be aware of having them, his professed tolerance does not convince the patient; the patient senses the analyst's real attitude without its being explicitly stated. He knows it from the way the analyst expresses something, from the traits he does and does not regard as undesirable. When, for instance, the analyst asserts that guilt feelings concerning masturbation have to be analyzed, he implies that he does not consider masturbation as "bad" and hence that it does not warrant guilt feelings. An analyst who calls a patient's trend "sponging," instead of referring to it simply as a tendency to be "receptive," implicitly conveys to the patient his judgment about it.

Tolerance is thus an ideal which can be only approximated, not realized. The more careful the analyst is in his choice of words, the more he will approximate it. But is tolerance, in the sense of refraining from value judgments, an ideal to be aimed at? The answer is ultimately a matter of personal philosophy and personal decision. My own opinion is that an absence of value judgments belongs among those ideals we should try rather to overcome than to cultivate. A limitless willingness to understand the inner necessities forcing the neurotic to develop and to maintain moral pretenses, para-

sitic desires, power drives and the like, does not prevent
my considering these attitudes as negative values interfering with real happiness. I rather suspect that for me
the conviction that attitudes like these are something to
be overcome is one of the incentives to understand them
fully.

Concerning the value of this ideal for therapy, I question whether it fulfills the expectations set on it.[10] The
expectation is that the analyst's tolerance will allay the
patient's fear of condemnation and thereby elicit a
greater freedom of thought and expression.

Despite its apparent plausibility this expectation is
invalid because it does not consider the exact nature of
the patient's fear of condemnation. The patient is afraid
not that an objectionable trend in him will be considered inferior, but that his personality as a whole will be
condemned because of such a trend. Also he fears that
this condemnation will be merciless and without consideration for what made him develop the undesirable
trend. Furthermore, while he may fear condemnation
for various special traits, his fear on the whole is indiscriminate. His anticipation of being condemned for
everything he does is due partly to the intensity of his
fear of people, and partly to the fact that his own system of values is unbalanced. He knows neither his real
values nor his real deficiencies, the former being represented in his mind by his illusory claims of perfection
and uniqueness, the latter being repressed. Hence he is
entirely insecure as to what he might be condemned
for; he does not know, for instance, whether it might be
for legitimate wishes concerning himself, for a critical

[10] Cf. Erich Fromm, "Die gesellschaftliche Bedingtheit der psychoanalytischen Therapie," Zeitschrift für Sozialforschung (1935).

attitude, for a sexual fantasy. In view of the fact that the neurotic's fear is of this character there can scarcely be any doubt that the analyst's pretense of objectivity is not only incapable of allaying the fear but is on the contrary bound to increase it. When the patient can never be certain about the analyst's attitude, when, in addition, he occasionally senses objections without their being admitted, his fear of potential condemnation is bound to be intensified.

Naturally, if these fears are to be banished they have to be analyzed. What helps to allay them is the patient's knowledge that the analyst, though considering certain traits undesirable, does not condemn him as a whole. Instead of tolerance, or rather pseudo-tolerance, there should be a constructive friendliness, in which recognition of certain deficiencies does not detract from the capacity to admire good qualities and potentialities. In therapy this does not mean a general patting the patient on the back, but rather a willingness to give credit to whatever good and genuine elements there are in a trend, at the same time that its dubitable aspects are pointed out. It is important, for instance, to distinguish explicitly between a patient's good critical faculties and the destructive use he makes of them, between his sense of dignity and his haughtiness, between his genuine friendliness—if there is any—and his pretense of being a particularly loving and generous person.

It might be objected here that all this does not matter much because the patient sees the analyst only through the spectacles of the emotions he has at a given time. It must not be forgotten, however, that it is only one part of the patient which sees the analyst as a dangerous monster or a superior being. Certainly these feelings may prevail at times, but there is another part always present, though not always noticeable, which preserves a clear feeling for reality. In later phases of the analysis a patient may realize explicitly that he feels in two ways about the analyst. He may say, for instance, "I know for certain that you like me and yet I feel as if you loathe me." Hence the patient's familiarity with the analyst's attitude is important not only for allaying his fear of condemnation but also in order that he may recognize his projections as such.

The history of psychiatry shows that as far back as ancient Egypt or Greece there have been two concepts of psychic disturbances: a medical scientific one and a moral one. If we may make a broad statement the moral concept has usually prevailed. It is to the merit of Freud, and also of his contemporaries, to have gained such a signal victory for the medical concept that—as it seems to me—it can never be eradicated.

Nevertheless, our knowledge of cause and effect in psychic ailments should not blind us to the fact that they do involve moral problems. The neurotic often develops particularly fine qualities, such as sympathy for the suffering of others, understanding of their conflicts, detachment from traditional standards, refined sensitivity to aesthetic and moral values, but he also develops certain traits of dubitable value. As a result of the fears, hostilities, feelings of weakness which are at the bottom of neurotic processes and are reinforced by them, he unavoidably becomes to some extent insincere, supercilious, cowardly, egocentric. The fact that he is not aware of these trends does not prevent them from existing nor does it—and this is what matters to the therapist—keep him from suffering from them.

The difference between our present attitude and that which prevailed before psychoanalysis is that we regard these problems now from another viewpoint. We have learned that the neurotic is inherently as little lazy, mendacious, grabbing, conceited, as anyone else, that the adverse circumstances of his childhood have forced him to build up an elaborate system of defenses and gratifications resulting in the development of certain unfavorable trends. Hence we do not consider him responsible for them. In other words, the contradiction between the medical and the moral concepts of psychic disturbances is less irreconcilable than it appeared to be: the moral problems are an integral part of the illness. As a consequence we should regard as belonging to our medical task the function of helping the patient in the clarification of these problems.

That the role they factually play in neuroses is not seen clearly in psychoanalysis is the result of certain theoretical presuppositions, mainly those implicit in the libido theory and the "super-ego" concept.

The moral problems actually presented are as a rule pseudo-moral, for they belong to the patient's need to appear perfect and superior in his own eyes. Hence the first step is to uncover the moral pretenses and to recognize their real functions for the patient.

His true moral problems, on the other hand, the patient is most anxious to hide. It is scarcely an exaggeration to say that he hides them more anxiously than anything else. The perfectionistic and narcissistic façade is indispensable for the very reason that it serves as a screen to conceal them. But the patient must be enabled to see their character distinctly, for otherwise he cannot be freed from the tormenting duplicity of his life nor from the resulting anxiety and inhibitions. For this reason the analyst should deal as candidly with moral issues as he does with sexual deviations. The patient can take a stand toward them only after having faced them squarely.

Freud realizes that the basic neurotic conflicts must eventually be solved by the patient's decision. Here too the question is whether this process should not be deliberately encouraged. Many patients, after having seen certain problems, take a stand spontaneously. When a patient recognizes the calamities ensuing from his peculiar kind of pride, for instance, he may spontaneously call it his false pride. Others, however, are too involved in their conflicts to make such judgments. In such cases it appears useful to indicate the eventual necessity for a decision. For example, if in one hour a patient expresses his admiration for persons who unscrupulously use any available means for success, and in another hour asserts that he does not care for success but is interested only in the subject matter of his work, the analyst should not only point out the contradiction implied but also indicate that eventually the patient will have to make up his mind as to what he really wants. I would, however, discourage quick and superficial decisions; the important point is to urge the patient to analyze what drives him in either direction and what he has to gain and renounce in either case.

If the analyst is to adopt these attitudes in therapy it is an essential prerequisite that his attitude to the patient be intrinsically friendly and that he has clarified his own problems. As long as he harbors certain pretenses himself, he is bound to protect them in the patient too. Not only should the analyst's own "didactic analysis" be extensive and thorough, but he must also subject himself to a never-ending self-analysis. If the task is primarily to unravel the patient's actual problems this self-understanding is, more than ever, an indispensable prerequisite for analyzing others.

I wish to conclude these remarks on psychoanalytical therapy by considering whether the new ways suggested have a bearing on the length of analysis.

The length of an analysis (as well as its chance of success) is dependent on a combination of factors, such as the amount of underlying anxiety, the amount of existing destructive tendencies, the extent to which the patient lives in fantasy, the scope and depth of his resignation and the like. In order to form a preliminary estimate as to probable length, various criteria can be used. Of these I pay most attention to the amount of energy available for constructive use in the past or present, the extent of positive realistic wishes concerning life, the strength of the superstructure. If these latter factors are favorable much help can be given through an active and direct tackling of the actual problems. I should say that more persons of this kind can be helped without a systematic analysis than is usually assumed.

Concerning chronic neuroses, I have tried to show in general the extent and kind of work which has to be done. Without going into much more detail it is impossible to give a picture of its intricacy. Both the amount and the difficulty of work make it impossible to do it quickly. Thus Freud's repeated statement remains true that possibilities for a quick cure of neuroses are commensurable with the severity of the illness.

Various suggestions have been made for shortening the process, such as setting a more or less arbitrary time at which to terminate the analysis, or carrying it on at intervals. Such attempts, although sometimes effective, do not and cannot possibly fulfill what is expected of them, because they entail no consideration of the work actually to be accomplished. There is in my opinion but one sensible means to shorten analysis: to avoid a waste of time.

I believe that there is no brief and easy recipe for attaining this aim. When we ask a mechanic how he manages to detect instantly a hidden defect in a machine, he tells us that his thorough knowledge of the machine makes it possible for him, through observation of the actual disturbance, to reach a conclusion as to its probable source, that in this way he does not lose time in searching in wrong directions. We must realize that despite the great work done in the past decades, our knowledge of the human soul is amateurish compared with a good mechanic's knowledge of the machine. Probably it will never be thus precise. But my experience with my own analyses, as well as with those supervised, leads me to believe that the more we understand of a psychic problem the less time we lose in arriving at a solution. Thus we may be justified in hoping that as our knowledge advances we shall not only be able to widen the range of problems to be reached by analysis, but we shall also be able to solve them within reasonable time limits.

When should an analysis be terminated? Again a warning is in place against seeking an easy solution by relying on outward signs or on isolated criteria, such as disappearance of gross symptoms, capacity for sexual enjoyment, change in the structure of dreams, or the like.

At bottom, the question again touches upon a personal philosophy of life. Do we intend to put out a finished product with all problems solved for good and all? If we consider this possible, do we believe it to be desirable? Or do we think of life as a process of development which does not end and should not end until the very last day of existence? As I have shown throughout this book, I believe that a neurosis arrests the individual's development by making him rigid in his pursuits and his reactions, that it traps him in conflicts which he cannot solve himself. Thus I hold that the aim of analysis is not to render life devoid of risks and conflicts, but to enable an individual eventually to solve his problems himself.

But when is the patient able to take his development into his own hands? This question is identical with the question as to the ultimate goal of psychoanalytical therapy. In my judgment, freeing the patient from anxiety is only a means to an end. The end is to help him to regain his spontaneity, to find his measurements of value in himself, in short, to give him the courage to be himself.

INDEX

Books That Live

THE NORTON IMPRINT ON A BOOK
MEANS THAT IN THE PUBLISHER'S
ESTIMATION IT IS A BOOK NOT FOR A
SINGLE SEASON BUT FOR THE YEARS

W · W · NORTON & COMPANY · INC ·

Norton Paperbacks on Psychiatry and Psychology

Adorno, T. W. et al. *The Authoritarian Personality.*

Alexander, Franz. *Fundamentals of Psychoanalysis.*

Alexander, Franz. *Psychosomatic Medicine.*

Bruner, Jerome S. *Toward a Theory of Instruction.*

Cannon, Walter B. *The Wisdom of the Body.*

Erikson, Erik H. *Childhood and Society.*

Erikson, Erik H. *Gandhi's Truth.*

Erikson, Erik H. *Identity: Youth and Crisis.*

Erikson, Erik H. *Insight and Responsibility.*

Erikson, Erik H. *Young Man Luther.*

Ferenczi, Sandor. *Thalassa: A Theory of Genitality.*

Field, M. J. *Search for Security: An Ethno-Psychiatric Study of Rural Ghana.*

Freud, Sigmund. *An Autobiographical Study.*

Freud, Sigmund. *Civilization and its Discontents.*

Freud, Sigmund. *The Ego and the Id.*

Freud, Sigmund. *Jokes and Their Relation to the Unconscious.*

Freud, Sigmund. *Leonardo da Vinci and a Memory of His Childhood.*

Freud, Sigmund. *New Introductory Lectures on Psychoanalysis.*

Freud, Sigmund. *On Dreams.*

Freud, Sigmund. *On the History of the Psycho-Analytic Movement.*

Freud, Sigmund. *An Outline of Psycho-Analysis Rev. Ed.*

Freud, Sigmund. *The Problem of Anxiety.*

Freud, Sigmund. *The Psychopathology of Everyday Life.*

Freud, Sigmund. *The Question of Lay Analysis.*

Freud, Sigmund. *Totem and Taboo.*

Horney, Karen (Ed.) *Are You Considering Psychoanalysis?*

Horney, Karen. *Feminine Psychology.*

Horney, Karen. *Neurosis and Human Growth.*

Horney, Karen. *The Neurotic Personality of Our Time.*

Horney, Karen. *New Ways in Psychoanalysis.*

Horney, Karen. *Our Inner Conflicts.*

Horney, Karen. *Self-Analysis.*

Inhelder, Bärbel and Jean Piaget. *The Early Growth of Logic in the Child.*

James, William. *Talks to Teachers.*

Kasanin, J. S. *Language and Thought in Schizophrenia.*

Kelly, George A. *A Theory of Personality.*

Klein, Melanie and Joan Riviere. *Love, Hate and Reparation.*

Levy, David M. *Maternal Overprotection.*

Lifton, Robert Jay. *Thought Reform and the Psychology of Totalism.*

Piaget, Jean. *The Child's Conception of Number.*

Piaget, Jean. *Genetic Epistemology.*

Piaget, Jean. *The Origins of Intelligence in Children.*

Piaget, Jean. *Play, Dreams and Imitation in Childhood.*

Piaget, Jean and Bärbel Inhelder. *The Child's Conception of Space.*

Piers, Gerhart and Milton B. Singer. *Shame and Guilt.*

Ruesch, Jurgen. *Disturbed Communication.*

Ruesch, Jurgen. *Therapeutic Communication.*

Ruesch, Jurgen and Gregory Bateson. *Communication: The Social Matrix of Psychiatry.*

Schein, Edgar et al. *Coercive Persuasion.*

Sullivan, Harry Stack. *Clinical Studies in Psychiatry.*

Sullivan, Harry Stack. *Conceptions of Modern Psychiatry.*

Sullivan, Harry Stack. *The Fusion of Psychiatry and Social Science.*

Sullivan, Harry Stack. *The Interpersonal Theory of Psychiatry.*

Sullivan, Harry Stack. *The Psychiatric Interview.*

Walter, W. Grey. *The Living Brain.*

Watson, John B. *Behaviorism.*

Wheelis, Allen. *The Quest for Identity.*

Zilboorg, Gregory. *A History of Medical Psychology.*